Adobe Photoshop Lightroom Classic

2024 Release

Classroom in a Book®
The official training workbook from Adobe

ISBN-13:   978-0-13-831814-7
ISBN-10:   0-13-831814-X

1 2024

WHERE ARE THE LESSON FILES?

Purchase of this Classroom in a Book in any format gives you access to the lesson files you'll need to complete the exercises in the book.

1 Go to *peachpit.com/LightroomCIB2024*.

2 Sign in or create a new account.

3 Click Submit.

⬤ **Note:** If you encounter problems registering your product or accessing the lesson files or web edition, go to *peachpit.com/support* for assistance.

4 Answer the questions as proof of purchase.

5 The lesson files can be accessed through the Registered Products tab on your Account page.

6 Click the Access Bonus Content link below the title of your product to proceed to the download page. Click the lesson file links to download them to your computer.

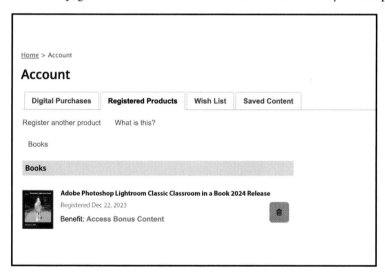

⬤ **Note:** If you purchased a digital product directly from *peachpit.com*, your product will already be registered. Look for the Access Bonus Content link on the Registered Products tab in your account.

CONTENTS

GETTING STARTED

Adobe Photoshop Lightroom Classic is the gold-standard workflow solution for the digital photographer—from importing, reviewing, organizing, and enhancing images to publishing photos, producing client presentations, creating photo books and web galleries, and outputting high-quality prints.

One of the benefits of using Lightroom Classic is that you get all of the power you've come to know and love from Adobe in an interface that is easy to use, getting you up to speed in no time.

Whether you're a home user, a professional photographer, a hobbyist, or a business user, Lightroom Classic enables you to stay in control of your growing photo library and to produce good-looking pictures and polished presentations for both web and print with little effort.

About Classroom in a Book

Adobe Photoshop Lightroom Classic Classroom in a Book 2024 Release is part of the official training series for Adobe graphics and publishing software developed with the support of Adobe product experts.

Each lesson in this book consists of a series of self-paced projects that give you hands-on experience using Adobe Photoshop Lightroom Classic.

If you're new to Lightroom Classic, you'll learn the fundamental concepts and skills that will help you master the application; if you've used earlier versions of Lightroom, you'll find that this Classroom in a Book® teaches advanced tips and techniques and covers the many new features and enhancements that Adobe Systems has introduced in the latest version.

What's new in this edition

This edition covers the many new features in Adobe Photoshop Lightroom Classic, such as interactive lens blur with the new Lens Blur panel, the ability to precisely adjust a single color using Point Color, and the ability to search your entire list of presets.

You'll discover enhancements to some of your favorite tools, including the Masking tool. With new Person Mask options, you can automatically select just clothing or facial hair to mask. And the new Denoise dialog box makes removing noise from your image easier and the results better.

You'll learn ways to organize your image library, streamline your workflow, and keep yourself organized by developing a solid workflow structure. And you'll meet guest photographers who offer you advice and inspiration.

Prerequisites

Before starting on the lessons in this book, make sure that you and your computer are ready by following the tips and instructions on the next few pages.

Requirements on your computer

You'll need about 6.78 GB of free space on your hard disk for all of the downloaded lesson files (see "Accessing the lesson files and Web Edition" on the facing page) and the work files that you'll create as you work through the exercises.

Required skills

The lessons in this book assume that you have a working knowledge of your computer and its operating system.

Make sure that you know how to use the mouse and the standard menus and commands, as well as how to open, save, and close files. Can you scroll (vertically and horizontally) within a window to see content that may not be visible in the display area? Do you know how to use context menus, which open when you right-click items?

If you need to review these basic and generic computer skills, see the documentation included with your Apple macOS or Microsoft Windows software.

Installing Lightroom Classic

● **Note:** This book describes and illustrates Lightroom Classic release 13.0.

Before you begin the lessons in *Adobe Photoshop Lightroom Classic Classroom in a Book 2024 Release*, make sure that your system is set up correctly and that you've installed the required software and hardware.

You must purchase the Adobe Photoshop Lightroom Classic software separately. For system requirements and detailed instructions for downloading, installing, and setting up the software, see the topics listed on the Lightroom Classic Get Started page at *https://helpx.adobe.com/lightroom-classic/get-started.html*.

Online content

Your purchase of this Classroom in a Book includes online materials provided by way of your Account page at *peachpit.com*. These include two useful bonus lessons called "Publishing Your Photos" and "An Overview of My Workflow."

Lesson files

To work through the projects in this book, you will need to download the lesson files by following the instructions below.

Web Edition

The Web Edition is an online interactive version of the book, providing an enhanced learning experience. Your Web Edition can be accessed from any device with a connection to the internet, and it contains:

*   The complete text of the book

*   Hours of instructional video keyed to the text

*   Interactive quizzes

Accessing the lesson files and Web Edition

⬤ **Note:** If you encounter problems registering your product or accessing the lesson files or web edition, go to *peachpit.com/support* for assistance.

You must register your purchase on *peachpit.com* to access the online content.

1 Go to *peachpit.com/LightroomCIB2024*.

2 Sign in or create a new account.

3 Click Submit.

4 Answer the question as proof of purchase.

5 The lesson files can be accessed from the Registered Products tab on your Account page. Click the Access Bonus Content link below the title of your product to proceed to the download page. Click the lesson file link(s) to download them to your computer.

   The Web Edition can be accessed from the Digital Purchases tab on your Account page. Click the Launch link to access the product.

⬤ **Note:** If you purchased a digital product directly from *peachpit.com*, your product will already be registered. Look for the Access Bonus Content link on the Registered Products tab in your account.

6 Create a new folder inside the Users/*username*/Documents folder on your computer, and then name the new folder **LRC2024CIB**.

7   If you downloaded the entire Lessons folder, drag that Lessons folder into the LRC2024CIB folder you created in step 6. Alternatively, if you downloaded folders for one or more individual lessons, first create a Lessons folder inside your LRC2024CIB folder, and then drag the individual lesson folder(s) into your LRC2024CIB/Lessons folder.

8   Keep the lesson files on your computer until you've completed all of the exercises.

The downloadable sample images are practice files, provided for your personal use in these lessons. It is illegal to use them commercially or to publish or distribute them in any way without written permission from Adobe Systems Inc. *and* the individual photographers who took the pictures.

Understanding Lightroom catalog files

The catalog file is the master digital notebook for all the photos in your library. This digital notebook includes the location of the master files, any metadata you've added in the process of organizing your images, and a record of every adjustment or edit you've made. Most users will keep all their photos in a single catalog, which can easily manage thousands of files. Some might want to create separate catalogs for different purposes, such as personal photos and business photos. Although you can create multiple catalogs, keep in mind that you can open only one catalog at a time in Lightroom Classic.

For the purposes of working with this book, you'll create a new catalog to manage the image files that you'll use in the lessons. This will allow you to leave the default catalog untouched while working through the lessons and will keep your lesson files together in one easy-to-remember location.

Creating a catalog file for working with this book

When Lightroom Classic starts for the first time, a catalog file named Lightroom Catalog.lrcat is automatically created on your hard disk. This default catalog file is created inside the folder *username*/Pictures/Lightroom.

● **Note:** In this book, the forward arrow character (>) is used to denote submenus and commands found in the menu bar at the top of the workspace or in context menus; for example, Menu > Submenu > Command.

You'll create your new work catalog file inside your LRC2024CIB folder, right beside the Lessons folder containing your downloaded work files.

1   Launch Lightroom Classic.

2   From the Lightroom menu bar, choose File > New Catalog.

3   Navigate to the LRC2024CIB folder you created on your hard disk.

4   Type **LRC2024CIB Catalog** in the Save As text box on macOS or the File Name text box on Windows, and then click Create.

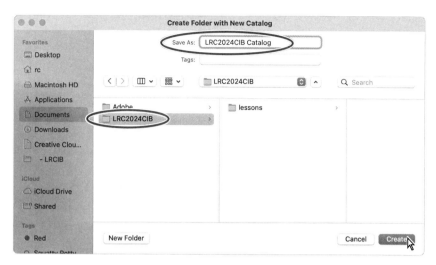

5   If you see a notification about backing up the current catalog before loading your
    new catalog, choose your preferred option to dismiss the message.

To be sure that you're always aware of which catalog you're working with as you
progress through the lessons in this book, you'll next set the preferences so that
you'll be prompted to specify your LRC2024CIB catalog each time you launch
Lightroom Classic. It is recommended that you keep this preference set as long
as you're working through the lessons in this book.

6   Choose Lightroom Classic > Preferences (macOS) or Edit > Preferences
    (Windows).

7   In the Preferences dialog box, click the General tab. From the Default Catalog
    menu, choose Prompt Me When Starting Lightroom.

● **Note:** In the
remainder of this book,
instructions that differ
for macOS users and
those working on
Windows systems are
given in a compact
format as follows:
the forward slash
character (/) is used
to separate equivalent
terms and commands
for macOS/Windows,
in the order shown here.

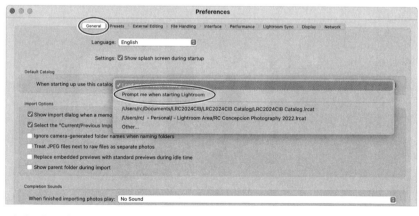

8   Click Close (macOS) or OK (Windows) to close the Preferences dialog box.

The next time you start Lightroom Classic, the Select Catalog dialog box will appear, giving you the opportunity to make sure that your LRC2024CIB Catalog file is selected before clicking Open to launch Lightroom.

Tip: Even if you've set Lightroom to load the most recent catalog by default, you can open the Select Catalog dialog box by holding down the Control+Option/ Ctrl+Alt keys immediately after you launch Lightroom.

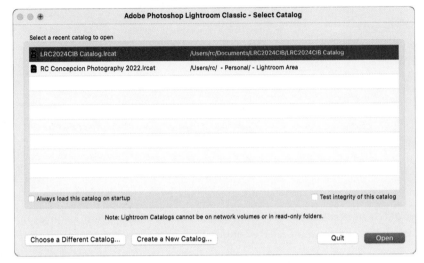

Getting ready to go mobile

Adobe Photoshop Lightroom Classic is integrated through Adobe Creative Cloud with Lightroom for mobile and Lightroom on the web, enabling you to sync photo collections between your desktop computer and a companion app on your mobile device. This means you can review, organize, and even edit your photos anywhere, anytime, and then share them online.

Whether you're working in Lightroom Classic on your desktop (or laptop) or Lightroom on your handheld device, any modifications made to a synced collection or the photos it contains will be updated on the other device. Lightroom syncs high-resolution Smart Previews to your mobile device, rather than your original photos. At a small fraction of the original file size, these Smart Previews won't take long to sync or use up all your storage space, which means that you can even work with raw images while you're away from your desktop computer.

Edits you make on the mobile device are synced back to the full-size originals in your Lightroom Classic catalog. Photos captured on your handheld device and added to a synced collection are downloaded to your desktop at full size. You can share your photos from your device to social media or via Lightroom on the web. Here's how to set this up:

1 Download and install Lightroom on your mobile device. You can download the app free from the Apple App Store (for iPad and iPhone) or from Google Play (for Android) on a trial basis; then, choose a subscription plan later.

2 Once you've installed Lightroom on your handheld device, see the section "Taking your collections on the road" in Lesson 4, "Managing Your Photo Library," for details on getting started with Lightroom.

Editing photos in Lightroom on the web is covered in Lesson 4, in the "Editing on the *lightroom.adobe.com* site" section. Sharing collections from Lightroom Classic via Lightroom on the web is explained in the "Syncing photos from Lightroom Classic" section in Lesson 4.

Subscription to Lightroom for mobile is free with either a full Creative Cloud subscription or the Photography plan. For subscription details, go to *www.adobe.com/ creativecloud/plans.html*.

Getting help

Help is available from several sources, each one useful to you in different circumstances.

Module-specific tips

The first time you enter any of the Lightroom Classic modules, you'll see module-specific tips that will help you get started by identifying the components of the Lightroom Classic workspace and stepping you through the workflow.

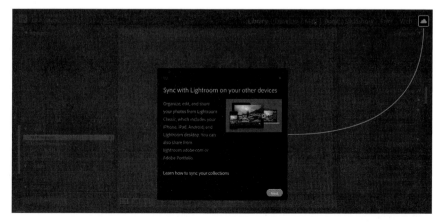

You can dismiss the tips if you want by clicking the Close button (x) in the upper-right corner of the floating tips window. You can call up the module tips at any time by choosing Help > [*Module name*] Tips.

In the Help menu, you can also access a list of keyboard shortcuts applicable to the current module.

Navigating Help in the application

The complete user documentation for Adobe Photoshop Lightroom Classic is available from the Help menu.

Note: You need to be connected to the internet to view Help in Lightroom.

1 Choose Help > Lightroom Classic Help or press the F1 key on your keyboard. Lightroom takes you to the online Help landing page. To search for a particular topic in the online Help, use the search bar at the upper right of the page. Enter a search term and press Return/Enter.

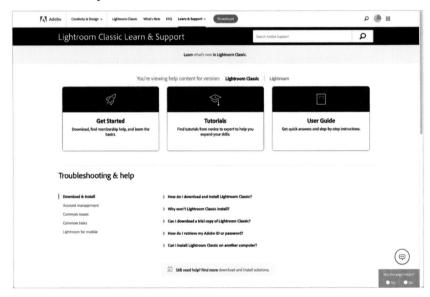

2 For quick access to the Lightroom Classic online user guide, press Command+Option+/ on macOS or Ctrl+Alt+/ on Windows.

3 Press Command+/ on macOS or Ctrl+/ on Windows to see a list of keyboard shortcuts for the current module. Press any key to hide it.

Accessing Help and support on the web

You can access Lightroom Classic Help, tutorials, support, and other useful resources on the web, even if Lightroom Classic is not currently running.

• If the application is running, choose Help > Lightroom Classic Help.

- If Lightroom Classic is not currently running, point your default web browser to *https://helpx.adobe.com/support/lightroom-classic.html*, where you can find and browse Lightroom Classic content on *adobe.com*.

Additional resources

Adobe Photoshop Lightroom Classic Classroom in a Book 2024 Release is not intended to replace the documentation that comes with the application or to be a comprehensive reference for every feature. Only the commands and options used in the lessons are explained in this book. For comprehensive information about program features and tutorials, please refer to these resources:

Adobe Photoshop Lightroom Classic Help and Support
You can search and browse Help and Support content from Adobe at *https://helpx.adobe.com/support/lightroom-classic.html*.

Adobe Support Community
Tap into peer-to-peer discussions, advice, and questions and answers on Adobe products at *https://community.adobe.com*.

Adobe Creative Cloud Learn
For inspiration, key techniques, cross-product workflows, and updates on new features, go to *https://helpx.adobe.com/lightroom-classic/tutorials.html*.

Adobe Photoshop Lightroom Classic product home page
See *www.adobe.com/products/photoshop-lightroom-classic.html*.

Adobe Creative Cloud: Discover
Visit *https://create.adobe.com* for how-to articles, challenges, and inspiration for design, photography, video, and more.

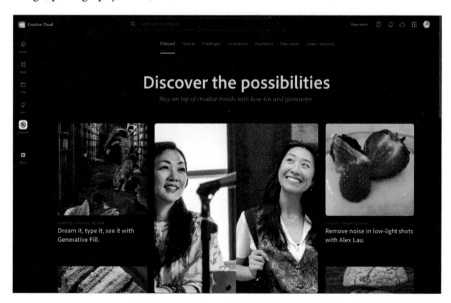

1 A QUICK TOUR OF LIGHTROOM CLASSIC

Lesson overview

This lesson starts with a quick look behind the scenes to show you how Lightroom Classic makes it easy to navigate, search, and manage your ever-growing image library and frees you to work on your photos without damaging the original files. The exercises then provide a hands-on introduction to Lightroom, familiarizing you with the workspace as they guide you through a typical workflow. In this lesson, you'll learn how to:

- Bring photos into Lightroom Classic.

- Review and compare photos.

- Sort and organize your image library.

- Adjust and enhance photos.

- Share your work.

 This lesson will take about 90 minutes to complete. To get the lesson files used in this chapter, download them from the web page for this book at *peachpit.com/LightroomCIB2024*. For more information, see "Accessing the lesson files and Web Edition" in the "Getting Started" section at the beginning of this book.

Note: The downloaded lesson images won't appear in Lightroom until you've imported them into the library catalog file; you'll do that in the exercise "Importing photos," after the overview that begins this lesson.

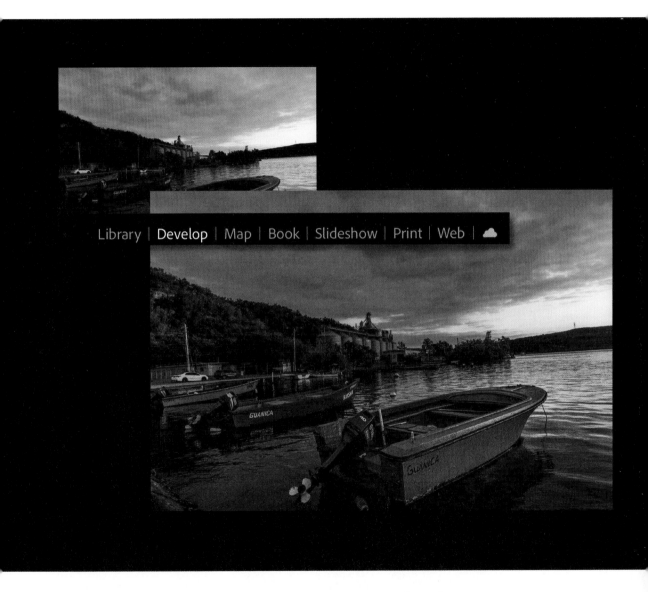

Whether you're a beginner or a professional,
Lightroom Classic delivers a complete desktop-based
workflow solution for today's digital photographer,
allowing you to work more efficiently and bring out
the very best in your images.

Understanding how Lightroom works

Working with Lightroom Classic will be easier and more productive if you have an overview of how Lightroom works—and how it differs from other image processing applications in the way it handles your pictures.

About catalog files

To work with a photo in Lightroom Classic, you must first bring it into your library catalog by importing it.

Think of the Lightroom catalog as a master notebook that keeps track of the location of your pictures (hard drive, external drives, network-attached storage device), as well as what you've done to these pictures (rank, sort, pick, develop, etc.). This digital notebook keeps track of all of the changes you make inside the catalog file and never touches the original images. This allows you to work with images more quickly and offers you better ways to organize and sort your growing photographic library.

A single catalog can easily manage thousands of files (my catalog file manages more than 350,000 images), but you're free to create as many catalogs as you wish and switch between them. The one thing to consider is that you will not be able to work with or search for images across multiple catalogs. Because of this, I recommend that you keep all of your images in one catalog.

Managing the photos in your catalog

Lightroom Classic lets you organize your photos right from the point of import: You can choose to add photos to your catalog without moving the image files from where they live on a hard drive, copy them to a new location while leaving the originals intact, or move them and delete the originals to avoid duplicating files. If you choose to copy or move your files during the import process, you have the option to select how folders are structured in your new location.

During this import process, Lightroom can rename your images, create backup duplicates (your digital negatives), attach keywords (I added "NAHJ"—National Association of Hispanic Journalists—to the photos here) and other metadata, and even apply develop presets—all before you've opened a single image!

● **Note:** You'll learn more about setting up import options in Lesson 2, "Bringing Photos into Lightroom Classic."

The Library module will let you organize your images and attach keywords and captions. Additionally, you can separate and organize your images by using pick flags and star and color ratings—on single images or on a group of images—in no time at all. Lightroom even gives you the option to sort images by places on a map or to sort by face. All of this information goes into your digital notebook, giving you access to it whenever you need it.

Managing files and folders

While all of this is quite useful, I'll add a word of caution. If you wish to rename or move an image file or folder that contains images that you've already imported into your catalog, you should always do so from within Lightroom so that the changes can be tracked in the catalog. If you make these changes outside of Lightroom, it will no longer be able to find those images (we'll talk about how to recover them later).

Non-destructive editing

While storing information about your images in a central catalog makes it easy to navigate, search, and manage your photo library, the greatest benefit of this catalog file is that your edits are *non-destructive*. When you modify or edit a photo, Lightroom makes a record of each step you take in the catalog file, rather than saving changes directly to the image. This ensures that the original raw image data is always safe. I like to think of it like this: the raw image data is the ingredients, but the recipe is what I save in my notebook (catalog file).

Non-destructive editing not only frees you to experiment with your photos without fear of losing information from the original files but also makes Lightroom a very powerful editing environment. All of your edits remain "live," so you can return at any time to undo, redo, or tweak any modification that you've made; Lightroom applies your edits permanently only to output copies—and it does that quickly.

Editing photos in another application

Should you wish to edit an image from your catalog using an external program, always launch the process from within Lightroom so that Lightroom can keep track of changes made to the file. For a JPEG, TIFF, or PSD image, you have the option to edit the original file or a copy—either with or without the adjustments that you've already applied in Lightroom. For other file formats, you can edit a copy to which your Lightroom adjustments have already been applied. The edited copy will automatically be added to your catalog.

▶ **Tip:** You can specify your favorite external editors in the External Editing preferences; your choices will appear in the Photo > Edit In menu. If you have Photoshop installed on your computer, it will be listed by default.

The Lightroom Classic workspace

Lightroom is split into seven main panels. At the center of the program is the preview and work area, and panel groups appear to the left and right of it. Directly above the work area and to the left is the identity plate. The Module Picker sits above and to the right. Finally, the area beneath the work area is the Toolbar, and below that, across the bottom of the workspace, is the Filmstrip.

● **Note:** The illustration at the right shows the macOS version of Lightroom. On Windows, the workspace is the same, except for minor differences between the two operating systems; on Windows, for example, the menu bar is located under the title bar, whereas on macOS it's anchored at the top of the screen.

This visual arrangement of panels is identical in all seven modules (tools for each part of your workflow). Only the contents of the panels vary from module to module.

The top panel

▶ **Tip:** The first time you enter any of the Lightroom modules, you'll see module tips that will help you get started by identifying the components of the Lightroom workspace and stepping you through the workflow. Dismiss the tips by clicking the Close button. To reactivate the tips for any module, choose [*Module name*] Tips from the Help menu.

The top panel displays an identity plate on the left and the Module Picker on the right. This identity plate can be customized to feature your own company name or logo and is temporarily replaced by a progress bar whenever Lightroom is performing a background process (clicking the progress bar brings up a menu that shows you the processes Lightroom is working on). To the right, you'll use the Module Picker to move between the different modules by clicking their names. Finally, the name of the currently active module is always highlighted in the Module Picker.

The work area

The main preview and work area sits at the center of Lightroom—you'll spend most of your time here. This is where you select, review, sort, compare, and apply adjustments to your images, and where you preview the work in progress. This center window will change as you move across modules, showing you book designs, slideshow presentations, web galleries, and print layouts as needed.

The Toolbar

Underneath the work area is the Toolbar, which offers a different set of tools and controls for each of the modules. You can customize the Toolbar for each module independently to suit your needs, choosing from a variety of tools and controls for switching viewing modes; setting ratings, flags, or labels; adding text; and navigating through preview pages. You can show or hide individual controls, or hide the Toolbar altogether until you need it.

▶ **Tip:** You can show and hide the Toolbar by pressing the T key.

Here, we see the Toolbar for the Library module, with the view mode buttons at the left and a selection of task-specific tools and controls that can be customized by choosing from the menu at the far right. The menu options change with the view.

Tools and controls that are currently visible in the Toolbar have a checkmark beside their names in the Select Toolbar Content menu. The order of the tools and controls from left to right in the Toolbar corresponds to their order from top to bottom in the menu. Most of the options presented in the Toolbar are also available as menu commands or keyboard shortcuts.

The Filmstrip

The Filmstrip gives you access to all of the images in your catalog or collection at any stage in your workflow. You can use the Filmstrip to quickly navigate through a selection of images or to switch between different sets of images without returning to the Library module.

▶ **Tip:** If you don't see the Filmstrip across the base of the workspace, choose Show Filmstrip from the Window > Panels menu, or press the F6 key.

You can work directly with the thumbnails in the Filmstrip—just as you do in the Library module's Grid view—to assign ratings, flags, and color labels; apply metadata and develop presets; and rotate, move, or delete photos.

By default, the Filmstrip displays the same set of images as the Grid view in the Library module; it can show every image in the library, the contents of a selected source folder or collection, or a selection filtered by a range of search criteria.

The side panels

● **Note:** This is the default configuration of the side panels but you can swap the panel groups in every module or just in the Develop module. Under the Lightroom Classic menu in macOS or the Edit menu in Windows, go to Preferences > Interface and select Swap Only Develop Left And Right Panel Groups or Swap Left And Right Panel Groups in the Panels section at the top.

As you move from module to module, the content of the side panels will change, offering you tools specific to that module. A quick way to think of this layout is that the panels in the left group of any module help you navigate to, preview, find, and select images, while panels in the right group allow you to edit or customize the settings for your selected photo.

In the Library module, for example, you'll use the panels on the left, below the Navigator preview (Catalog, Folders, Collections, and Publish Services), to locate and group the images you want to work with or share and the panels on the right, below the Histogram panel (Quick Develop, Keywording, Keyword List, Metadata, and Comments), to apply changes to your selected photo.

In the Develop module, you'll choose develop presets on the left and fine-tune their settings on the right. In the Slideshow, Print, and Web modules, you'll select a layout template on the left and customize its appearance on the right.

Left panels, Develop module.   Right panels, Develop module.   Left panels, Web module.   Right panels, Web module.

Customizing the workspace

As you spend more time working through Lightroom, you'll notice that you won't work with every single panel. Thankfully, you have the option to quickly modify the layout of each panel to fit your specific workflow. Keep in mind that the configuration of each layout is on a module-by-module basis. This is a good thing, as your needs will vary as you move across the modules.

Click the outer margin at the top, sides, and bottom of the workspace (the black bar with the gray triangle at its center), or use the commands and shortcuts listed in the Window > Panels menu, to show or hide any of the panels that surround the work area. Right-click the side and bottom margins, and in the menu, you can set the side panels or the Filmstrip to show and hide in response to your pointer movements so that information, tools, and controls appear only when you need them. You can also drag to adjust the width of the side panel groups or the height of the Filmstrip panel as needed.

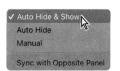

You can expand any of the panels on the right and left sides by clicking the triangle beside its name. Right-click any panel header to access a menu where you can hide panels you seldom use, creating more space for those you access more often, or reduce clutter by choosing Solo Mode so that all the panels other than the one you're working with close automatically.

The View > Grid View Style menu and the Library View Options dialog box (View > View Options) allow you to customize the appearance of the thumbnail image cells in the Grid view. You can have thumbnails displayed in either compact or expanded cells, and you can specify how much information about the images will be shown for each view style.

If you use a second monitor, click the Second Window button (the rectangle with a "2" inside, located at the upper left of the Filmstrip) to set up an additional view that is independent of the module and view mode on your main monitor. You can use the view picker at the top of the secondary display, or right-click the Second Window button to access its menu, to customize the view and the way it responds to your actions in the main workspace.

Tip: Make sure you check out the downloadable content to see a video on how to customize your workspace. See the "Getting Started" section at the beginning of the book for how to access it.

Tip: Lightroom Classic allows you to reorganize the panels in the Develop module. We'll cover how (and why) to set up your own panel configuration in Lesson 5, "Developing Basics."

Tip: To choose from a more limited set of display options for the thumbnails in the Filmstrip, right-click the Filmstrip and choose View Options from the menu.

The Lightroom Classic modules

▶ **Tip:** The Sync icon at the right of the Module Picker allows you to check the amount of storage you have used online and pause the syncing of images with the cloud.

Lightroom Classic has seven modules: Library, Develop, Map, Book, Slideshow, Print, and Web. Each module offers a set of tools for a different phase of your workflow: the Library module for importing, organizing, and publishing your photos; the Develop module for correcting, adjusting, and enhancing images; and specialized modules for creating stylish presentations for screen, print, or web.

Use the Module Picker, or the commands and keyboard shortcuts listed in the Window menu, to move between each of these modules as you work.

Library ⌕ Develop | Map | Book | Slideshow | Print | Web | ☁

The Lightroom Classic workflow

The Lightroom Classic interface makes it easy to manage every stage of your workflow, from image import to the final print.

- **Import:** In the Library module, you can import images from your memory card, hard disk or other storage media, or directly into your Lightroom catalog from your camera through a tethering session.

- **Organize:** You can attach keywords and other metadata to your photos during the import process, making this task much quicker. Once the photos have been added to your catalog, use the Library and Map modules to manage them—to tag, sort, and search your image library and create collections to group your photos. You can even share these collections online with others, providing feedback on your images.

- **Process:** Crop, adjust, correct, retouch, and apply effects to your images one at a time or en masse in the Develop module.

- **Create:** In the Book, Slideshow, Print, and Web modules, you can put together polished presentations and layouts to showcase your work.

- **Output:** The Book, Slideshow, Print, and Web modules each have their own output options and export controls. The Library module hosts the Publish Services panel for sharing your images online. With each of these, you have the opportunity to export the right image, at the right resolution, for the right task.

In the exercises that follow, you'll go through a typical workflow as you familiarize yourself with the Lightroom Classic workspace.

▶ **Tip:** If you wish to process your images further in your favorite pixel-based editor as part of your workflow, you can launch an external application from inside the Library or Develop modules and Lightroom will keep track of the changes that you make.

Importing photos

You can import photos into your Lightroom Classic library from your hard disk, from your camera or memory card reader, or from external storage media. (We'll cover this in a lot more detail in Lesson 2.)

Before you start on the exercises, make sure you've set up the LRC2024CIB folder for your lesson files and created the LRC2024CIB Catalog file to manage them, as described in "Accessing the lesson files and Web Edition" and "Creating a catalog file for working with this book" in the "Getting Started" section at the beginning of this book.

If you haven't already, log in to your peachpit.com account to download the files for this lesson, or follow the instructions under "Accessing the lesson files and Web Edition" in the "Getting Started" section.

1 Start Lightroom Classic. In the Select Catalog dialog box, make sure that the file LRC2024CIB Catalog.lrcat is selected in the list of recently opened catalogs, and then click Open.

2 Lightroom Classic will open in the screen mode and workspace module that were active when you last quit. If necessary, switch to the Library module by clicking Library in the Module Picker at the top of the workspace.

3 Choose File > Import Photos And Video. If the Import dialog box appears in compact mode, as shown here, click the Show More Options button at the lower left of the dialog box to access all of the options available in the expanded Import dialog box.

The layout of the header bar of the Import screen reflects the steps in the import process: working from left to right, first specify the source location of the files you wish to import; next, select the appropriate type of import; and then designate a destination (for Copy and Move imports) and set batch processing options.

4 In the Source panel at the left of the expanded Import dialog box, navigate to the Lessons folder inside the LRC2024CIB folder on your hard disk.

5 Select the lesson01 folder. Click the Check All button at the lower left of the preview grid to ensure that all of the images in the lesson01 folder are selected for import.

Note: If you can't see the Module Picker, choose Window > Panels > Show Module Picker, or press the F5 key. Note that in macOS, the function keys are assigned to specific operating system functions by default and may not work as expected in Lightroom. If you find this to be the case, either press the fn key (not available on all keyboards) together with the F5 key or change the keyboard behavior in the system preferences.

Note: When first choosing Import Photos And Video, Lightroom Classic may ask to access parts of your system before opening the Import dialog box.

6   In the import options just above the thumbnail previews, click Add so that the imported photos will be added to your catalog without being moved or copied.

7   In the File Handling panel at the right of the expanded Import dialog box, choose Minimal from the Build Previews menu. Disable the Build Smart Previews option and enable Don't Import Suspected Duplicates.

8   In the Apply During Import panel, choose None from both the Develop Settings menu and the Metadata menu, and then type **Lesson 01, Aguada** (including the comma) in the Keywords text box. Make sure that your import is set up as shown here, and then click Import.

Thumbnails of the Lesson 1 images appear in the Grid view of the Library module and also in the Filmstrip at the bottom of the workspace. If you don't see the Filmstrip, press the F6 key or choose Window > Panels > Show Filmstrip.

Reviewing and organizing

When you're working with a library with many images, you'll need to be able to find exactly what you're looking for quickly. Lightroom provides multiple tools that make organizing and finding your files easy.

I make it a habit of going through my images immediately to sort them into groups and place them into collections. Investing a little time on the front end can help you later by making it easier to find what you need.

You've already taken the first step toward structuring your catalog by tagging the lesson images with the keyword *Aguada* as they were imported.

Tagging photos with keywords is an intuitive and versatile way to organize your catalog. Tags let you sort and search your library based on whatever words you choose to associate with your images, making it easy to find the files you need, regardless of how they are named or where they are located.

About keywords

Keywords are labels (such as *desert* or *Dubai*) that you can attach to your images to make them easy to find and organize. Shared keywords create virtual groupings within your library, linking photos by association, although the image files may actually be stored in many separate locations.

Assign one or more keywords to your images and you can easily retrieve them by searching your library using the Metadata and Text filters located in the Filter bar across the top of the work area.

You can use keywords to sort your photos into photographic categories, organizing them according to content by tagging them with the names of people, places, activities, or events. The key here is to tag your images with general keywords to start and then add more refined keywords later in the organizational process.

Attach multiple keywords to your images to make retrieving the pictures you want even easier. For example, you could quickly find all the photos that you've tagged with the keyword *Dubai* and then narrow the search to only those that are also tagged *desert*. The more tags you attach to your photos, the more chances you have of finding exactly the right image when you need it.

For more on working with keywords, see Lesson 4, "Managing Your Photo Library."

Culling your images

Once your images are imported, it's a good idea to do a quick sort. The goal here is to flag images that you know were not successful as rejected, and flag images that you believe were successful as picked images. We'll talk about this method later in more detail, but let's quickly go over it here.

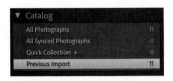

Tip: Press Command+Return/ Ctrl+Enter to see your images large in a slide-show. The slideshow plays according to the current settings in the Slideshow module and will repeat until you press the Esc key to return to the Library.

1 Press the spacebar or double-click an image to see it larger. Then, press Shift+Tab to hide all of the panels around the main work area. Once those panels are hidden, press the L key to dim everything onscreen except your image by 80%, known as Lights Out mode. Pressing the L key again will dim everything outside your image to 100% black.

Dimming the interface allows you to simply focus on the image that is in front of you. At this point you are trying to make only one choice: is this image successful or not?

2 Press the P key on your keyboard to flag the image currently displayed in your slideshow as a pick (⚐), press the X key to flag it as rejected (⚑), or press the U key to remove any flags. Press the right arrow key to move to the next image. Flag several of the Lesson 1 images as picks, and mark at least one as a reject.

The most important thing to remember is that if you have to think for a second about whether the image should be picked or rejected, skip it by pressing the right arrow key.

3 Press the Esc key to return to Grid view and then press L again to leave Lights Out mode.

Now, in the Library module, you can use the Filter bar above the thumbnail grid to search your images by text or metadata, and then refine your search by filtering for one or more of the searchable attributes—flag status, edits, rating, label color, or file type—so that only those photos you want are displayed in the Grid view and the Filmstrip. For now we want to show only the images that are unflagged.

4 If the Filter bar is not already visible above the work area, open it by choosing View > Show Filter Bar. Click Attribute, and in the Attribute bar, select the center Unflagged option (the gray flag, circled above).

5 Repeat the process of hiding your panels (if you showed them again after leaving Lights Out mode) and turning off your interface so you can focus on marking each image as a pick or as rejected. You'll know when you are finished with the

culling process when your image no longer changes. From here, press the L key to turn the lights back on, press Shift+Tab to bring back the panels, and deselect the Unflagged option in the Attribute bar. You can choose to display flags, along with other information, in the image cells in the Library views and in the Filmstrip. Images flagged as rejects appear grayed out, while those marked as picks are indicated by a white border. If you accidentally reject the wrong image, simply click your rejected image and press U to unflag it.

6   Stars can also help you rank your images in order of importance. To quickly assign a rating to the image that's currently displayed, press a number from 1 (for one star) to 5 (for five stars) on your keyboard. To remove the rating, press 0. You can attach only one rating to each photo; assigning a new rating will replace the old one. For the purposes of this exercise, mark three or four images with either 3, 4, or 5 stars.

▶ **Tip:** Whenever you use your keyboard to mark a photo in the impromptu slideshow, the rating, flag, or label you assign appears briefly in the lower-left corner of the screen to confirm your action.

Rating stars are displayed below the thumbnail images in the Grid view and in the Filmstrip, as shown in the illustration above.

Finally, color labels can be very useful to mark images for specific purposes or projects. You might use a red label for images you plan to crop, green for those that need correction, or blue to identify photos you wish to use in a particular presentation.

7   To assign a color label to the image currently displayed, use the number keys. Press 6 on your keyboard to assign a red color label, press 7 for yellow, 8 for green, or 9 for blue. There's no keyboard shortcut to assign a purple color label. To remove a color label, simply press the same number again. Assign different color labels to several of the images, and then remove one.

In the Library module's Grid view, and in the Filmstrip, a photo with a color label will be framed in that color when it's selected and surrounded by a tinted image cell background when it's not, as shown at the right.

Remember, you can go back into the Library Filter and find specific images using all of these criteria. For example, can you find a picked image that is a 5-star image and also assigned a color label of Green?

Select all three of those markers and you will see an image that matches those criteria. If an image is not available, make sure to rank one with all three before you apply the filter.

Working with collections

Once you've marked specific images with flags, ratings, or color labels, you can group the resulting photos as a *collection*. A collection is an organized set of images from anywhere in your Lightroom catalog. While we'll get into this in more detail in a later lesson, I think collections are a cornerstone of your organization and merit getting under your belt as soon as possible. Here's a quick look at the different types of collections:

- **Quick Collection:** A temporary holding collection in the Catalog panel, where you can assemble a selection of images on an ad hoc basis.

- **"Standard" collection:** A more permanent grouping of images in the Collections panel.

- **Smart collection:** A selection of images automatically filtered from your library according to specific criteria.

- **Collection set:** A container that allows you to store multiple collections or other collection sets in it. It is largely used for organization.

For this exercise, you'll create a standard collection.

1 Ensure that Previous Import is selected in the Catalog panel. Choose View > Sort > File Name; the Grid view and the Filmstrip should display all images. If you cannot see all of your images, make sure that you deselect any attributes or click None in the Library Filter bar.

Tip: A selected image is highlighted in the Grid view and the Filmstrip by a narrow white border (or a colored border if the image has a color label) and a lighter cell background color. If more than one photo is selected, the active photo is shown with an even lighter background. Some commands will affect only the active photo, while others affect all selected photos.

Note: Don't worry if your Grid view doesn't show all the information seen here. We'll discuss the different View Options later in this lesson.

Once you import more images, the Previous Import folder will update, and you'll no longer be able to isolate this particular group of images by selecting that entry in the Catalog panel. In this case, you could still retrieve this group by selecting its folder in the Folders panel or searching the Lesson 01 keyword, but it isn't as easy to retrieve a group of photos that don't share a keyword or that are spread across separate folders. Because of this, it's best to create a collection, a virtual grouping that is permanently listed in the Collections panel, allowing you to access that same set at any time with a single click.

2   Before we create this collection, press Command+A/Ctrl+A to select all of the images in the Grid view.

3   Click the plus sign (+) icon at the upper right of the Collections panel and choose Create Collection. In the Create Collection dialog box, type **Lesson 01 - Aguada** as the collection name. Under Location, leave the Inside A Collection Set option disabled. Under Options, ensure that Include Selected Photos is selected and the other options are unselected; then click Create.

Your new collection is now listed in the Collections panel. The listing includes an image count showing that this collection contains 11 photos.

Rearranging and deleting images in a collection

One drawback to working with images in the Previous Import or All Photographs folder (listed in the Catalog panel) is that you don't have many options for reorganizing your images. The thumbnails are ordered either by capture time (the default) or by the other choices in the Sort menu in the Toolbar.

With a collection, however, you're free to rearrange the images in any order in either the Grid view or the Filmstrip, and you can even remove them from the working view without deleting them from the catalog.

1   If your new collection is not already selected in the Collections panel, click to select it now. Choose Edit > Select None or press Command+D/Ctrl+D.

2   In the Filmstrip, Command-click/Ctrl-click to select the fourth and sixth images and drag the selection over the dividing line between the first and second thumbnails in the Filmstrip. Release the mouse button when the black insertion line appears.

> **Tip:** Collections can be nested using collection sets. For example, you could create a Portfolio collection set and then create nested collections for Portraits, Scenic, Product Shots, Black & White, and so on. Each time you import an outstanding new image, add it to one of these collections to slowly build up your photo portfolio.

> **Tip:** You can drag the thumbnail of one of your selected images, rather than the image cell frame, to move it.

The selected photos snap to their new positions in the Grid view and the Filmstrip.

3 Deselect the photos by clicking an empty area in the main work area. Click to select the first thumbnail in the Grid view and drag it over the border between the fifth and sixth images. Release the mouse button when the black insertion line appears. In the Toolbar, the Sort criterion has changed to Custom Order.

4 Choose Edit > Select None if any images are selected. Click the third image in the grid (lesson01-0002) to select it. Then, right-click the selected image and choose Remove From Collection from the menu.

In the Collections panel (and in the header bar of the Filmstrip) the image count shows that the new collection now contains only 10 images.

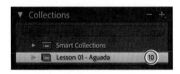

Although you've removed a photo from the collection, it has not been deleted from your catalog. The Previous Import and All Photographs folders in the Catalog panel still contain all 11 images. A collection contains only links to the files in your catalog; deleting a link does not affect the file in the catalog.

There are two benefits to using images in collections. First, you can add an image to as many collections as you like since they are simply references to images in your Lightroom catalog, not copies. Second, if you make any change to one of the images in a collection, all of the other instances of that image in other collections will be changed as well. This allows for better picture housekeeping and gives you more opportunities to experiment with your work. We'll go into more examples of how to make collections really work for you in Lesson 4.

▶ **Tip:** Should you wish to edit the same image differently in two collections, you'll first need to make a virtual copy—an additional catalog entry for the image—for inclusion in the second collection. You'll learn about this in Lesson 5.

Comparing photos side by side

Sometimes you'll need the ability to compare images to one another to find the best in a series. Lightroom's Compare mode will prove very useful here:

Tip: If at any point you want to check metadata from your images, press I to cycle through your chosen info overlays.

1   Press Command+D/Ctrl+D to deselect all images. Select two images in the Filmstrip, and then click the Compare View icon in the Toolbar, choose View > Compare, or press C on your keyboard to switch to Compare view.

2   The Select photo is active by default on the left. The right arrow key on your keyboard will let you move the next photo in the Filmstrip into the Candidate position. Keep pressing the right arrow to cycle through the other images.

3   Press the Tab key on your keyboard, and then press F5 to hide the side and top panels so that your photos can be displayed at a larger size in the Compare view.

4   Once you find an image that should replace the selected image, click the Swap icon in the Toolbar below the Candidate image to swap the Candidate and Select

Tip: If you're on a Mac without a full-size keyboard, press the fn key and then the F5 key.

images. Go back to using the arrows to compare the new Select photo with other candidates from the collection.

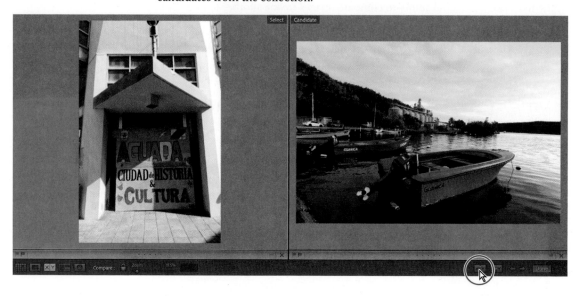

5   Once you have the image you want, click the Done button at the right end of the Toolbar. The Select image will appear in the single-image Loupe view.

Comparing several photos

While Compare view lets you compare two images, Survey view is better when you are trying to pick the best image out of a series. In Survey view, you can compare several photos at once and narrow your selection until only the best one remains.

▶ **Tip:** Having a group of images side by side can be helpful in selecting a 5-star image or an image that needs to be flagged for editing. You can continue to use flags, stars, and color labels to classify your images while in Survey view.

1   Choose Edit > Select None. In the Filmstrip, Command-click/Ctrl-click any five images and then click the Survey view icon (next to the Compare view icon) in the Toolbar. Alternatively, choose View > Survey or press N on your keyboard.

Survey view displays all of the selected images; the more images you select, the smaller the individual previews in Survey view. The active image has a thin border around it; to activate a different photo, you can either click its thumbnail in the Filmstrip or click the image directly in the work area.

2   If you have two images you'd like to compare more directly, simply drag one next to the other. The rest of the images will shuffle automatically.

3   As you move the pointer over each image, a Deselect Photo icon (⊠) appears in the lower-right corner. Click this icon to remove a photo from the selection in Survey view.

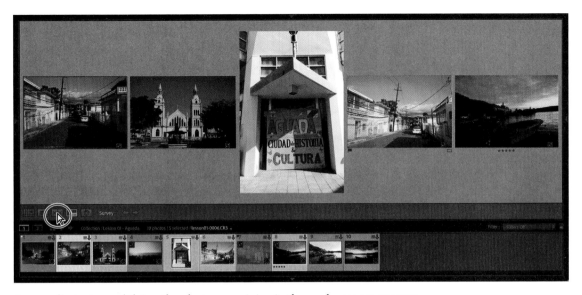

As you eliminate candidates, the photos remaining in the work area are progressively resized and shuffled to fill the space available. When you eliminate a photo from Survey view, the image is simply dropped from the selection, not removed from the collection.

▶ **Tip:** If you eliminate a photo accidentally, choose Edit > Undo Deselect Photo to return it to your Survey view, or Command-click/Ctrl-click the image in the Filmstrip. You can easily add a photo to the selection in the same way.

4 Eliminate photos from Survey view until your selection is narrowed down to a single image, and then press E on your keyboard to switch to the single-image Loupe view.

5 Press Shift+Tab (twice, if necessary) to show all of the workspace panels. Press G on your keyboard to return to the Grid view. Choose Edit > Select None.

Developing and editing

Once the images you want to edit are selected, it's time to bring out the very best in them. While the Develop module is extremely powerful, you can start your edits right inside the Library module with Quick Develop.

The Quick Develop panel offers simple controls for basic color correction and tonal adjustment, and a choice of preset crop and develop settings. For a finer degree of control, the Develop module offers an extended suite of sophisticated image processing tools in a more comprehensive and convenient editing environment.

Using Quick Develop in the Library module

In this exercise you'll quickly improve the color and tonal balance of an image and then tweak the results with the controls in the Quick Develop panel.

1   Select the Lesson 01 - Aguada collection to see all 10 images.

⬤ **Note:** If you can't see any images in your collection, check the Library Filter bar to make sure None is selected.

⬤ **Note:** If the Filmstrip is not visible, choose Window > Panels > Show Filmstrip or press F6 on your keyboard.

2   In the Filmstrip or Grid view, hold the pointer over the seventh picture in the group, lesson01-0008. You'll see basic image details displayed in a tool tip. Click the thumbnail to select it; the filename is also displayed in the status bar at the top of the Filmstrip. Press U to unflag the image.

3   Double-click the selected image in the Filmstrip to see it enlarged in Loupe view. Expand the Histogram and Quick Develop panels in the right panel group (if they're not already expanded) by clicking the arrow beside each panel's name.

▶ **Tip:** You can change your background color in Loupe view, Compare view, or Survey view by right-clicking the background behind the image(s) and choosing a new color.

▶ **Tip:** To make more space for the image in Loupe view, use the Show/Hide commands under the Window > Panels menu to hide the left panels, the Module Picker, and the Filmstrip. Commands for showing/hiding the Toolbar and Filter bar are listed in the View menu.

As you can see from both the image preview and the histogram, in this photo, everything is a bit underexposed and lacks midtone contrast, giving it a dull, flat look. The color could also use some work. Let's see how much better we can make it.

4   Click the Auto Tone Control button in the Quick Develop panel and watch the tone distribution curve shift in the Histogram panel.

Although the automatic adjustment isn't perfect, it could be an improvement. A lot of tone and color detail has been recovered from the darker shadows. These changes are reflected in the histogram, which has been pushed over to the right. The tonal balance, while drastically different, could still use some more work.

5 Click the triangle to the right of the Auto button to expand the Tone Control area. Click the right-most button (the right-facing double arrow) twice for Contrast control and the left-most button twice for Highlights. Click the right-most button once for Shadows, Clarity, and Vibrance. Finally, set the White Balance menu to Auto, and then click the triangle to the right of the menu to expand the White Balance area and click the leftmost button once for Temperature. This will give the photo a slightly cool, less yellow look.

● Note: Your results may look different and setting numbers may vary based on your monitor's calibration and whether you are working in macOS or Windows.

The adjusted image has more detail than the original in both the brightest and most shadowed areas, and the overall contrast and color is much better. Press D to switch to the Develop module and see how much we were able to get back from this raw file by pressing the backslash (\) key to toggle between a before and after view. Press E to get back to the Library module.

Working in the Develop module

The controls in the Quick Develop panel let you change settings but don't show you absolute values for the adjustments you make to your images.

In our example, there is no way to tell which parameters were modified by the Auto tone adjustment or how much they were shifted. For finer control, and a more comprehensive editing environment, you need to move to the Develop module.

1 Keeping the image from the previous exercise selected, switch to the Develop module now by doing one of the following:

- Click Develop in the Module Picker at the top of the workspace.

- Choose Window > Develop.

- Press Command+Option+2/Ctrl+Alt+2.

2 If necessary, press F7 to expand the left panel group, and then expand the History panel there and the Basic panel in the right panel group by clicking the triangle beside each panel's name. Collapse any other panels that are currently open, except the Navigator on the left and the Histogram on the right.

The History panel not only lists every modification you've made to a photo—even Quick Develop adjustments made in the Library module—but also enables you to return the image to any of its previous states.

The most recent White Balance adjustment you applied is at the top of the History list. The entry at the bottom of the list records the date and time of import. Clicking this entry will revert the photo to its original state. As you move the pointer over each entry, the Navigator displays a preview of the image at that stage of development.

The Basic panel displays numerical values for the adjustment settings that were unavailable in the Quick Develop panel. For our image in its most recent state, Exposure is set to +1.71; Contrast is set to +47; and Highlights, Shadows, Whites, Blacks, Clarity, Vibrance, and Saturation are set to −89, +76, +13, −29, +20, +32, and −1, respectively. Don't be concerned if your settings differ from these fractionally.

3 In the History panel, click the entry for the first modification you made to this photo—Auto Settings—and inspect the settings in the Basic panel.

For this image, clicking the Auto button modified all but one setting in the Tone area and only Vibrance and Saturation under Presence, but applying Auto tone to another photo may affect fewer settings and produce very different adjustment values.

4 Click the top entry in the History list to return the photo to its most recent state.

5 In the Toolbar (View > Show Toolbar), click the small triangle to the right of the Before/After button and choose Before/After Left/Right from the menu.

▶ **Tip:** In Lightroom Classic, you can clear the history of your file from the step you have selected. This command is located below Copy History Step Settings To Before when you right-click a step.

By comparing the Before and After images, you can see how much you've improved the photo with just a few clicks. Now let's look at how much difference your manual Quick Develop adjustments made after applying Auto tone.

6 Leaving the most recent White Balance adjustment activated in the History panel, right-click the entry for the Auto Settings adjustment, and choose Copy History Step Settings To Before from the menu.

● **Note:** If you don't see the Before/After button in the Toolbar, click the triangle at the right of the Toolbar and choose View Modes in the Toolbar menu.

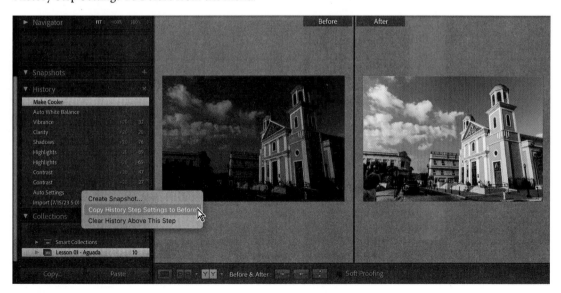

There's much more to learn about the correction and adjustment tools in the Develop module, but we'll leave that for later. For now, you'll straighten this slightly tilted photo and then crop it.

Straightening and cropping an image

Note: Lightroom Classic has a dedicated Edit tool to the left of the Crop tool just below the Histogram panel. This allows you to quickly get out of any localized adjustment and back to the Basic panel for editing.

1 Press D on your keyboard to switch to Loupe view in the Develop module.

2 Click the Crop Overlay tool (circled on top here), located just below the Histogram in the right panel group, or press the letter R. The Crop Overlay tool enables you to both crop and straighten an image.

3 A panel with tool-specific controls opens below the tool strip. Click the Straighten tool (circled at right). The pointer changes to a crosshairs cursor, and the level icon follows your movement across the image preview.

4 With the Straighten tool, drag a line that follows the top of the building on the left. Release the mouse button and the image is rotated so that your line becomes horizontal and the Straighten tool returns to its place in the Crop Overlay tool options (as shown here). If you are not satisfied with the result, undo the step (Command+Z/Ctrl+Z) and try again. You also can use the text box beside the Straighten tool slider to indicate a rotation, or you can drag the slider itself.

Lightroom overlays a cropping rectangle on the straightened photo positioned to achieve as large a crop as possible with the original aspect ratio while trimming away the angled edges. I went with a –3.40 rotation in the end.

▶ **Tip:** To maintain the original aspect ratio of an image when you crop it manually, make sure that Original is selected from the cropping Aspect menu and that the aspect ratio is locked.

If you wish to adjust the crop, you can drag any of the eight handles on the cropping rectangle. To assist with manual cropping, you can choose from a variety of grid overlays in the Tools > Crop Guide Overlay menu, or hide the grid by choosing Tools > Tool Overlay > Never Show.

5 When you're done, apply the crop by clicking the Crop Overlay tool or the Close button at the lower right of the tool options, or press Return/Enter. You can reactivate and adjust the crop at any time by clicking the tool again.

Adjusting lighting and tonal balance

Previously, we used the Quick Develop tone controls to adjust a picture. Let's go into the Develop module's Basic panel with another picture to see just how much tone we can pull out of an image.

1 While in the Develop module, press F6 and F7 (or use the Window > Panels menu) to show the Filmstrip and hide the left panels. In the Filmstrip, click to select lesson01-0009.dng, a set of boats in Guanica, Puerto Rico.

This image is (slightly) underexposed, although it has some really bright spots, the color is a little muted, and it lacks detail and focus.

2 Check the histogram at the top of the right panels for an idea of what you're working with. A lot of the pixels sit to the left side of the exposure graph here.

3 In the Basic panel, click the Auto adjustment button at the upper right of the Tone area, noting the effect on the histogram curve as well as the image in the work area.

The image looks quite a bit better with one button click. From a histogram point of view, the range is pushed toward the middle, thus the brightening,

> **Tip:** If there is one reason to make sure you are shooting images in a raw format, this is it. (I converted my raw files to DNG, which is Adobe's digital negative format and which we'll talk more about later.) The raw files out of your camera hold an incredible amount of information. It's up to us to get the most out of them in Lightroom!

and it seems a little more spread out, giving us increased contrast. This is a good starting point, but I think we can make it even better.

4 In the Basic panel, note that the Auto tone adjustment affected all six of the settings in the Tone area, as well as Vibrance and Saturation under Presence.

As the automatic adjustment moved this photo in the right direction, you can now use these settings as a starting point and then make manual adjustments to tweak the tonal balance, as you did with the simplified Quick Develop controls in the previous exercise.

5 Watch the change in the histogram, as well as the photo, as you move the Highlights slider to the left, or type in the text box, to reduce the value to −100.

Reducing the highlights may seem counterintuitive, but it has effectively drawn image data inward from the ends of the histogram curve toward the center, reducing the tonal range most affected by the trough. We can then use Exposure, Shadows, and Contrast to push that trough out to an acceptable range and finish with Whites, Temperature, and Tint.

6 Set Exposure to +0.69. Decrease Shadows to +54, Contrast to +6, Highlights to −68, Whites to +8, and Blacks at −17. This brings out a little more detail in the image.

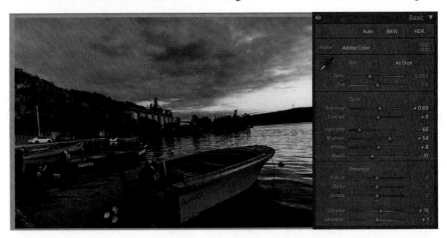

At this point, I think the Auto tone adjustment made the image look good, so these tweaks should finalize the tonal changes to the image. If you feel your image is too blue, you can drag the Temp slider to the right to warm it up a bit. The Tint slider is used to add green or magenta to the image. We'll talk more about how to set your white balance properly in Lesson 5.

7 Press F7, or use the Window > Panels menu, to show the left panels. In the History panel, click back and forth between the current state at the top of the

list, the Import state at the bottom, and the Auto Settings entry just above it, comparing the changes in the histogram as well as the results in the Loupe view. When you're done, leave the image open in Loupe view for the next exercise.

Original photo.

Auto tone.

Auto tone with manual adjustments.

Creating effects with the Radial Filter tool

To focus the viewer's attention, let's add a vignette. You can use the Radial Filter tool to create off-center custom vignettes by applying local adjustments to a selected area in an image through a feathered (soft-edged) elliptical mask.

There is a centered post-crop vignette in the Effects panel, but you can place the center of a Radial Filter adjustment anywhere in the photo, focusing the viewer's attention on whichever part of the image you choose.

By default, your local adjustments are applied to the area outside the ellipse, leaving the inside unaffected, but the Radial Filter's Invert option enables you to reverse the focus of the filter.

By applying multiple Radial Filter adjustments, you can treat the inside and outside areas differently, as shown here; highlight more than one area in the same image; or create an asymmetrical vignette.

In this exercise, you'll learn how to work with the Radial Filter tool as you set up a more complex effect that will add a little more color and atmosphere to our photo. You'll start by setting up a combination of adjustments that will be applied to the photograph through your first Radial Filter.

Note: Lightroom Classic 2024 added new features to the Masking tool that make it even more powerful. We'll cover them in depth in Lesson 6, "Advanced Editing."

1 Click the Masking tool below the Histogram in the right panel group, and in the masking options, select the Radial Gradient tool.

Once it is activated, a panel of tool options appears below the mask options. If necessary, double-click the Preset label in the section above the Tone sliders to reset those sliders to 0.

2 I want to bring the tone in the left center more into focus. Set the Temp slider to +10, set the Tint to −6, increase the Contrast setting to +27, increase Highlights to 51, and increase Whites to +100. Set the Feather control to 50.

3 Drag in the Loupe view with the Radial Gradient tool's crosshairs cursor, starting from a point near the center lower left of the boat. When you've created an oval and positioned and scaled it as shown in the illustration at the right, release the mouse button.

Tip: Radial Gradient adjustments scale from the center by default. Hold down Option/Alt to scale from one side.

Once created, the active Radial Filter adjustment is displayed with a circular *pin* at its center and four round control handles around its circumference. Whenever the tool is active, you can select an existing filter for editing by clicking its central pin, reposition it by dragging the pin, and resize the adjustment area or change its shape by dragging any of the round control handles.

By default, the Radial Filter adjustments are applied evenly across the unmasked parts of the image like an overlay. If needed, you can set up the Range control (at the bottom of the Point Color options) so the adjustments are applied only to a specific brightness (luminance) or a specific color in the image. We'll talk more about this in Lesson 6.

Tip: To prevent a reset all of the sliders every time you create a new mask, select Reset Sliders Automatically near the top of the tool options panel.

4 In the Color options, below the Tint control, you can use the Hue slider to adjust the overall hue of the area. Drag it to +14.

5 To give some added detail and emphasis to the image, we can add a little more detail. Texture will increase the contrast in the image, making it appear a little sharper as well. The Texture slider gives you a much better effect on the small contrast areas in an image without any of the drawbacks that Clarity would bring. Drag the Texture slider to a value of 35. Drag the Noise slider to −100 to reveal some of the grain of the original image.

Tip: If the colors you see onscreen differ significantly from those illustrated, consider calibrating your display. See the macOS/Windows Help for instructions. Slighter differences may be a result of conversion from RGB to CMYK color for printing.

The image is almost complete, but there are four bright spots that appear at the top right that may be distracting in a print. To get rid of them, we'll quickly tour the Healing tool in Lightroom Classic.

Using the Healing tool

Try as we may to prevent it, there will always be spots in our images that need to be removed. A spot can come from particles that have collected on your sensor after changing lenses several times (or in this case, a bright spot in the clouds). Blemishes can also be things in a picture that you don't want to call attention to, like a hand that doesn't belong in the frame or a telephone pole that appears to be coming out of someone's head. Lightroom's Healing tool provides you with tools that help see imperfections better and remove them quickly.

1   Activate the Healing tool (the third tool from the left, directly under the Histogram) by clicking it or pressing the letter Q on your keyboard.

2   The Healing tool has three options: Heal, Clone, and Content-Aware Remove. Clone allows you to make a direct copy from one area to another. Heal attempts to blend the pixels to create a more natural look. Content-Aware Remove does a great job of using AI technology to remove trouble spots in an image. Depending on your Mode choice, you

Tip: Press the bracket keys ([,]) to decrease or increase the brush size of the Healing tool.

also can control the size of the brush, the softness of the brush's edge (Feather), and how opaque your result is (Opacity).

3   To better see spot problems in an image, click the Visualize Spots option at the bottom of the toolbar. The image is inverted in black and white, making it easier

to see any spots. You can adjust the image contrast with the slider to the right. Adjust the slider until you see the spots at the top of the image.

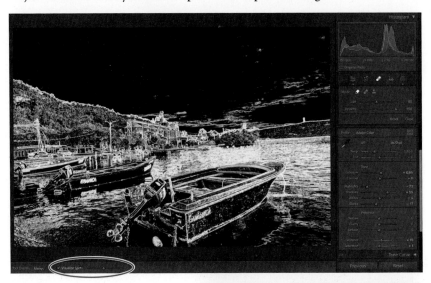

4   After selecting the Content-Aware Remove option, adjust the brush to the size of the spot and click once right over the spot; Lightroom uses content-aware technology to remove the spot. When it does, a circle appears with the Content-Aware icon (it looks like an eraser). If you're not happy with the result, hold down the Command/Ctrl key and drag over a portion of the image that you want to use as a source for the repair.

5   The great part about the Healing tool is that it's not just limited to spots. Deselect Visualize Spots. Now, drag over a non-round object in the photo (like where you can see the buoy in the water) and a highlighted stroke will appear. Release the mouse button and Lightroom will use Content-Aware to fix it. As before, you can always adjust the result after the fact.

With the new Content-Aware Remove technology and experimentation, it's like we were never even there.

With the image complete, it's time to send this picture off. Click the Edit icon at the left end of the tool strip below the Histogram panel or click Close at the bottom of the Healing tool's options.

Sharing your work by email

Now that you've edited and enhanced your photos, the final step in your workflow is to present them to your client, share them with friends and family, or publish them for the world to see on a photo-sharing website or in your own web gallery. In Lightroom Classic, it takes only minutes to create a sophisticated photo book or slideshow, customize a print layout, publish your photos online, or generate a stylish interactive gallery ready to be uploaded directly to your web server from within Lightroom.

Lessons 8–10 (about creating photo books, slideshows, and prints of your images) and the online bonus lesson, "Publishing Your Photos," provide much more detail on the many Lightroom Classic tools and features that make it simple to create professional-looking presentations, layouts, and galleries to showcase your photos. In this exercise, you'll learn how you can attach your finished images to an email without leaving Lightroom Classic.

1   Press G to return to Grid view, and then press Command+D/Ctrl+D or choose Edit > Select None. In the Filmstrip, Command-click/Ctrl-click to select the two photos that you've edited in this lesson, lesson01-0008.dng and lesson01-0009.dng.

● **Note:** For Windows
users: If you have not
specified a default
email application in
Windows, the sequence
of dialog boxes you
see may differ slightly
from that described and
illustrated here (from
macOS). The process is
basically the same, but
you may need to refer
to steps 8, 9, and 10 to
set up an email account
with Lightroom before
returning to this step.

2 Choose File > Email Photos.

Lightroom automatically detects the default email application on your computer
and opens a dialog box where you can set up the address, subject, and email account
for your message and specify the size and quality of the attached images.

3 Click the Address button to open your Lightroom address book. Click New
Address, enter a contact name and email address, and click OK.

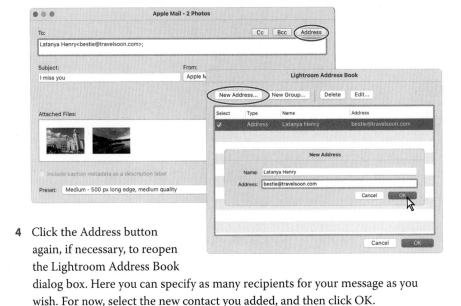

4 Click the Address button
again, if necessary, to reopen
the Lightroom Address Book
dialog box. Here you can specify as many recipients for your message as you
wish. For now, select the new contact you added, and then click OK.

5 Next, type a subject line for your email.

6 Choose your image size and quality options from the Preset menu at the bottom.

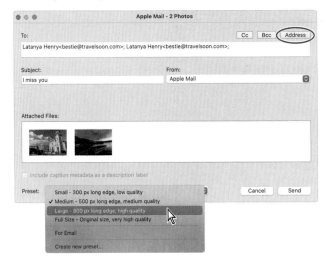

7 If you intend to use your default email application, you're ready to click Send and add your message in the standard email window.

8 If you'd prefer to connect directly to a web-based mail service, you need to set up an account. In the From menu, choose Go To Email Account Manager.

9 In the Lightroom Email Account Manager dialog box, click the Add button at the lower left. In the New Account dialog box, enter your email account name, choose your service provider, and then click OK.

10 Enter your email address and password under Credential Settings in the Lightroom Email Account Manager dialog box, and then click Validate.

Lightroom uses your credential settings to verify your account online. In the Lightroom Email Account Manager dialog box, a green light indicates that your web-based email account is now accessible by Lightroom.

11 Click Done to close the Lightroom Email Account Manager. Type a message in the text box above the thumbnails of your attached images; change the font, text size, and text color if you wish; and then click Send.

Review questions

1 What is non-destructive editing?

2 What are the seven Lightroom workspace modules, and how does each relate to your workflow?

3 How many Healing tools are in Lightroom Classic? What makes each of them different?

4 How can you increase the viewing area without resizing the application window?

5 What advantage is there to grouping images in a collection rather than by keyword?

6 What is the difference between editing a photo using the Quick Develop panel in the Library module and editing it in the Develop module?

7 How can I adjust what Lightroom Classic selected as a result for the Content-Aware Remove tool?

Review answers

1 Non-destructive editing means that whatever modifications you make to an image in your library—cropping, rotation, corrections, retouching, or effects—Lightroom records the editing information only in the catalog file. The original image data remains unchanged, like a digital negative.

2 The Lightroom workflow begins in the Library module: a hub where you'll import, organize, sort, and search your photos; manage your growing catalog; and keep track of the images you publish. You can leverage GPS metadata to organize your photos by location in the Map module. Move to the Develop module for a comprehensive editing environment with all of the tools you need to correct, retouch, and enhance digital images and ready them for output. The Book, Slideshow, Print, and Web modules each provide a range of stylish preset templates together with a suite of powerful, intuitive controls to help you customize them so that you can quickly create sophisticated layouts and presentations to share and showcase your work in its best light.

3 There are three different Healing tools in Lightroom Classic. The Clone tool replaces a problem area with another area of your choosing. The Healing tool creates a blending of the surrounding areas to remove a blemish. The Content-Aware Remove tool uses Content-Aware match technology to remove imperfections.

4 You can hide any of the panels and panel groups surrounding the center work area. The working view automatically expands into the space available. The work area is the only part of the Lightroom workspace that you cannot hide from view.

5 The difference between grouping images in a collection and applying shared keywords is that, in a collection, you can change the order of the photos displayed in the Grid view and the Filmstrip and easily remove an image from the group.

6 The Quick Develop panel gives you simple controls for basic color correction and tonal adjustment, as well as a choice of preset crop and develop settings. The Develop module offers a finer degree of editing with sophisticated image processing tools in a more comprehensive and convenient editing environment.

7 If you do not like the results of the Content-Aware Remove tool, you can hold down the Command/Ctrl key and draw an area for the tool to sample from.

PHOTOGRAPHY SHOWCASE
MARY BEL

"I used a camera and Photoshop as a way to…turn my emotional feelings into something physical that others can see."

My photographic journey began while going through a divorce. I wanted to pick up photography as a hobby, but felt I needed practice before working with models or families. I watched countless tutorials, read magazines, and attended various workshops in order to increase my knowledge of photography. I just jumped in and started practicing the techniques I learned on myself. I wanted to escape the turmoil of my personal life by making images. After a long day of work, cooking dinner, helping kids with homework, and putting them to bed, I locked myself in my bedroom, placed my camera on a tripod, and used a remote to fire the trigger. I had so much fun experimenting with speedlights, gradually moving the light off the camera. Then, over time, I added modifiers in order to mold the light.

I always desired to be a painter or illustrator, but was never any good at drawing. So I used a camera and Photoshop as a way to digitally add myself into places and also turn my emotional feelings into something physical that others can also see. I started sharing these images on Facebook, where they resonated with so many people. Thus, I kept documenting my journey of self-discovery and healing through self-portraits. Today, my self-portrait fine art prints have been displayed at Miami Art Week, I have been a featured artist in Orlando art galleries, I won a Photoshop World Guru Award, and I received a Sony Alpha Female+ grant. Today, I am a very proud instructor for KelbyOne and enjoy doing commercial photography.

www.marybelphotography.com/
instagram.com/marybelphotography/

2 BRINGING PHOTOS INTO LIGHTROOM CLASSIC

Lesson overview

Lightroom Classic allows a great deal of flexibility when importing photos: You can download them directly from a camera, import them from an external drive, or transfer them between catalogs on separate computers. During the import process, you can organize folders, add keywords and metadata to make your photos easier to find, make backup copies, and even apply editing presets. In this lesson, you'll learn how to:

- Import images from a camera or card reader.

- Import images from a hard disk or removable media.

- Evaluate images before importing.

- Organize, rename, and process images automatically.

- Implement a backup strategy.

- Set up automatic importing and create import presets.

- Acquire images from other catalogs and applications.

 This lesson will take about 90 minutes to complete. To get the lesson files used in this chapter, download them from the web page for this book at *peachpit.com/LightroomCIB2024*. For more information, see "Accessing the lesson files and Web Edition" in the "Getting Started" section at the beginning of this book.

esson02-007.cr3
2/19/22 1:25:23 PM
192 x 5464

Embedded Preview

Lightroom Classic helps you to begin organizing and managing your growing photo library. From the moment you click the Import button, you can make backups, create and organize folders, inspect images at high magnification, and add keywords and other metadata that will save you hours of sorting and searching your image library later—and all this before your photos even reach your catalog!

Getting started

Before you begin, make sure you've set up the LRC2024CIB folder for your lesson files and downloaded the lesson02 folder from your Account page at peachpit.com to the LRC2024CIB\Lessons folder, as described in "Accessing the lesson files and Web Edition" in the "Getting Started" section at the start of this book. Also, be sure you have created the LRC2024CIB Catalog file to manage the lesson files, as detailed in "Creating a catalog file for working with this book," also in the "Getting Started" section.

1 Start Lightroom Classic. In the Select Catalog dialog box, make sure that LRC2024CIB Catalog.lrcat is selected, and then click Open.

▶ **Tip:** If you can't see the Module Picker, choose Window > Panels > Show Module Picker, or press the F5 key. If you're working on macOS, you may need to press the fn key together with the F5 key or change the function key behavior in the system preferences.

2 Lightroom Classic will open in the screen mode and workspace module that were active when you last quit. If necessary, switch to the Library module by clicking Library in the Module Picker at the top of the workspace.

Lightroom is your digital notebook

Before we begin, I want to share with you an analogy that I think helps explain what Lightroom does in terms of organization. I'll come back to this analogy from time to time throughout the book.

Imagine you are sitting at home when someone knocks on the door and gives you a box of pictures. They ask you to store the pictures for safekeeping, so you take the box into your home and place it on top of your desk in the living room. To remember where you placed those pictures, you pull out a notebook and write down that they are in a box on the desk in the living room.

There's another knock at the door, and another box of pictures appears. You take these pictures and place them inside one of the drawers in your bedroom. You want to remember where they are, so you write it down in your notebook. More boxes of pictures appear, and you continue to place them in different areas of your house, writing down the location of each box of pictures in your notebook—there are lots of boxes of pictures, and you don't want to forget!

That notebook becomes the central record of where the boxes of pictures are stored in your home.

Now, imagine that you're bored one day while at home, and you take the pictures that are in the box on top of the desk in the living room and place them in a particular order. You want to make a note of this change, so you write down in your notebook that the pictures on top of the desk in the living room have been organized in a specific fashion.

The notebook you've been using serves as the master record of the location of each box of pictures inside your home, as well as a record of all of the changes you've made to each picture.

That notebook is your Lightroom catalog—your Lightroom catalog is a digital notebook that keeps track of where your images are and what you have done to them.

Lightroom doesn't store your images; it stores information about your images in the catalog. This catalog includes a ton of information about each image (or video), including where the file lives on your drives; the camera settings at capture; any descriptions, keywords, ratings, and so on, that you apply in Lightroom's Library module; and a running list of every edit you make in Lightroom's Develop module.

When you think of your Lightroom catalog, just think of a digital notebook that's keeping track of where you put your pictures and what you are doing with them.

The import process

Lightroom Classic has a number of options for importing your images. You can import directly from a digital camera or card reader, your hard disk, or any external storage media, or you can transfer them from another Lightroom catalog or from other applications. You can import at the click of a button, use a menu command, or simply drag and drop. Lightroom can launch the import process as soon as you connect your camera, or import automatically whenever you move files into a specified folder. Wherever you're acquiring photos from, it will be important to become familiar with the Import dialog box.

The top section of the Import dialog box presents the basic steps in the import process, arranged from left to right: choose an import source, specify how Lightroom is to handle the files you're importing, and then—if you choose to copy or move the source files—set up an import destination. If these are all of the details that you require to import the images, you can leave the dialog box set to compact mode. To access even more information, you can click the triangle at the lower left to expand to the full dialog box.

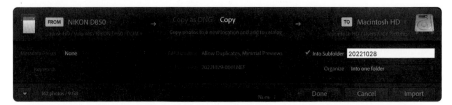

In expanded mode, the Import dialog box looks and works like the Lightroom Classic workspace modules. The Source panel at the left accesses your files on any available drive. The Preview area in the center displays images from the source as thumbnails in Grid view or enlarged in Loupe view. Depending on the type of import, the right panel group offers a Destination panel that mirrors the Source panel, and a set of controls for processing your images while they're being imported.

Importing photos from a digital camera

While this section outlines the process of importing from a camera pretty clearly, I recommend you try this with some sample images of your own. Take your camera and make 10–15 images of anything, really; just have something on the memory card that we can use for the import process.

The first step is to ensure the Lightroom preferences are set so that the import process is triggered automatically whenever you connect your camera or a memory card to your computer.

1   Choose Lightroom Classic > Preferences (macOS)/Edit > Preferences (Windows). In the Preferences dialog box, click the General tab. Under Import Options, select Show Import Dialog When A Memory Card Is Detected.

Some cameras generate folder names on the memory card. If you don't find these folder names helpful for organizing your images, select Ignore Camera-Generated Folder Names When Naming Folders. You'll learn more about folder naming options later in this lesson.

2   Click the Close button or OK to close the Preferences dialog box.

3   Connect your digital camera or card reader to your computer, following the manufacturer's instructions.

4   This step may vary depending on your operating system and the image management software on your computer:

•   In Windows, if the AutoPlay dialog box or settings pane appears, select the option to open image files in Lightroom Classic. If you wish, you can set this as the default by going to Settings > Devices > AutoPlay from the Start menu.

•   If you have more than one Adobe image management application—such as Adobe Bridge—installed on your computer and the Adobe Downloader dialog box appears, click Cancel.

•   If the Import dialog box appears, continue to step 5.

•   If the Import dialog box does not appear, choose File > Import Photos And Video, or click the Import button below the left panel group.

5 If the Import dialog box appears in compact mode, click the Show More Options button at the lower left of the dialog box to see all of the options in the expanded Import dialog box.

The top panel of the Import dialog box—visible in both the compact and expanded modes—presents three steps in the import process, arranged from left to right:

- Selecting the source location of the images you want to add to your catalog.

- Specifying how you want Lightroom to handle the files you're importing.

- Setting the destination to which the image files will be copied, with the option to choose any develop presets, keywords, or other metadata that you would like applied to your photos as they are added to your catalog below this panel.

Your camera or memory card is now shown as the import source in the FROM area at the left of the top panel and under Devices in the Source panel at the left of the Import dialog box.

Depending on your computer setup, it's possible that your camera's memory card will be recognized as a removable storage disk. If this is the case, you may see some differences in the options available in the Import dialog box, but it shouldn't affect anything.

● **Note:** If your memory card is recognized as a removable disk, the Move and Add options may not be disabled as illustrated here and on the next page; these import options are discussed later in this lesson.

6 If your memory card is listed as a removable disk—rather than a device—in the Source panel, click to select it from the Files list and make sure that Include Subfolders is selected.

7 From the import type options in the center of the top panel, choose Copy so that the photos are copied from your camera to your hard disk and then added to your catalog, leaving the original files on your camera's memory card.

Lightroom displays a brief description of the action that will be taken for whichever option is currently selected.

8 Move your pointer over each of the options shown in the bar across the top of the Preview pane to see a tool tip describing the option. For now, leave the default All Photos option selected, and don't click the Import button yet.

A checkmark in the upper-left corner of an image cell indicates that the photo will be imported. By default, all of the photos on your memory card will be selected for import. If you do not want to import an image, you can exclude it by clicking its checkbox to deselect it.

▶ **Tip:** Use the slider below the right side of the preview pane to change the size of the thumbnails.

You can select multiple images and then change all of their checkmarks simultaneously. To select a contiguous range of images, select the first image in the range by clicking the thumbnail or the surrounding image cell, and then hold down the Shift key and select the last image in the series. To select individual additional images, Command-click/Ctrl-click their thumbnails. Click the checkmark of any selected image to change the import status for the entire selection.

Notice that at the top of the import dialog, Copy is selected rather than Add. Keep in mind that, during the import process, Lightroom does not actually import the image files themselves; it only adds entries to the Lightroom catalog to record their locations. Because you're copying the files, you'll need to specify a destination.

If you were to select Add rather than Copy, you wouldn't have to specify a destination folder; the photos would stay where they are already stored. However, because memory cards are expected to be erased and reused, they should not be the permanent home for your pictures. Thus, you're not offered the Add and Move options when you import from a camera—Lightroom expects to copy your photos from your memory card to a more permanent location.

The next step, then, is to specify a destination folder to which your photos should be copied. This is the time to give some thought to how you intend to organize your photos on your hard drive. For now, leave the Import Photos dialog box open; you'll choose a destination folder and deal with the rest of the import options in the following exercises.

Organizing your copied photos in folders

By default, Lightroom tries to organize your images in the Pictures folder. You can choose any other location, but as a general rule, it is a good idea to keep all of your images organized into one location—no matter where that is. Nailing down that location (or workflow) early will help a ton in finding missing images (we'll talk about the workflow later in the book).

Before beginning the lessons in this book, you created a folder named LRC2024CIB inside your Users/*username*/Documents folder on your computer. This folder already contains subfolders for your LRC2024CIB Catalog file and for the image files used for the lessons in this book. For the purposes of this exercise, you'll create another subfolder inside the LRC2024CIB folder as the destination for the images that you import from your camera's memory card:

1   In the right panel group of the Import dialog box, collapse the File Handling, File Renaming, and Apply During Import panels; then, expand the Destination panel.

2   In the Destination panel, navigate to and select your LRC2024CIB folder; then, click the plus sign (+) button at the left of the Destination panel header and choose Create New Folder.

3   In the Browse For Folder/Create New Folder dialog box, navigate to and then select your LRC2024CIB folder, if it's not already selected. Click the New Folder button, type **Imported From Camera** as the name for your new folder, and then click Create/press Enter.

4   Make sure the new Imported From Camera folder is selected in the Browse For Folder/

Create New Folder dialog box, and then click the Choose/Select Folder button to close the dialog box. Note that the new folder is now listed and selected in the Destination panel.

The name of the new destination folder also appears in the TO area at the right of the top panel of the Import dialog box.

The Organize menu, near the top of the Destination panel, offers various options to help you organize your photos into folders as you copy them onto your hard disk:

- **Into One Folder** With the current settings, the images would be copied into the new Imported From Camera folder. Instead, you could select Into Subfolder to create a new subfolder for each import from your camera and type a name into the text box to the right. Here, I typed in the date with no punctuation added.

- **By Date:** *[Date Format]* These options are all variations on organizing your photos by capture date. Your images would be copied into one or more subfolders, depending on your choice of date format. Choosing the format "2023/09/09," for example, would result in one folder per year, containing one folder per month, containing one folder per day for each capture date. Or, choosing 2023 September 9 simply creates one folder per date.

> ◗ **Note:** If your memory card has been recognized as a removable disk, you may also see the Organize option By Original Folders; this option will be discussed later in this lesson.

Think about which system of folder organization best suits your needs before you import photos from your camera, and then maintain that system for all your camera imports. It will make your photos easier to find.

5 For the purposes of this exercise (and what I recommend to everyone as a default), choose Into One Folder from the Organize menu.

6 Select the Into Subfolder option at the top of the panel, type **Lesson 2 Import** in the adjacent text box as the new subfolder's name, and press Return/Enter. The subfolder should then appear inside the folder you chose in the bottom section of the Destination panel.

Backup strategies

Your next choice is whether to make backup copies of the images from your camera at the same time as Lightroom creates primary copies in the location you've just

About file formats

Camera raw formats Camera raw file formats contain unprocessed data from a digital camera's sensor. Most camera manufacturers save image data in a proprietary camera format. Lightroom reads the data from most cameras and processes it into a full-color photo. You can use the controls in the Develop module to process and interpret the raw image data for your photo. For a list of supported cameras and camera raw formats, see *https://helpx.adobe.com/photoshop/camera-raw.html*.

DNG format The Digital Negative (DNG) file format is a publicly available archival format for raw files generated by digital cameras. DNG addresses the lack of an open standard for raw files created by individual camera models, ensuring that photographers will be able to access their files in the future. You can convert proprietary raw files to DNG in Lightroom. For more information about the DNG file format, visit *https://helpx.adobe.com/photoshop/digital-negative.html*.

TIFF format Tagged-Image File Format (TIFF, TIF) is used to exchange files between applications and computer platforms. TIFF is a flexible bitmap image format supported by virtually all paint, image-editing, and page-layout applications. Also, virtually all desktop scanners can produce TIFF images. Lightroom supports large documents saved in TIFF format (up to 65,000 pixels per side). However, most other applications, including older versions of Photoshop (pre-Photoshop CS), do not support documents with file sizes greater than 2 GB. The TIFF format provides greater compression and industry compatibility than Photoshop document (PSD) format and is the recommended format for exchanging files between Lightroom and Photoshop. In Lightroom, you can export TIFF image files with a bit depth of 8 bits or 16 bits per channel.

JPEG format Joint Photographic Experts Group (JPEG) format is commonly used to display photographs and other continuous-tone images in web photo galleries, slideshows, presentations, and other online services. JPEG retains all color information in an RGB image but compresses file size by selectively discarding data. A JPEG image is automatically decompressed when opened. In most cases, the Best Quality setting produces a result indistinguishable from the original.

PSD format PSD is the standard Photoshop file format. To import and work with a multi-layered PSD file in Lightroom, the file must be saved in Photoshop with the Maximize PSD and PSB File Compatibility option activated. You'll find this option in the Photoshop file handling preferences. Lightroom saves PSD files with a bit depth or 8 bits or 16 bits per channel.

PNG format Portable Network Graphic (PNG) files will import, but transparency will appear white.

CMYK files Lightroom imports CMYK files, but edits and output are performed in the RGB color space.

Video files Lightroom will import video files from most digital cameras. You can tag, rate, filter, and include video files in collections and slideshows. Video files can be trimmed, and also edited with most of the Quick Edit controls. Click the camera icon on the video file's thumbnail to launch an external viewer such as QuickTime or Windows Media Player.

File format exceptions Lightroom doesn't support the following file types: Adobe Illustrator® files, Nikon scanner NEF files, or files with dimensions greater than 65,000 pixels per side or larger than 512 megapixels.

Note: To import photos from a scanner, use your scanner's software to scan to TIFF or DNG format.

Creating import presets

When you import photos on a regular basis, you'll probably find that you're setting up the same configurations of options over and over. Lightroom Classic enables you to streamline your import workflow by saving your preferred settings as import presets. To create an import preset, set up your import in the expanded Import dialog box, and then choose Save Current Settings As New Preset from the Import Preset menu below the Preview pane.

Type a descriptive name for your new preset, and then click Create.

Your new preset will include all of your current settings: the source, import type (Copy as DNG, Copy, Move, or Add), file handling and renaming options, develop and metadata presets, keywords, and destination. You might set up one preset to move photos from a memory card to your computer, and another preset to import from a memory card to a network-attached storage device. You could even create separate import presets tailored to the characteristics of different cameras so you can quickly apply your favorite noise reduction, lens correction, and camera calibration settings during the import process, saving yourself time in the Develop module later.

Using the Import dialog box in compact mode

Once you've created the presets you need, you can speed up the process even more by using the Import dialog box in compact mode, where you can use your import preset as a starting point and then change the source, metadata, keywords, and destination settings, as required.

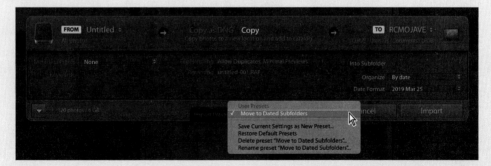

specified and adds them to the library catalog. For some, it's a good idea to create backup copies on a separate hard disk or on external storage media so you don't lose your images if your hard disk fails or you accidentally delete them.

1   In the right panel group of the Import dialog box, expand the File Handling panel and select the Make A Second Copy To option.

2   Click the small triangle to the right and select Choose Folder to specify a destination for your backup copies.

3   In the Browse For Folder/ Choose Folder dialog box, navigate to the folder in which you want to store the backup copies of your images, and then click Choose/Select Folder.

Keep in mind that the purpose of this backup is mainly as a precaution against loss of data due to disk failure or human error during the import process; it's not meant to replace the standard backup procedure you have in place—or should have in place—for the files on your hard disk.

For the most part, I don't use this backup option; I rely instead on a combination of my computer's backup system (Time Machine) and the use of my network-attached storage device. This is part of my personal workflow strategy, which I'll share with you and explain later in the book.

Renaming files as they are imported

The cryptic filenames created by digital cameras are not particularly helpful when it comes to sorting and searching your photo library. Lightroom can help by renaming your images for you as they are imported. You can choose from a list of predefined naming options or create your own customized naming templates.

▶ **Tip:** An option you should consider, if it's supported by your camera, is to set the camera to generate filenames with unique sequence numbers. When you clear your memory card, or change cards, your camera will continue to generate unique sequence numbers rather than starting the count from 1 again. This way, the images you import into your library will always have unique filenames.

1   In the Import dialog box's right panel group, expand the File Renaming panel and select Rename Files. Choose Custom Name - Sequence from the Template menu, type a descriptive name in the Custom Text box, and then press the Tab key on your keyboard. A sample name at the bottom of the File Renaming panel shows how your settings will be applied for the first image imported. You can enter a number other than 1 in the Start Number text box; this is useful if you're importing more than one batch of images from the same shoot or series (often from multiple memory cards).

2 Click the small triangle to the right of the Custom Text box; your new text has been added to a list of recently entered names. You can choose from this list if you import another batch of files that belong in the same series. This not only saves time and effort, but also ensures that subsequent batches are named identically. To clear the list, choose Clear List from the menu.

3 Choose Custom Name (x of y) from the Template menu. Note that the sample name at the bottom of the File Renaming panel updates to reflect the change.

4 Choose Edit from the Template menu to open the Filename Template Editor. Choose Custom Name - Sequence from the Preset menu.

In the Filename Template Editor dialog box, you can set up a filename template that makes use of metadata information stored in your image files—such as filenames, capture dates, or ISO settings—adding automatically generated sequence numbers and any custom text you specify. A filename template includes placeholders—or *tokens*—that will be replaced by actual values during the renaming process. A token is highlighted in blue on macOS and framed by curly brackets on Windows.

▶ **Tip:** For more information on using the Filename Template Editor, please refer to Lightroom Help.

You could rename your photos 20230917-0001, and so on, by setting up a filename template with a date token and a four-digit sequence number token, separated by typed hyphens, as shown at the right. Let's remove the Custom Text token from the template we chose by selecting and deleting it. Then click Insert next to Date (YYYYMMDD).

5 Choose Save Current Settings As New Preset from the Preset menu at the top.

6 Type **Date and 4 Digit Sequence** for your preset name, click Create, and then click Done.

Despite all of the options available for renaming your images during the import process, there's only so much information you can squeeze into a single filename. While you may be tempted to be descriptive in your filenames, consistency is key for your archive, and the more streamlined you keep it, the better. This simple organization of dates and sequences in the actual files will pay off in speed and efficiency. Lightroom's strength is in its ability to find your images through the use of things like metadata, keywords, and collections. In these areas, you can be a lot more descriptive than the limited confines of the filename.

Tips for naming your files and folders

We've talked about the importance of naming your files and folders to better organize your photos, and I gave you an example of how to name them. Here are some tips and suggestions for renaming:

- Name your files and folders similarly to make it easier to find the photos you want later.
- Start the name of every file with the year and then add a month and day.
- Use lowercase when naming your files and folders.
- If you believe it is necessary, add a descriptive word about the shoot after the date, and keep it as short as possible.
- If you need to add a space in your name, use an underscore (_) instead of a space.
- At the end of the filename, add C1, C2, C3, and so on, for card 1, card 2, card 3. This helps when you have a shoot that spans multiple memory cards.

For example, if I want to import images that I took of my family on October 4, 2023, my folder would be named *20231004_family*. If I shot only one card during that shoot, the filename would be *20231004_family_c1_sequential file number*. Is the filename long? Yes. Does it give you all of the information about the shoot? Absolutely.

Here's the practical reason for adding the C1 to your filenames: Every now and then, during a Lightroom import, you will run into a file that looks like the one here. While it may make for an interesting art project, it's actually something a lot more sinister. It is a corrupt picture, a quick sign that the card you used may not be as reliable as you thought. Memory cards, like everything else, can fail over time, and you cannot afford to lose an important shoot because of it. If you are importing from multiple cards, how do you tell which one is the bad one?

As soon as I purchase a memory card, I make it a point to label it using those C numbers. Then, I add that C number to the filename. The moment I see a potential problem with an image, I can look at the name and know exactly which card failed so I can take that card out of rotation…and give it to a friend. Kidding! Simply labeling your memory cards and adding that C1 or C2 to your filenames can go a long way to helping you troubleshoot. Anal? Yes. Vital? Absolutely.

You'll learn about working with metadata, keywords, and collections in the following exercises and in Lesson 4, "Managing Your Photo Library."

7 For now, click Import if you want to bring your photos into the LRC2024CIB catalog or Cancel to close the Import dialog box without importing any images.

You have now completed this exercise on importing photos from a digital camera or a memory card. You'll learn about the other options that are available in the Import dialog box in the exercises to follow.

Importing images from a hard disk

When you import photos from your hard disk or from external drives, Lightroom Classic offers you more options for organizing your image files than are available when importing from a camera.

You can still choose to copy your images to a new location during the import process, as you did in the previous exercise, but you also have the option to add them to your catalog without moving them from their current location. You might choose to do this if the images you want to import are already well organized in a folder structure on your drive.

For images that are already located on your hard disk, you have an extra option: to move them to a new location and remove them from their original location at the same time as they are added to your catalog. This option might appeal if the images on your hard disk are not already well organized.

1 To import the images for this exercise from your hard disk, you can choose File > Import Photos And Video, press Shift+Command+I/ Shift+Ctrl+I, click the Import button below the left panel group in the Library module, or drag the folder onto Lightroom's Library module.

2 In the Source panel at the left of the Import dialog box, navigate to the Lessons folder inside the LRC2024CIB folder on your hard disk. Click the lesson02 folder and select Include Subfolders at the upper right of the panel (it's best to leave this on unless you have some images you don't want to import).

> **Tip:** The same commands apply for importing images from a CD, DVD, or other external storage media.

An image count in the lower-left corner of the Import dialog box shows that the lesson02 folder contains a total of 13 photos with a combined file size of 846 MB.

3 From the import type options in the center of the top panel, click Add so that your photos will be added to your catalog without being moved—an option that is not available when importing images from a camera. Do not click Import yet!

4 Use the scrollbar at the right of the Preview pane to view all of the images in the lesson02 folder. Drag the Thumbnail slider below the Preview pane to the left to reduce the size of the thumbnails so that you can see as many of the images as possible in the Preview area.

5 In the Source panel, notice the Include Subfolders option. This checkbox allows you to add images from within subfolders, which is handy to have with larger image collections you may be importing.

Before we go any further, let's review each of the import type options above the Preview area.

6 Click each of the import type options in turn, from left to right:

- Copy As DNG will have Lightroom make copies of your images in DNG file format, which will be stored in a new location and then added to your catalog. You'll notice that for the Copy As DNG, Copy, and Move options, the right panel group offers the same suite of panels—File Handling, File Renaming, Apply During Import, and Destination.

- Click Copy to have Lightroom create copies of your images in a new location and then add them to your catalog, leaving the originals in their current locations. You can set a destination for your copies in the Destination panel, as you did in the previous exercise. Expand the Destination panel and click the Organize menu. When you use either the Copy As DNG, Copy, or Move option to import images from your hard disk or from external storage media, the Organize menu offers you the option to copy your photos into a single folder, into subfolders based on the capture dates, or into a folder structure that replicates the original arrangement.

Note: Expand the File Handling and Apply During Import panels to see the options available.

- Click Move to have the images moved to a new location on your hard disk, arranged in whatever folder structure you choose from the Organize menu, and then deleted from their original locations.

- Click Add to add the images to your catalog without moving or copying them from their current locations or altering the folder structure in which they are stored. For the Add option, the right panel group offers only the File Handling and Apply During Import panels; you cannot rename the original source images during import, and there's no need to specify a destination because the files remain where they are.

Applying metadata

Lightroom uses information attached to files to enable you to quickly find and organize your photos. This information is known as *metadata*. Some of this metadata is automatically added to the file at the point of creation (shutter speed, ISO, camera type, and so on), and some of it can be added after the fact (keywords, your name, and so on).

You can search your image library and filter the results by all of this metadata, as well as things like flag status, color label, shooting settings, or any combination of a wide range of other criteria.

You can also choose specific information about your images from this metadata and have Lightroom display it as a text overlay applied to each image in a slideshow, web gallery, or print layout.

Let's add some important information into our files quickly and make sure we don't have to reinvent the wheel every time. For this, we'll use metadata presets.

1 In the Apply During Import panel, choose New from the Metadata menu.

2 Let's create a metadata preset that includes your copyright information in each file. In the New Metadata Preset dialog box, for Preset Name, type *[year]* **Copyright**. Then, enter your copyright information into the IPTC Copyright fields and contact information into the IPTC Creator fields. This should give anyone online enough information to get a hold of you should someone find your image interesting and want to use it. It does happen at times.

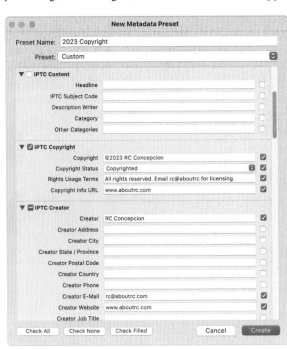

3 Click Create to close the New Metadata Preset dialog box, and then confirm that your new metadata preset is selected in the Metadata menu.

4 Also in the Apply During Import panel, choose None from the Develop Settings menu and type **Taming West** in the Keywords text box.

5 In the File Handling panel, choose Embedded & Sidecar from the Build Previews menu. Check that your settings are the same as those shown in the illustration here, and then click Import.

The images from the lesson02 folder are imported into your library catalog, and thumbnails of the images appear in both the Grid view and the Filmstrip in the Library module.

6 Right-click the lesson02-0009 image in the Grid view and choose Go To Folder In Library from the menu.

In the Folders panel in the left panel group, the lesson02 folder is highlighted, and the image count indicates that it contains 13 photos.

Right-clicking the folder at this point gives you options to update folder locations, or even find the folder of images inside of Finder (on macOS) or Explorer (on Windows). This comes in handy when you are missing folders, but we'll talk more about that later in the book. For now, choose Show In Finder/Show In Explorer to see the folder.

Importing via drag and drop

Perhaps the easiest way to add photos to your image library is to simply drag a selection of files—or even an entire folder—directly into Lightroom Classic.

1   The Finder/Explorer window, where you can see the lesson02A folder, should still be open from the previous exercise. Position the window so that you can see the Grid view in the Lightroom Classic workspace behind it.

2   Drag the lesson02A folder from the Finder/Explorer window onto the Grid view.

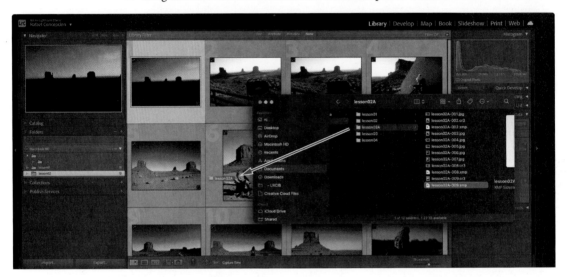

In the Import dialog box, the lesson02A folder is now selected in the Source panel, and the photos it contains are displayed in the Preview area.

3   In the Apply During Import panel, choose your new Metadata preset and type **The Valley** in the Keywords box. Don't click Import just yet.

Evaluating photos before importing

Lightroom Classic makes it easy to decide which of your photos you wish to import by providing an enlarged Loupe view in the Import dialog box; you can examine each image in detail so that you can choose between similar images or exclude a photo that is out of focus.

1 Double-click any of the thumbnails to see the photo in Loupe view, or select any thumbnail and click the Loupe view button at the left of the Toolbar below the preview pane; the image is enlarged to fit the preview area, and the pointer becomes a magnifying glass cursor. Depending on the size of your display and/or the application window, you may first see a Zoom Out cursor.

2 If necessary, click the image again to further magnify the image to a zoom ratio of 1:1. Use the Zoom slider below the preview pane to see even more detail. Drag the enlarged image in the preview pane to pan the view so that you can inspect portions of the photo that are not currently visible.

While you're examining the photo in Loupe view, you can select or deselect the Include In Import option in the Toolbar below the image preview.

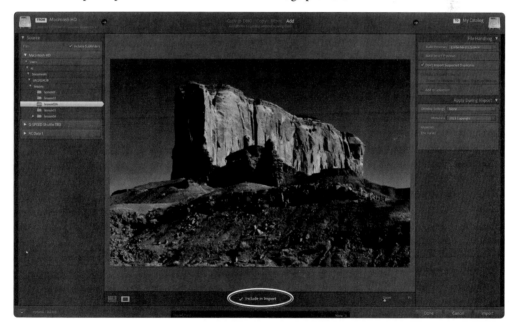

3 Click the enlarged preview to return to the Fit view, where the entire image is visible. Double-click the image, or click either the Loupe view button or the Grid view button beside it, to return to the thumbnail display.

Let's go ahead and keep all of the images selected in this folder.

Images that are already imported

Lightroom does a great job trying to keep your collection organized and free from duplicates. During the import process, there is an option in the File Handling panel on the right side that prevents you from importing images that have already been added to your Lightroom catalog. It's a great idea to keep this selected.

When you try to import from a memory card or folder that you have already imported from, any of the images that are duplicates (that are already in your Lightroom catalog) appear in gray and are not selected for import. (Here, I added four already-imported images to my lesson02B folder as an example.) If the card or folder has new images, those images are visible and will already be selected, so you specify where you would like them imported.

▶ **Tip:** While I suggest you stagger your shoots across multiple memory cards, you don't need to buy four memory cards. You can stagger shoots across as many cards as you own. Think of this as a workflow suggestion, but I can't tell you how many times this has saved me from losing images.

As a general rule, I advise photographers never to format their memory cards until after they have used up all of the cards they own. For example, if I have four memory cards (A, B, C, and D) and I make images on card A, I will import that card into Lightroom but will not format it. At the next shoot, I use card B and repeat the process. The following shoot? Card C.

Should something go wrong on my computer, I have a much better chance of recovering the images from the memory cards if I stagger the formatting in this manner. Working this way, you may forget to format a card and shoot with one that you've already imported. Thankfully, Lightroom is there to catch these kinds of things. Go ahead and import the images from the lesson02A folder.

Importing and viewing video

Lightroom Classic will import many common digital video files from digital still cameras, including AVI, MOV, MP4, AVCHD, and HEVC. Choose File > Import Photos And Video or click the Import button in the Library module; then set up your import in the Import dialog box, just as you would for photos.

In the Library module Grid view, you can scrub backward and forward in your video clips by simply moving the mouse over the thumbnails, making it easy to select the clip you want. Double-click a thumbnail to preview the video in Loupe view; drag the circular current time indicator in the playback control bar to scrub through the video manually.

Setting distinctive thumbnail images (poster frames) for your videos can make it easier to find the clip you want in the Grid view. Move the current time indicator to the frame you want; then, click the Frame button in the control bar and choose Set Poster Frame. Choose Capture Frame from the same menu to convert the current frame to a JPEG image that will be stacked with the clip. To shorten a video clip, click the Trim Video button. The playback control bar expands to display a timeline view of the clip where you can drag the start and end markers to trim the clip as desired.

● **Note:** HEVC (MOV) video files are supported for import and playback on macOS High Sierra (10.13) or later and Windows 10 or later.

Importing to a specific folder

From within the Library module, you can import photos directly to a folder in the Folders panel without needing to specify a destination in the Import dialog box.

1   In the Folders panel, right-click the lesson02A folder and choose Import To This Folder from the menu.

This automatically brings up the Import dialog box. Notice that the Destination is already selected for you.

2   In the Source panel, notice that you have your hard drive, any connected memory cards, and any network drives available as your import source.

3   All of the other panels are available for you to use. From here, you can still apply metadata templates, change the filename, add keywords, and so forth. Click Cancel when done.

This feature is useful when you are working with multiple memory cards and want to have all of them available to import to a shoot. That said, Lightroom does a great job of remembering the last location you saved to, so you may find that you rely on this a lot less than you'd think.

Importing from a watched folder

Designating a folder on your hard disk as a *watched folder* can be a very convenient way to automate the import process. Once you've designated a folder that is to be watched, Lightroom will detect any photos that are placed or saved into it and then automatically move them to a specified location and add them to the catalog. You can even have Lightroom rename the files and add metadata in the process.

1   Choose File > Auto Import > Auto Import Settings. In the Auto Import Settings dialog box, click the first Choose button to designate a watched folder. Navigate to your desktop, create a new folder, name it **Watch This**, and then click Choose/ Select Folder.

Importing a Photoshop Elements catalog

Lightroom Classic makes it easy to import photographs and videos from Photoshop Elements 6 and later on Windows, and from Photoshop Elements 9 and later on macOS.

The media files from your Photoshop Elements catalog are imported complete with keywords, ratings, and labels—even your stacks are preserved. Version sets from Photoshop Elements are converted to stacks in Lightroom Classic, and your albums become collections.

1   In the Lightroom Classic Library module, choose File > Import A Photoshop Elements Catalog.

    Lightroom searches your computer for Photoshop Elements catalogs and displays the most recently opened catalog in the Import Photos From Photoshop Elements dialog box.

2   If you wish to import a Photoshop Elements catalog other than that selected by default, choose it from the menu.

3   Click Import to merge the photo library and all catalog information from your Photoshop Elements catalog to your Lightroom Classic catalog.

If you're migrating from Photoshop Elements to Lightroom Classic, or intend to use the two applications together, refer to the Adobe tutorial "Automatically import photos from Photoshop Elements to Lightroom Classic" for useful tips and info:
https://helpx.adobe.com/lightroom-classic/help/import-photos-various-sources.html.

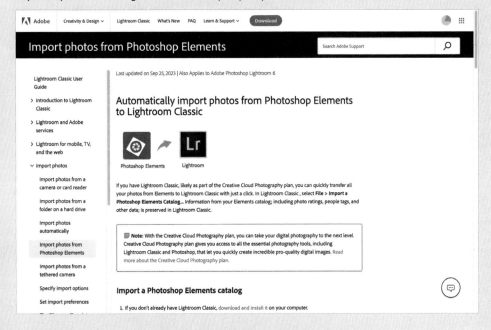

2 Now that you have designated a watched folder, you can select Enable Auto Import at the top of the Auto Import Settings dialog box.

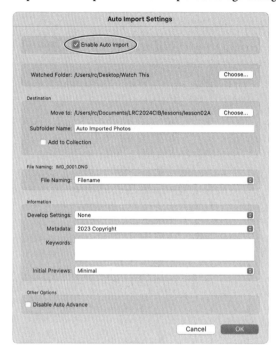

3 Under Destination, click the Choose button to specify a folder to which Lightroom will move your photos when adding them to the library catalog. Navigate to and select the lesson02A folder, and then click Choose/Select Folder. Type **Auto Imported Photos** in the Subfolder Name text box.

▶ **Tip:** Once you've set a watched folder, you can activate or disable Auto Import at any time, without opening the Auto Import Settings dialog box, by choosing File > Auto Import > Enable Auto Import. A checkmark beside this menu command indicates that the Auto Import feature is currently enabled.

4 Under Information, select the metadata preset that we made in the previous exercise, choose None from the Develop Settings menu, and choose Minimal from the Initial Previews menu. Click OK to close the Auto Import Settings dialog box.

5 Switch to Finder/Windows Explorer and navigate to the lesson02B folder. Open the Watch This folder and drag the image files inside this watched folder.

When Lightroom has finished importing, you'll notice that the images are automatically placed into the Auto Imported folder we created in the Auto Import Settings dialog box. Looking at the Watch This folder, you'll see that it is now empty.

In Lightroom, if you navigate to the lesson02A folder, you'll notice that there are several more pictures that have been added to that folder.

You'll find that this watched folder feature is commonly used by photographers who are performing tethered shooting using the manufacturer's software to control the camera. Dedicated to supporting photographers every step of the way, Lightroom also handles this type of shooting quite well. Want to learn more about tethered shooting? We'll cover that in the next section.

Specifying initial previews
when importing

As photos are imported, Lightroom can immediately display a photo's embedded preview or display higher-quality previews as the program renders them. You can choose the rendered size and quality for previews using the Standard Preview Size and Preview Quality menus on the File Handling tab of the Catalog Settings dialog box (choose Lightroom Classic > Catalog Settings/Edit > Catalog Settings). Please keep in mind that embedded previews are created on the fly by cameras and are not color managed; therefore, they don't match the interpretation of the camera's raw files made by Lightroom. Previews rendered by Lightroom are color managed.

In the Import Photos dialog box, choose one of the four Build Previews options:

- **Minimal** displays images using the smallest previews embedded in the photos; Lightroom renders standard-size previews as needed.

- **Embedded & Sidecar** displays the largest possible preview available from the camera; it's slower than a Minimal preview but faster than a Standard preview.

- **Standard** displays previews as Lightroom renders them. Standard-size previews use the ProPhoto RGB color space.

- **1:1** displays a one-to-one view of the actual pixels.

You can also choose to build Smart Previews during the import process. Smart Previews are compressed, high-resolution previews that allow you to work on your photos even when the originals are offline. They support editing at high magnification, though they are a fraction of the size of the source files. Generating Smart Previews for a large import takes time, but adds a lot of flexibility to your workflow.

Tethered shooting

Many modern digital cameras support tethered shooting, a process where you connect—or tether—your digital camera to your computer and save images to the computer's hard disk rather than to the camera's memory card. With tethered shooting, you can view a photo on your computer screen immediately after you shoot it—a vastly different experience from seeing it on your camera's LCD screen.

▶ **Tip:** Please refer to Lightroom Classic Help to see a list of cameras currently supported for integrated tethered shooting.

For a range of DSLR cameras, including many models from Canon and Nikon, you can capture photographs directly into Lightroom Classic without the need for any third-party software. If your camera allows tethered shooting but is not on the list of models supported by Lightroom Classic, you can still capture images into your Lightroom Classic library using either the image capture software associated with the camera or any of a number of third-party software solutions.

You can have Lightroom name the photos, add metadata, apply developing settings, and organize them in your library then and there. If necessary, you can adjust your camera settings (white balance, exposure, focus, depth of field, and others), or even change cameras, before taking the next shot. The better the quality of the captured image, the less time you'll need to spend adjusting it later.

Tethered shooting with a supported camera

1 Connect your camera to the computer.

2 In the Library module, choose File > Tethered Capture > Start Tethered Capture.

3 In the Tethered Capture Settings dialog box, type a name for your shooting session. Lightroom will create a folder with this name inside the destination folder of your choice; this session folder will appear in the Folders panel.

Note: Depending on your camera model and the operating system your computer uses, you may also need to install the necessary drivers for your camera.

4 Choose a naming scheme for your shots, select a destination folder, and specify any metadata or keywords that you want Lightroom to apply as the newly captured images are imported.

5 Click OK to close the Tethered Capture Settings dialog box. The tethered capture control bar appears.

The control bar displays the model name of the connected camera, the name you entered for the shooting session, and the current camera settings, all of which you can change. You can choose from a wide range of Develop presets in the Develop Settings menu at the right. You can trigger the shot with your camera's shutter button by clicking the large circular button at the right of the control bar or by pressing F12 on your keyboard.

Tip: To collapse the control bar to just the shutter button, hold down the Option/Alt key and click the Close button at the upper right. Repeat to expand the control bar again.

As you shoot, the images captured will appear in both the Grid view and the Filmstrip. To see each captured photo as large as possible, switch to the Loupe view and hide unwanted panels or choose Window > Screen Mode > Full Screen And Hide Panels.

Viewing imported photos in the work area

In the Library module, the main display area—the work area—in the center of the application window is where you select, sort, search, review, and compare images. The Library module work area offers a choice of view modes to suit a range of tasks, from organizing your photos to choosing between similar shots.

1 If you're not already in the Library module, switch to it now. Select All Photographs in the Catalog panel to see all of the images you have imported.

Note: You'll learn more about using the Filter bar controls in Lesson 4.

Depending on your workspace setup in the Library module, you may see the Filter bar across the top of the work area. You can use filters to limit the images that are displayed in the Grid view and the Filmstrip so that you'll see only those photos with a specified rating or flag status, or with particular metadata content.

The Toolbar, located at the bottom of the work area, is common to all of the workspace modules, but contains different tools and controls for each.

2 If the Filter bar is not already visible, show it by pressing the backslash key (\) on your keyboard or by choosing View > Show Filter Bar. Press the backslash key again or choose View > Show Filter Bar to hide it again.

3 If the Toolbar is not already visible, press T to show it. Press T again to hide it. Switch to the Develop module. If the Toolbar is not already visible, press T to show it. Switch back to the Library module. In the Library module, the Toolbar is still hidden; Lightroom remembers your Toolbar setting for each module independently. Press T to show the Toolbar in the Library module.

4 Double-click an image in Grid view to switch to Loupe view. The Loupe view is available in both the Library and Develop modules, but the controls available in the Loupe view Toolbar differ for each of these modules.

5 To hide or show individual tools, click the white arrow at the right end of the Toolbar and choose their names from the menu. Tools that are currently visible in the Toolbar have a checkmark in front of their names.

> **Tip:** If you activate more tools than can be displayed in the width of the Toolbar, you can increase the Toolbar's width by hiding the side panel groups or disabling tools that you don't need at the moment.

Setting Grid and Loupe view options

You can choose from many options in the Library View Options dialog box to customize the information Lightroom Classic displays for each image in the Grid and Loupe views. For the Loupe view overlay and thumbnail tool tips, you can activate two sets of options and then use a keyboard shortcut to switch between them.

1 Press G to switch to Grid view in the Library module. Press Shift+Tab to hide all of the panels and focus on your grid of images.

2 Choose View > View Options. The Library View Options dialog box appears with the Grid View tab already selected. Position the Library View Options dialog box so you can see some of the images in the Grid view.

3 At the top of the Grid View tab, deselect Show Grid Extras. This disables most of the other options.

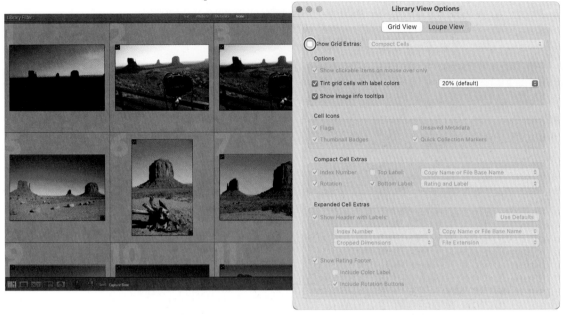

4 The only options still available are Tint Grid Cells With Label Colors and Show Image Info Tooltips. If they're not already activated, select both of these options. As this lesson's images have not yet been assigned color labels, activating the first option has no visible effect in the Grid view. Right-click any image—you can do this while the Library View Options dialog box is open—and choose a color from the Set Color Label menu.

In the Grid view and the Filmstrip, a color-labeled image that is currently selected will show a thin colored frame around the thumbnail; a color-labeled image that is not selected has a tinted cell background.

5   Position the pointer over a thumbnail in the Grid view or the Filmstrip; a tool tip appears. In macOS you'll need to click anywhere in the Lightroom Classic workspace window to bring it to the front before you can see the tool tips.

By default, the tool tip will display the filename, the capture date and time, and the cropped dimensions. You can specify the information to be displayed in the tool tip by choosing from the Loupe View options.

6   On macOS, if the Library View Options dialog box is now hidden behind the main application window, press Command+J to bring it back to the front.

7   On the Grid View tab, select the Show Grid Extras option and choose Compact Cells from the menu beside it. Experiment with each setting to see its effect in the Grid view display. Select and deselect the settings for Options, Cell Icons, and Compact Cell Extras. Position the pointer over the various icons in the image cells to see tool tips with additional information.

8   Under Compact Cell Extras, click the Top Label menu to see the long list of choices available. For some choices, such as Title or Caption, nothing will be displayed until you add the relevant information to the image's metadata.

9   Now choose Expanded Cells from the Show Grid Extras menu. Experiment with the Expanded Cell Extras options to see the effects in the Grid view. Click any of the Show Header With Labels menus to see the many choices available to customize the information that is displayed in the cell headers.

10 Click the Loupe View tab. The work area switches to Loupe view so you can preview the changes you'll make in the Library View Options dialog box.

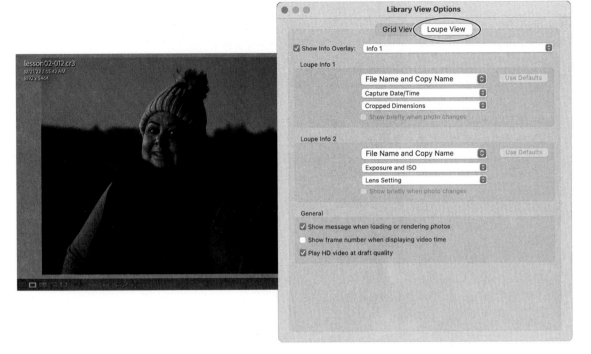

● **Note:** When you choose an information item such as Capture Date And Time, those details are drawn from the image metadata. If the image's metadata does not contain the specified information, nothing will be displayed for that item. For both the Grid and Loupe view options you can choose the information item Common Attributes, which will display the flag status, star rating, and color label for each image.

For the Loupe view, you can select the Show Info Overlay option to display image information in the upper-left corner of the view. Choose items from the menus in Loupe Info 1 and Loupe Info 2 to create two different sets of information, and then choose either set from the Show Info Overlay menu.

You can reset either group to its default state by clicking its Use Defaults button. Select Show Briefly When Photo Changes instead of Show Info Overlay to show the info overlay for only a few seconds when a new image is displayed in the Loupe view. Select the Show Message When Loading Or Rendering Photos option to display a notification in the lower part of the view while the image preview is updated.

11 Click the Close button to close the Library View Options dialog box.

12 Choose which of the two information sets will be displayed by choosing an option from the View > Loupe Info menu or by pressing the I key to cycle the info overlay through Loupe Info 1, Loupe Info 2, and its disabled state.

13 Switch to Grid view. From the View > Grid View Style menu, you can choose whether to display additional information using either the Compact Cells layout or the Expanded Cells layout. Press the J key to cycle through the cell layouts.

Review questions

1 When would you choose to copy imported images to a new location on your hard disk, and when would you want to add them to your library catalog without moving them?

2 What is DNG?

3 When would you use the Import dialog box in compact mode?

4 Why would you use tethered shooting in Lightroom Classic?

5 How can you specify the information displayed for images in the Grid and Loupe views?

Review answers

1 When importing photos from a camera or memory card, the images need to be copied to a more permanent location, as memory cards are expected to be erased and reused. Copying or moving images also might be useful when you want Lightroom to organize the files into a more ordered folder hierarchy during the import process. Images that are already arranged in a useful way on the hard disk or removable media can be added to the library catalog in their current locations.

2 The Digital Negative (DNG) file format is a publicly available archival format intended to address the lack of an open standard for raw files generated by cameras. Converting raw files to DNG in Lightroom will help ensure that you'll be able to access your raw files in the future even if the original proprietary format is no longer supported.

3 Once you've created import presets to suit your workflow, you can speed up the import process by using the Import dialog box in compact mode. Use your import preset as a starting point, and then modify the settings as required.

4 When shooting tethered into Lightroom, you can see the images much larger on your computer screen than on the LCD on your camera, allowing you to adjust your camera settings as you shoot to reduce the amount of postproduction work needed.

5 You can choose from the many options in the Library View Options dialog box (View > View Options) to customize the information Lightroom Classic displays for each image in the Grid and Loupe views. For the Loupe view and thumbnail tool tips, you can define two sets of options and then press the I key to switch between them. From the View > Grid View Style menu you can switch between Compact or Expanded Cells and activate or disable the display of information for either style.

PHOTOGRAPHY SHOWCASE
GREGORY HEISLER

I'm eternally grateful that I have eyeballs. Wired to my brain. Ducted through my heart.

I'm endlessly fascinated by how light follows this path and produces an emotional tug on how people and things look. It's never neutral. Capturing light as it exists, reproducing it from memory, and creating it from scratch are the challenges I relish in eliciting an immediate response from the viewer. It is how I approach making an image. It's my way in; once I envision the light, the rest falls into place. I know how the picture will look.

Light is all the camera sees, but it never sees it the way I do in my mind. So I need to be the interpreter, translating the language of the light into the more limited language the camera can understand; otherwise, there's a heartbreaking disparity between what I can see and imagine and what I actually get.

Traditionally, camera settings were the primary tool for interpreting light. Conventional darkroom techniques allowed a further measure of control. Then the addition of flash or continuous illumination offered the opportunity to completely reinterpret, reshape, or re-create the light. Now, Lightroom and Photoshop have presented us with incredibly sophisticated tools to work with the light after the image has been captured.

This can be used to create fantastical effects and fiction, or to faithfully restore the image as seen or experienced, which is essentially a documentary pursuit. This is why I believe it is essential to understand and master these applications. It is critical for the photographer to make these post-production decisions. They are not purely aesthetic. They affect the narrative in an immediate and powerful way. Only the photographer knows what was originally seen, felt, and experienced. Only the photographer knows the intention driving the image.

Only the photographer can be its true author, and light is the key.

gregoryheisler.com
instagram.com/eyeballcalisthenics

MUHAMMAD ALI

ROBERT BALLARD

DENZEL WASHINGTON

HARRY BELAFONTE

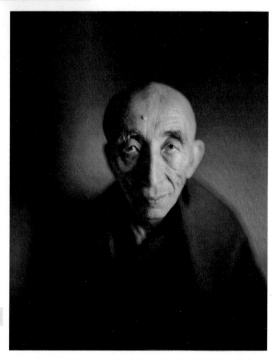

KUSHOK BAKULA

3 EXPLORING THE LIGHTROOM WORKSPACE

Lesson overview

Whether you prefer to use menu commands and keyboard shortcuts or buttons and sliders, whether you use one monitor or two, you can set up the Lightroom Classic workspace to suit the way *you* work. Customize each module to always have your favorite tools and controls at hand, arranged as you like them. In this lesson you'll explore the Library module and a variety of view modes, tools, and techniques for reviewing your images and navigating your catalog. In the process, you'll become familiar with the interface elements and skills that are common to all of the workspace modules. You'll learn how to:

- Adjust the workspace layout, use the Navigator panel and the Filmstrip, and work with a second display.

- Work with the different image preview and screen modes.

- Use keyboard shortcuts.

- Compare, flag, and delete photos.

- Assemble groups of images using the Quick Collection.

 This lesson will take about 90 minutes to complete. To get the lesson files used in this chapter, download them from the web page for this book at *peachpit.com/LightroomCIB2024*. For more information, see "Accessing the lesson files and Web Edition" in the "Getting Started" section at the beginning of this book.

Make working with Lightroom Classic even more pleasurable, and ultimately more productive, by personalizing the workspace so that you always have your favorite tools and controls at hand. Here we are simulating how a photo will look in a sample magazine layout, which we cover in this chapter.

Getting started

Note: This lesson assumes that you have a basic working familiarity with the Lightroom Classic workspace. If you need more background information, refer to Lightroom Classic Help or review the previous lessons.

Before you begin, make sure you've set up the LRC2024CIB folder for your lesson files and created the LRC2024CIB Catalog file to manage them, as described in "Accessing the lesson files and Web Edition" and "Creating a catalog file for working with this book" in the "Getting Started" section at the beginning of this book.

If you haven't already done so, download the lesson03 folder from your Account page at peachpit.com to the LRC2024CIB\Lessons folder, as detailed in "Accessing the lesson files and Web Edition" in the "Getting Started" section.

1   Start Lightroom Classic.

2   In the Select Catalog dialog box, make sure the file LRC2024CIB Catalog.lrcat is selected under Select A Recent Catalog To Open, and then click Open.

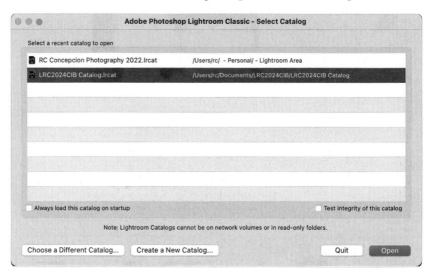

Note: If you can't see the Module Picker, choose Window > Panels > Show Module Picker, or press the F5 key. If you're working on macOS, you may need to press the fn key together with the F5 key or change the function key behavior in the system preferences.

3   Lightroom Classic will open in the screen mode and workspace module that were active when you last quit. If necessary, switch to the Library module by clicking Library in the Module Picker at the top of the workspace.

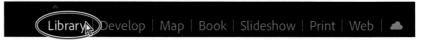

Importing images into the library

The first step is to import the images for this lesson into the Lightroom library.

1   In the Library module, click the Import button below the left panel group.

2 If the Import dialog box appears in compact mode, click the Show More Options button at the lower left of the dialog box to see all of the options in the expanded Import dialog box.

▶ **Tip:** The first time you enter any of the Lightroom Classic modules, you'll see tips that will help you get started by identifying the components of the workspace and stepping you through the workflow. Dismiss the tips by clicking the Close button. To reactivate the tips for any module, choose [*Module name*] Tips from the Help menu.

3 Under Source at the left of the expanded Import dialog box, locate and select your LRC2024CIB\Lessons\lesson03 folder. Ensure that all 20 photos in the lesson03 folder are selected for import (deselect the mag-cover.png file).

4 In the import options above the thumbnail previews, select Add so that the imported photos will be added to your catalog without being moved or copied. Under File Handling at the right of the expanded Import dialog box, choose Embedded & Sidecar from the Build Previews menu and leave the Don't Import Suspected Duplicates option selected. Under Apply During Import, choose None from the Develop Settings menu, choose your copyright in the Metadata menu, and type **Lesson 03 - Mayaguez** in the Keywords text box. Make sure that your import is set up as shown here, and then click Import.

The 20 images are imported and now appear in both the Library module's Grid view and the Filmstrip across the bottom of the Lightroom Classic workspace.

Viewing and managing your images

The Library module is where every Lightroom Classic workflow begins, whether you're importing new images or finding a photo that's already in your catalog. The Library module offers a variety of viewing modes and an array of tools and controls to help you evaluate, sort, and group your photos. During import, you applied common keywords to the selection of images as a whole. Now, even as you review your newly imported photos for the first time, you can begin to add more structure to your catalog, flagging picks and rejects and assigning ratings, tags, and labels.

Lightroom's search and filter features enable you to leverage the metadata that you attach to your photos. You can search and sort the images in your library by any attribute or association and then create collections to group them, making it easy to retrieve exactly the photos you want, no matter how big your catalog.

In the Library module's left panel group, you'll find panels where you can access and manage the folders and collections containing your photos. The right panel group presents controls for adjusting your images and working with keywords and metadata. Above the work area is the Filter bar, where you can set up a custom search. The Toolbar below the work area provides easy access to your choice of tools and controls, and the Filmstrip presents the images in the selected source folder or collection, no matter which view is active in the work area.

Adjusting the workspace layout

You can customize the layout of the flexible Lightroom Classic workspace to suit the way you prefer to work on any task in your workflow, freeing up screen space as you need it and keeping your favorite controls at your fingertips. In the next exercises, you'll learn how to modify the workspace on the fly and use the various screen display modes, skills that are applicable to any of the Lightroom modules.

Resizing panels

When you need more space to work, you can quickly change the width of the side panel groups and the height of the Filmstrip panel by simply dragging, or you can hide any of these elements.

1   Move the pointer over the right edge of the left panel group; the cursor changes to a horizontal double arrow. Drag to the right and release the mouse button when the panel group has reached its maximum width.

The central work area contracts to accommodate the expanded panel. This is useful if you have a set of collections that has a long name and you want to see it.

2   Click Develop in the Module Picker to switch to the Develop module. You'll notice that the left panel group returns to the width it was when you last used the Develop module.

Lightroom Classic remembers your customized workspace layout for each module independently, so the workspace is automatically rearranged to suit the way you work for each stage of your workflow as you move between modules.

3   Press the G key to switch back to Grid view in the Library module.

4   In the Library module, drag the right edge of the left panel group to return the group to its minimum width.

▶ **Tip:** You can't change the size of the top panel, but you can hide or reveal it just like the side panel groups and the Filmstrip. You'll learn about showing and hiding panels in the next exercise.

5   Move the pointer over the top edge of the Filmstrip panel; the cursor changes to a double arrow. Drag the top edge of the Filmstrip down as far as it will go.

The work area expands to fill the available space. This arrangement keeps the Filmstrip visible while increasing the space available for the Grid view when you're selecting photos or when reviewing images in Loupe, Compare, and Survey views.

6   Switch to the Develop module. The Filmstrip remains unchanged as you move between modules. Whichever module you switch to, the Filmstrip will remain at its current height until you resize it.

▶ **Tip:** For the side panel groups, double-clicking the border will produce a different result. This is discussed in the next section, "Showing and hiding panels or panel groups."

7   Move the pointer over the top edge of the Filmstrip panel, and it changes to a vertical double-arrow cursor. Double-click the top edge of the Filmstrip to reset the panel to its previous height, then switch back to the Library module.

8   Drag the top border of the Filmstrip to its maximum height. The thumbnails in the Filmstrip are enlarged and, if necessary, a scroll bar appears along the bottom of the Filmstrip. Scroll to view all of the thumbnails; then double-click the top edge of the Filmstrip with the vertical double-arrow cursor to reset the panel to its previous height.

Showing and hiding panels or panel groups

By adjusting the size of the side panel groups and the Filmstrip, you can allocate more space for the controls you access most frequently and reduce the prominence of features you use less often. Once you've set up the workspace as you like it, you can maximize your working view as needed by temporarily hiding any, or all, of the surrounding panels.

1 To hide the left panel group, click the Show/Hide Panel Group arrow icon in the left margin of the window. The panel group disappears, and the arrow icon is reversed to face right.

2 Click the reversed Show/Hide Panel Group arrow to reinstate the left panel group.

You can use the arrows in the top, right, and bottom margins of the workspace to show and hide the top panel, the right panel group, and the Filmstrip.

3 Deselect the menu option Window > Panels > Show Left Module Panels or press the F7 key to hide the left panel group. To show the group again, press F7 or choose Window > Panels > Show Left Module Panels. Deselect the menu option Window > Panels > Show Right Module Panels or press the F8 key to hide the right panel group. To show the group again, press F8 or choose Window > Panels > Show Right Module Panels.

4 Deselect the menu option Window > Panels > Show Module Picker or press the F5 key to hide the top panel. To show it again, press F5 or choose Window > Panels > Show Module Picker. To hide the Filmstrip, press the F6 key or deselect the menu option Window > Panels > Show Filmstrip. To show it again, press F6 or choose Window > Panels > Show Filmstrip.

5 To hide or show both side panel groups at once, press the Tab key or choose Window > Panels > Toggle Side Panels. To hide or show the top panel and the Filmstrip as well as the side panel groups, press Shift+Tab or choose Window > Panels > Toggle All Panels.

Lightroom Classic offers options that make the workspace even more flexible and convenient by showing and hiding panels or panel groups automatically in response to your movements with the pointer, so information, tools, and controls will appear only when you need them.

6 Right-click the Show/Hide Panel Group arrow in the left margin of the workspace. Choose Auto Hide & Show from the menu.

7 Hide the left panel group by clicking the Show/Hide Panel Group arrow, and then move the pointer over the arrow in the left margin of the workspace. The left panel group automatically slides into view, partially covering the work area. You can click to select catalogs, folders, and collections; the left panel group will remain visible as long as the pointer remains over it. Move the pointer outside the left panel group

▶ Tip: You don't need to be accurate when you click the Show/Hide Panel Group arrows. In fact, you can click anywhere along outer margins of the workspace to hide and show panels.

● Note: On macOS, some function keys are assigned to specific operating system functions by default. If pressing a function key in Lightroom Classic does not work as expected, either press the fn key (not available on all keyboard layouts) together with the respective function key or change the keyboard behavior in the system preferences.

and it will disappear again. To show or hide the left panels independently of the current settings, press the F7 key.

8 Right-click the Show/Hide Panel Group arrow in the left margin of the workspace window and choose Auto Hide from the menu. Now the panel group disappears when you are done with it and does not reappear when you move the pointer into the workspace margin. To show the left panel group again, click in the workspace margin or press the F7 key.

9 To turn off automatic show and hide for this panel, right-click the Show/Hide Panel Group arrow in the left margin of the workspace and choose Manual from the menu.

10 To reset the left panel group to its default behavior, choose Auto Hide & Show in the menu. If either of the left or right panel groups is still hidden, press the F7 key or the F8 key, respectively, to show it again.

Lightroom remembers your panel layout for each module independently, including your choice of show and hide options. The options you choose for the Filmstrip and the top panel, however, remain unchanged as you move between modules.

Expanding and collapsing panels

Up to this point in our lesson, we've dealt with the left and right panels only as groups. Now you'll learn to work with the individual panels within the groups.

1 If you are not already in the Library module, switch to it now. Create more space to work with the side panel groups by hiding both the top panel and the Filmstrip. (See step 4 in the previous exercise.)

In the Library module, the left panel group contains the Navigator, Catalog, Folders, Collections, and Publish Services panels. Each panel within a group can be *expanded* to show its content or *collapsed* so that only the panel header is visible. A triangle next to the panel name indicates whether a panel is expanded or collapsed.

Tip: You don't need to be accurate when you click the triangle. Clicking anywhere in the panel header will do, as long as you don't click any other control that might be located there, such as the plus sign (+) in the header of the Collections panel.

2 To expand a collapsed panel, click the triangle beside its name; the triangle turns downward, and the panel expands to show its content. Click the triangle again to collapse the panel.

Folders within a panel—such as the Smart Collections folder in the Collections panel—can also be expanded and collapsed by clicking the triangle next to the folder name.

3 Open the Window > Panels menu; panels that are currently expanded and fully visible in the panel group show a checkmark in front of their names. Choose any panel from that menu and toggle its display status.

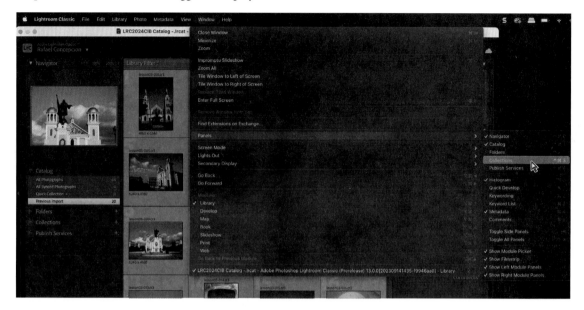

4 In the Window > Panels menu, look at the keyboard shortcuts for expanding and collapsing the individual panels.

- For the panels in the left group, the keyboard shortcuts begin with Control+Command/Shift+Ctrl followed by a number. The panels are numbered from the top down, so press Control+Command+0/Shift+Ctrl+0 for the Navigator panel, Control+Command+1/Shift+Ctrl+1 for the Catalog panel, and so on.

- For the right panel group, the keyboard shortcuts begin with Command/Ctrl followed by a number. Press Command+0/Ctrl+0 to collapse the Histogram panel. Press the same keyboard shortcut again to expand it. These keyboard shortcuts may be assigned to different panels in another module, but this shouldn't be too confusing if you remember that, whatever module you're in, the panels are always numbered from the top of the group, starting at 0.

- Using keyboard shortcuts is a great way to streamline your workflow, so it's worthwhile to note the shortcuts listed beside the menu commands you use.

5 Press Command+/ (macOS) or Ctrl+/ (Windows) to see a list of all of the keyboard shortcuts for the currently active module. When you're done, click anywhere on the list to dismiss it.

With one click, you can expand or collapse all panels other than the topmost in each group, or have all panels other than the top panel in the group and the one you're working with close automatically. The top panel in each group has a special role and is not affected by these commands.

6 To collapse all panels in either of the side groups, right-click the header of any panel other than the top panel in the group and then choose Collapse All from the menu. If the top panel is already expanded, it will stay open.

7 To expand all of the panels in either group, right-click the header of any panel—other than the top panel in each group—and choose Expand All from the menu. Once again, the top panel remains unaffected.

▶ **Tip:** Option-click/Alt-click the header of any panel to quickly activate or disable the Solo mode.

8 To collapse all of the panels in a group other than the one you're working with, right-click the header of any panel—other than the top panel in the group—and choose Solo Mode from the menu. Only one panel will remain expanded. The triangles beside the panel names change from solid to dotted when Solo mode is activated. Click the header of a collapsed panel to expand it. The previously expanded panel collapses automatically.

Hiding and showing panels

If you use some panels in a group less often than others, you can hide them from view to create more space to expand the panels you use most frequently.

1 To show or hide an individual panel, right-click a panel header and choose the panel. Currently visible panels have checkmarks in front of their names.

2 To show all of the panels that are currently hidden in either of the side panel groups, right-click the header of any panel other than the top panel in the group and choose Show All from the menu.

You can't access the panel group menu by right-clicking the header of the Navigator or Histogram panel; if you've hidden all of the panels other than the topmost in either side group, you can make the panel you want visible again by choosing its name from the Window > Panels submenu.

Toggling screen modes

Whichever of the Lightroom Classic modules you're working in, you can choose between several *screen modes* to suit the way you prefer to work. In the default mode, the workspace appears inside an application window that you can resize and position onscreen. If you prefer, you can expand the workspace to fill the screen, either with or without the menu bar, or switch to a full-screen preview to see the photo you're working on without any distracting workspace elements.

1 Choose Window > Screen Mode > Normal to ensure you're in the default mode.

In Normal screen mode, the Lightroom Classic workspace appears inside an application window. You can resize and reposition the application window just as you are used to doing with other applications.

2 Move the pointer over any edge or corner of the application window. When the pointer changes to a horizontal, vertical, or diagonal double arrow, drag to reduce the size of the application window.

3 On macOS, click the green Zoom button at the left of the title bar; on Windows, click the Maximize button, located at the upper right of the window. The application window expands to fill the entire screen, although the title bar may remain visible. While the window is maximized, it's no longer possible to resize it, as you did in step 2, or reposition it by dragging the title bar.

4 Click the green Zoom button/Restore Down button to restore the window to the size you established in step 2.

5 Choose Window > Screen Mode > Full Screen, and the workspace fills the entire screen. The menu bar is hidden, as is the Dock on macOS or the taskbar on Windows. Move the pointer to the top edge of the screen to see the menu bar. Choose Window > Screen Mode > Full Screen And Hide Panels. Alternatively, use the keyboard shortcut Shift+Command+F/Shift+Ctrl+F.

The Full Screen And Hide Panels mode is a good choice to quickly maximize the space available for the main work area, whether you're working with the thumbnail grid or a single image in the Loupe view. You can still access any of the hidden panels when needed—using either keyboard shortcuts or your mouse—without changing the view.

6 Press Shift+F repeatedly, or choose Window > Screen Mode > Next Screen Mode, to cycle through the working modes. As you switch between the screen modes, you'll notice that the panels around the work area remain hidden. To reveal all panels, press Shift+Tab. Press T to show or hide the Toolbar.

7 Press the F key to see a full-screen preview of the selected image at the highest magnification possible, without the distraction of workspace elements; then, press F again to return to Normal screen mode.

Switching views

In each Lightroom Classic module, you have a different set of working views to suit the various phases of your workflow. You can switch between viewing modes as you work by choosing from the View menu, using the keyboard shortcuts listed there, or clicking a view mode button at the left of the Toolbar below the work area.

In the Library, you can move between several viewing modes. Press the G key or click the Grid view button in the Toolbar to see thumbnails of your images while you search; apply flags, ratings, and labels; or create collections. Use the keyboard shortcut E or click the Loupe view button to inspect a single photo at a range of magnifications. Press C or click the Compare view button to see two images side by side. Click the Survey view button in the Toolbar or use the keyboard shortcut N to evaluate several images at once. The Toolbar displays a different set of controls for each view mode. For the purposes of this lesson, we'll ignore the fifth view button in the Toolbar, which is used in the process of tagging faces in your photos; you'll learn about using the People view in Lesson 4, "Managing Your Photo Library."

1 If you're not already in the Grid view, click the Grid view button. Adjust the size of the thumbnails to your liking by dragging the Thumbnails slider.

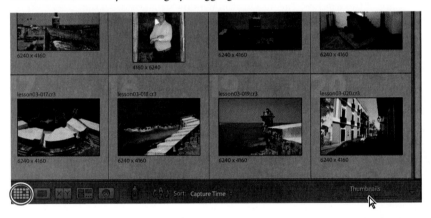

Note: The order of the tools and controls from top to bottom in the menu corresponds to the order you see them from left to right in the Toolbar.

2 Click the triangle at the right end of the Toolbar and ensure that View Modes is activated in the menu. If you're working on a small screen, you can disable any of the other options except Thumbnail Size for this lesson.

Tools and controls that are currently visible in the Toolbar have a checkmark beside their names in the menu.

3 Review the section "Setting Grid and Loupe view options," at the end of Lesson 2, and specify which items of information you would like to see displayed with each photo in the Grid view image cells.

Working in Loupe view

The Loupe view displays a single photo at a wide range of zoom levels. In the Develop module, where high magnification enables fine editing, the Loupe view is the default; in the Library module, you'll use it while evaluating and sorting your images. You can use the Navigator panel to set the level of magnification and to find your way around a zoomed image that's mostly out of frame. As with the Loupe view, you'll find the Navigator panel in both the Library and Develop modules.

1   In the Grid view or the Filmstrip, select a photo, and then click the Loupe view button in the Toolbar or press the E key. Alternatively, simply double-click the thumbnail in the Grid view or the Filmstrip.

2   If necessary, expand the Navigator panel at the top of the left panel group. The zoom controls in the upper-right corner of the Navigator panel enable you to switch quickly between preset magnification levels. You can choose from Fit, Fill (in a menu), 100%, 200%, or choose another zoom percentage from a menu.

▶ **Tip:** In the Library View Options dialog box, activate Show Info Overlay if you wish to display text details overlaid on your image in the Loupe view.

You can toggle between zoom levels by choosing View > Toggle Zoom View, by pressing Z on your keyboard, or simply by clicking the photo in the work area.

To better understand what happens when you use the Toggle Zoom View command, you should be aware that the magnification controls are organized into two groups: Fit and Fill make up one group, while the percent zoom settings are in the second. The Toggle Zoom View command toggles the Loupe view between whichever magnification levels were last used in each group.

▶ **Tip:** Lightroom now includes a Scrubby Zoom option that you can take advantage of in the Develop module. We'll cover how to use it in Lesson 4.

3   Click Fit in the zoom controls in the upper-right corner of the Navigator panel. Now click the 100% control. Choose View > Toggle Zoom View, or press Z. The zoom setting reverts to Fit. Press the Z key; the zoom setting reverts to 100%.

4   Choose Fill from the Fit menu in the Navigator panel header, and then choose 300% from the menu at the far right.

5   Click the image in the Loupe view. The zoom setting reverts to Fill. The difference between zooming this way and using the Toggle Zoom View command is that the zoomed view will now be centered on the area you clicked. Press Z to zoom to 300%. Click the Fill menu and choose Fit.

Lightroom now has another way to zoom in to pictures: by dragging out a box around the area you want to zoom in to. Doing this changes the third column to a custom percentage that you can toggle back and forth from using the Z key.

6   Hold down the Command/Ctrl key and drag a selection out over the image. A selection area appears, showing the area you'll zoom in to. The image then zooms to the specific percentage now showing in the third column in the Navigator header, and you can toggle between that and Fit/Fill by pressing the Z key. You can move to 100% by pressing **Command+Option+0/Ctrl+Alt+0**.

7 Using keystrokes to navigate an image can be helpful when inspecting the entire image in close detail. Press the Home key (fn+Left Arrow on a macOS laptop) to move the zoom rectangle to the upper left of the image, and then press the Page Down key (fn+Down Arrow) to scroll through the magnified image one section at a time. When you reach the bottom of the photo, the zoom rectangle jumps over to the top of the next column. To start in the lower-right corner of the image, press the End key (fn+Right Arrow), and then use the Page Up key (fn+Up Arrow).

8 Show the Filmstrip, and then select another photo with the same orientation and click in the Navigator preview to move the zoom rectangle to a different part of the image. Return to the previous image, and the zoom rectangle returns to its previous position for that photo. Choose View > Lock Zoom Position, and then repeat the first part of this step; the position of the zoom rectangle is now synchronized. This can be useful when comparing detail across similar photos.

9 Choose View > Lock Zoom Position again to disable it, and then click Fit in the header of the Navigator panel.

The zoom controls and the Navigator panel work the same way for the Loupe view in both the Library and Develop modules.

Using the Loupe view overlays

When you're working in Loupe view in the Library or Develop modules, or during a tethered capture session, you can show configurable overlays that can be useful for setting up a layout, aligning elements, or making transformations.

1 Select lesson03-019.cr3 in the Filmstrip. Choose View > Loupe Overlay > Grid and then choose View > Loupe Overlay > Guides. To hide both the grid and guides, choose Show in the same submenu; choose it again to show them.

The Layout Image option for the Loupe overlay can be useful when you're choosing a photo—or shooting one in tethered capture mode—that is intended for use in a printed layout, in a web page design, or as a title screen for a slide show. You can create a layout sketch, with a transparent background, in PNG format, and then choose the Layout Image option.

Let's say, for example, we want to review a series of images and simulate what they would look like on a magazine cover.

2 Choose View > Loupe Overlay > Choose Layout Image.

Note: The Loupe Overlay Layout Image feature is the only instance in which Lightroom supports PNG transparency. Otherwise, transparent layers show as white.

3 Navigate to the lesson03 folder and choose the mag-cover.png that I designed. This image is set as a transparent PNG file, so you should be able to see the layout as an overlay on the picture.

4 Hold down the Command/Ctrl key to bring up overlay controls, allowing you to reposition the layout image, change the opacity of the layout or matting (the area around the layout), and use a vertical and horizontal guide to align the text with the image. Choose View > Loupe Overlay > Show to hide the grid, guides, and layout image.

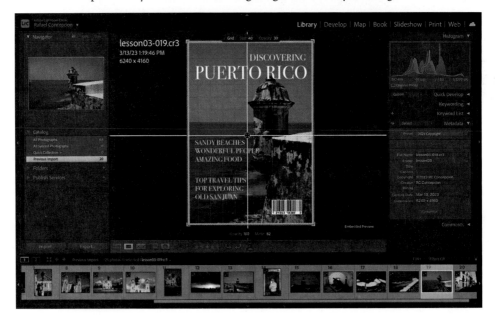

Comparing photos

As the name suggests, the Compare view is ideal for examining and evaluating images side by side.

1   In the Filmstrip, select any pair or group of similar photos; then, click the Compare View button in the Toolbar, or press the C key.

The first image that you selected becomes the *Select* image, which is displayed in the left pane of Compare view; the image displayed in the right pane is called the *Candidate*. In the Filmstrip, the Select image is marked with a white diamond icon in the upper-right corner of the image cell, whereas the Candidate image is indicated by a black diamond.

To use the Compare view to make a choice from a group of more than two photos, select your favored choice first to place it as the Select image, and then add other photos to the selection by Command-clicking/Ctrl-clicking them (for non-contiguous photos) or Shift-clicking the last one (for contiguous photos). Click the Select Previous Photo and Select Next Photo buttons (the left and right arrows on the right side of the Toolbar) or press the left and right arrow keys on your keyboard to move between the Select and Candidate photos. Should you decide that the current Candidate is better than the Select image, you can reverse their positions by clicking the Swap button in the Toolbar.

> **Tip:** To make the preview area (and thus your images) larger, hide the Module Picker and left panels by pressing F5 and F7 or clicking the white arrows at the top and left edges of the workspace.

2   To compare fine detail in the images, zoom in by dragging the Zoom slider in the Toolbar. You'll notice that the images zoom together. Drag either of the images in the Compare view and they move in unison. The closed lock icon to the left of the Zoom slider indicates that the view focus of the two images is locked.

In some situations, this may prove to be inconvenient, for instance, with photos of the same subject shot at different zoom levels or differently composed.

3   To pan the Select and Candidate images independently, click the Link Focus (lock) icon to unlink them, and then drag either image to pan the view.

A thin white line surrounds whichever photo in the Compare view is currently the active image (the image that will be affected by the Zoom slider or the controls in the right panel group).

4   Click the photo on the right to make it active, and then alter the zoom ratio.

5   Press Shift+Tab twice to show all panels. Click the lock icon to relink the views, and adjust the zoom to the zoom you like best.

6   Change the active image—the image to which your edits will be applied—by clicking the photo on the left, and then expand the Quick Develop panel. In the Tone Control section, experiment with the adjustment buttons to improve the image. Here we clicked the right double-arrow button for Highlights three times, and then the right double-arrow for Exposure and Vibrance once each to get to the result on the left, but see what you can get by experimenting with it.

Using the controls in the Quick Develop panel while you're working in Compare view can help you choose between images. Applying a develop preset or making Quick Develop adjustments can help you assess how an image will look once it's edited and adjusted. You can then either undo your Quick Develop operations and move to the Develop module to edit the image with greater precision or use the modifications you've already made as a starting point.

Using Survey view to narrow a selection

The last of the four viewing modes in the Library module, the Survey view lets you see multiple images together on one screen and then refine your selection by dropping one photo after another from the view.

1 Make sure the Previous Import folder is selected as the image source in the Catalog panel. In the Filmstrip, select four of the city shots. Click the Survey view button (the fourth from the left) in the Toolbar, or press the N key. If you need more space in the center work area, hide the side panels.

2 Navigate between the images by pressing the arrow keys on your keyboard or click the Select Previous Photo (left arrow) and Select Next Photo (right arrow) buttons in the Toolbar. The active image is surrounded by a thin border.

3 Position the pointer over the image you like least and click the Deselect Photo (X) icon that appears in the lower-right corner of the thumbnail to drop this photo from the Survey view selection.

As you eliminate candidates, the remaining photos are progressively resized and shuffled to fill the space available in the work area.

▶ **Tip:** If you have eliminated a photo accidentally, choose Edit > Undo Deselect Photo to return it to the selection, or simply Command-click/Ctrl-click its thumbnail in the Filmstrip. You can add a new photo to the selection in the Survey view in the same way.

Dropping a photo from the Survey view doesn't delete it from its folder or remove it from the catalog; the dropped image is still visible in the Filmstrip—it has simply been deselected. You can see that the images that are still displayed in the Survey view are also the only ones that remain selected in the Filmstrip.

4   Continue to eliminate photos from the Survey view. For the purposes of this exercise, deselect all but one favorite. Keep the last image selected in the Survey view for the next exercise.

Flagging and deleting images

Now that you've narrowed down a selection of images to one favorite in the Survey view, you can mark your choice with a flag.

Flagging images as either picks or rejects as you review them is an effective way to quickly sort your work; flag status is one of the criteria by which you can filter your photo library. You can also quickly remove images flagged as rejects from your catalog using a menu command or keyboard shortcut.

A white flag denotes a pick, a black one with an X marks a reject, and a neutral gray flag indicates that an image has not been flagged.

▶ **Tip:** Press the P key on your keyboard to flag a selected image as a pick, the X key to flag it as a reject, or the U key to remove any flags.

1   Still in the Survey view, move the pointer over the remaining photo to see the flag icons just below the lower-left corner. The grayed icons indicate that the image is not yet flagged. Click the flag on the left. The flag turns solid, which marks this image as a pick. In the Filmstrip, you can see that the thumbnail now displays a white flag in the upper-left corner of the image cell.

2   If you decide you don't like the image, press the X key instead. The black reject flag icon appears at the lower-left corner of the image in the Survey view and at the upper left of the image cell in the Filmstrip. The thumbnail of the rejected image is dimmed in the Filmstrip.

3   Choose Photo > Delete Rejected Photos or press Command+Delete/Ctrl+Backspace. Then, click Remove/Remove From Lightroom to remove the rejected photo from your catalog without also deleting the master file from your hard disk.

Having been removed from the Lightroom library catalog file, the rejected image is no longer visible in the Filmstrip. Press Command+Z/Ctrl+Z to restore the image, select it, and press the P key to switch it to a pick.

4   Press the G key or click the Grid view icon in the Toolbar to see all of the images as thumbnails in the Grid view. Press F7 to see the left panels again, if necessary.

Grouping images in the Quick Collection

A collection is a convenient way to keep a group of photos together in your catalog, even when the image files are actually located in different folders on your hard disk. You can create a new collection for a particular presentation or use collections to group your images by category or any other association. Your collections are always available from the Collections panel, where you can access them quickly.

The Quick Collection is a temporary holding collection: a convenient place to group images as you review and sort your new imports or while you assemble a selection of photos drawn from different folders in your catalog.

In the Grid view or the Filmstrip, you can add images to the Quick Collection with a single click and remove them just as easily. Your images will stay in the Quick Collection until you clear it or convert it to a more permanent collection listed in the Collections panel. You can access the Quick Collection from the Catalog panel so that you can return to work with the same selection of images at any time.

Moving images into or out of the Quick Collection

1 Expand the Catalog panel in the left panel group, if necessary, to see the listing for the Quick Collection.

● **Note:** If you don't see the numbers in the cells, press the J key to cycle through the different views.

2 In the Grid view or the Filmstrip, select images 6, 8, 9, and 14.

3 To add the selected photos to the Quick Collection, press the B key or choose Photo > Add To Quick Collection.

In the Catalog panel, the image count beside the Quick Collection indicates that it now contains four images. Click the Quick Collection to see the four images. If you have activated the Thumbnail Badges and Quick Collection Markers options in the Library View Options dialog box, each of the four images is marked with a gray dot in the upper-right corner of its thumbnail in the Grid view. The same markers are also shown in the Filmstrip, unless the thumbnail size is too small.

▶ **Tip:** If you don't see the Quick Collection marker when you move your pointer over a thumbnail, make sure that Show Extras and Show Badges are activated in the View > Grid View Style menu. Choose View > View Options and activate both Thumbnail Badges and Quick Collection Markers under Cell Icons in the Library View Options dialog box.

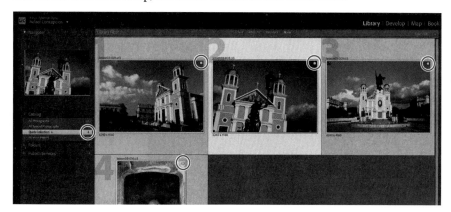

You can remove all of the selected photos from the Quick Collection by simply clicking the marker on one of the thumbnails or by pressing the B key.

4   For this exercise, you'll remove only the fourth image from the Quick Collection. First, deselect the other three images; then with only the fourth image selected, press the B key. Your Quick Collection's image count has been reduced to three.

Converting and clearing the Quick Collection

1   With the Quick Collection selected in the Catalog panel, the Grid view now displays only three images. Until you clear the Quick Collection, you can easily return to this group of images to review your selection.

Now that you've refined your selection, you can move your grouped images to a more permanent collection.

2 Choose File > Save Quick Collection.

3 In the Save Quick Collection dialog box, type **Old Town** in the Collection Name box. Select the Clear Quick Collection After Saving option, and click Save.

4 In the Catalog panel, you can see that the Quick Collection has been cleared; it now has an image count of 0. If necessary, expand the Collections panel so that you can see the listing for your new collection, which displays an image count of 3.

5 In the Folders panel, click the lesson03 folder. The Grid view once more shows all of the lesson images, including those in your new collection.

Designating a target collection

By default, the Quick Collection is designated as the *target collection*; this status is indicated by the plus sign (+) that follows the Quick Collection's name in the Catalog panel. The target collection is the collection to which a selected image is added when you press the B key or click the circular marker in the upper-right corner of the thumbnail, as you did in the previous exercise.

You can designate a collection of your own as the target collection so that you can use the same convenient techniques to add and remove photos quickly and easily.

1 Right-click the entry for your new Old Town collection in the Collections panel, and choose Set As Target Collection from the menu. The name of your collection is now followed by a plus sign (+).

2 Select the Previous Import folder in the Catalog panel, and then select image 10 (or Command-click/Ctrl-click to select multiple images) in the Grid view.

3 Make sure the Collections panel is open, and then watch as you press the B key on your keyboard; the image count for the Old Town collection increases as the selected image is added. Press B again to remove it.

4 Right-click the Quick Collection in the Catalog panel and choose Set As Target Collection. The Quick Collection once again displays the plus sign (+).

Working with the Filmstrip

No matter which module or view you're working in, the Filmstrip across the bottom of the Lightroom Classic workspace provides constant access to the images in your selected folder or collection.

As with the Grid view, you can quickly navigate through the images in the Filmstrip using the arrow keys on your keyboard. If there are more images than will fit in the visible Filmstrip, you can either use the scroll bar below the thumbnails, drag the Filmstrip by the top edge of the thumbnail frame, click the arrows at either end of the Filmstrip, or click the thumbnails at either end to access photos that are currently out of view.

Across the top of the Filmstrip, Lightroom Classic provides a convenient set of controls to help streamline your workflow.

At the far left, you'll find buttons for working with two displays, with pop-up menus that enable you to set the viewing mode for each display independently.

To the right of these buttons is the Grid view button and arrow buttons for navigating between the different folders and collections you've recently been viewing.

Next is the Filmstrip Source Indicator, where you can see at a glance which folder or collection you're viewing, how many photos it contains, how many images are currently selected, and the name of the active image or the photo that is currently under your pointer in the Filmstrip. Click the Source Indicator to see a menu listing all of the image sources that you've accessed recently.

Hiding the Filmstrip and adjusting its size

You can show and hide the Filmstrip and adjust its size, as you can with the side panel groups, to make more screen space available for the image you're working on.

1   Click All Photographs in the Catalog panel. Then, click the triangle in the lower border of the workspace window or press F6 to hide and show the Filmstrip. Right-click the triangle to set the automatic show and hide options.

2   Position the pointer over the top edge of the Filmstrip; the cursor becomes a double arrow. Drag the top edge of the Filmstrip up or down to enlarge or reduce the thumbnails. The narrower you make the Filmstrip, the more thumbnails it can display.

Using filters in the Filmstrip

As you'll see, when you have only a few photos in a folder, it's not difficult to see all of the images at once in the Filmstrip. However, when you're working with a folder containing many images, it can be inconvenient to scroll the Filmstrip looking for the photos you want to work with.

You can use the Filmstrip filters to narrow down the images displayed in the Filmstrip to only those that share a specified flag status, rating, or color label, or any combination of these attributes.

Note: If you don't see the flags, right-click anywhere in the Filmstrip image cells and choose View Options > Show Ratings And Picks.

1   In the Filmstrip, you can see that three of the images in All Photographs display the white Pick flag that you assigned earlier. Take a look at the other options available in the Filmstrip menu. Many of the commands apply to the image or images currently selected; others affect the Filmstrip itself.

2   From the Filter menu at the upper right of the Filmstrip, choose Flagged. Only the images with white flags are displayed in the Filmstrip.

3   The white flag icon is now highlighted among the Filter controls in the top bar of the Filmstrip. Click the word *Filter* at the left of the flag icons to see the attribute filter options displayed as buttons in the Filmstrip header.

You can activate or disable any of the filters you saw in the Filter menu by clicking the respective Filter buttons. You can set up a combination of filters and save it as a custom preset by choosing Save Current Settings As New Preset from the menu.

4   Click the white flag button to deactivate the active filter or choose Filters Off from the Filter menu to disable all filters. The Filmstrip once more displays all of the images in the folder. Click the word *Filter* again to hide the filter buttons.

You'll learn more about using filters in Lesson 4.

Changing the sorting order of the thumbnails

Use the Sort Direction icon and the Sort menu in the Toolbar to change the display order of the thumbnail images in the Grid view and the Filmstrip.

1   If the sorting controls are not currently visible in the Toolbar, choose Sorting from the tools menu at the right of the Toolbar.

2   Choose Pick from the Sort menu. Be sure the letters before *Sort* are listed as A to Z, rather than Z to A.

The thumbnails are rearranged in both the Grid view and the Filmstrip to display the rejected images first, then the unflagged images, and then any images with the white Pick flag.

3   Click the Sort Direction control to reverse the sorting direction of the thumbnails. The images with the white Pick flag now appear first in the order (if we had any rejected images, they would be last).

When you've grouped images in a collection, you can manually rearrange their order however you wish. This can be particularly useful when you're creating a slide-show, print layout, or web gallery that you want to save, as the images will be placed in the collection created when you save the project according to their sort order.

4 Expand the Collections panel and click the
   Old Town Collection that you created earlier in
   this lesson. Choose Capture Time from the Sort
   Criteria menu.

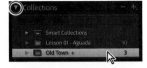

5 In the Filmstrip, drag the third image to the left and release the mouse button
   when you see a black insertion bar appear after the first thumbnail.

▶ **Tip:** You can also
change the order of
the photos in a collec-
tion by dragging the
thumbnail images in
the Grid view.

The image snaps to its new location in both the Filmstrip and the Grid view. The
new sorting order is also apparent in the Toolbar; your manual sorting order has
been saved and is now listed as Custom Order in the Sort menu.

6 Choose File Name from the Sort menu; then return to your manual sorting by
   choosing Custom Order.

Using a secondary display

Click the lesson03 folder in the Folders panel so we have more images to work with. If you have a second monitor connected to your computer, you can use it to display an additional view that is independent of the module and view mode currently active on your main monitor. You can choose to have the secondary view displayed in its own window that can be resized and repositioned or have it fill your second screen. Use the view picker at the top of the secondary display or window to switch between Grid, Loupe, Compare, Survey, and Slideshow views.

If you have only one monitor connected to your computer, you can open the additional view in a floating window that you can resize and reposition as you work.

1   To open a separate view—whether you're using one or two monitors—click the Second Window button (it looks like a monitor with a 2 in it), located at the upper left of the Filmstrip.

▶ **Tip:** You can use keyboard shortcuts to change the view in the secondary window— Shift+G for Grid, Shift+E for Loupe, Shift+C for Compare, and Shift+N for Survey. If the second window is not already open, you can use these keyboard shortcuts to quickly open it in the desired viewing mode.

2   In the top panel of the secondary window, click Grid or press Shift+G.

3   Use the Thumbnails slider in the lower-right corner of the secondary window to change the size of the thumbnail images. Use the scroll bar on the right side, if necessary, to scroll to the end of the Grid view.

Although it's possible for the secondary window to show a different enlarged photo from the main window, the Grid view in the secondary window always shows the same images as the Grid view and the Filmstrip in the main window.

The Source Indicator and menu at the left of the secondary window's lower panel work the same way as they do in the Filmstrip, and the top and bottom panels can be hidden and shown, just as they can in the main window.

4   Click to select any thumbnail in the secondary window's grid, and then click Loupe in the view picker at the left of the top panel. Check the picker at the right of the top panel to make sure that Normal mode is active.

● **Note:** If your secondary display is open in a window rather than on a second screen, you may need to change the focus for any keyboard input by clicking inside the main window or on its title bar.

When the secondary window is in Normal mode, the Loupe view displays the active image from the Grid view and the Filmstrip in the main window.

5   Use the left and right arrow keys on your keyboard to select another photo in the Grid view. The new selection becomes the active image, and the secondary window is updated accordingly.

6   Click Live in the mode picker at the right of the secondary window's top panel.

In Live mode, the secondary window shows the image that is currently under your pointer in the main window—whether that image is a thumbnail in the Filmstrip or the Grid view or enlarged in the Loupe, Compare, or Survey view.

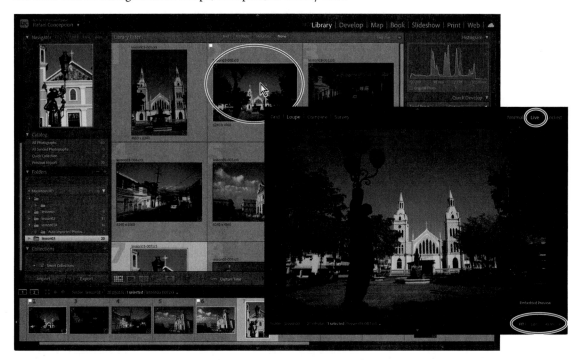

You can set a different zoom level for the secondary window in Loupe view by choosing from the picker at the lower right of the secondary window.

7   Select an image in the Filmstrip; then switch the secondary window to Locked mode by clicking Locked in the mode picker at the right of the top panel. The current image will now remain fixed in the secondary display until you return to Normal or Live mode—regardless of the image displayed in the main window.

8   Change the zoom level for the secondary window by choosing from the picker at the right of the lower panel: click Fit/Fill, 100%, or choose a zoom percentage from the menu at the far right.

9   Drag the zoomed image to reposition it in the secondary window, and then click the image to return to the previous zoom level.

10 (Optional) Right-click the image to choose a different background color or texture from the menu. These settings will apply to the secondary window independently of the options chosen for the main window.

11 Select Compare in the view picker at the left of the secondary window's top panel. The selected image and the next image in the Grid view or in the Filmstrip in the main window automatically become the Select and Candidate images, but you can select two or more images to replace them.

12 As in the main window, the image on the left of the Compare view is the Select image; the image on the right is the Candidate. To change the Candidate photo, make sure the Candidate pane is active, and then click the Select Previous Photo or the Select Next Photo button. If you have more than two images selected, only images from the selection are considered as Candidates. To replace the Select image with the current Candidate, click the Make Select button.

13 In the main window, select three or more images, and then click Survey in the top panel of the second window. Use the Survey view to compare more than two images at once. To remove an image from the Survey view, move the pointer over the unwanted image and click the Deselect Photo button that appears in the lower-right corner of the image.

14 Choose Show in the Window > Secondary Display menu to deselect it, or click the Close button to close the secondary window.

Review questions

1 Name the four working views in the Library module, and explain how they're used.

2 What is the Navigator?

3 How do you use the Quick Collection?

4 What is the target collection?

Review answers

1 The four working views are Grid, Loupe, Compare, and Survey. Press the G key or click the Grid view button in the Toolbar to see thumbnails of your images while you search, apply flags, ratings, and labels, or create collections. Use the keyboard shortcut E or click the Loupe view button to inspect a single photo at a range of magnifications. Press C or click the Compare view button to see two images side by side. Click the Survey view button in the Toolbar or use the keyboard shortcut N to evaluate several images at once or refine a selection.

2 The Navigator is an interactive full-image preview that helps you move around easily within a zoomed image in Loupe view. Click or drag in the Navigator preview to reposition the view while a white rectangle indicates the portion of the magnified image that is currently visible in the workspace. The Navigator panel also contains controls for setting the zoom levels for the Loupe view. Click the image in Loupe view to switch between the last two zoom levels set in the Navigator panel.

3 To create a Quick Collection, select one or more images and then press the B key or choose Photo > Add To Quick Collection. The Quick Collection is a temporary holding area; you can continue to add—or remove—images until you are ready to save the grouping as a more permanent collection. It resides in the Catalog panel.

4 The target collection is the collection to which a selected image will be added when you press the B key or click the circular marker in the upper-right corner of the thumbnail. By default, the Quick Collection is designated as the target collection; this status is indicated by the plus sign (+) that follows the Quick Collection's name in the Catalog panel. You can designate a collection of your own as the target collection so that you can use the same convenient techniques to add and remove photos quickly.

PHOTOGRAPHY SHOWCASE
LATANYA HENRY

"The ability to capture a photo has given me the opportunity to connect with people across the world and across language barriers."

I got my first camera when I was 10 years old—a Kodak 110 that I took everywhere.

I grew up with a love for exploring the world through a camera and for documenting all of the important people and moments around me. I loved having a catalog of snapshots in time, preserving memories for years to come.

Later, I found that portrait photography allowed me to connect with new people and to help them see their unique beauty. However, wedding photography reignited my passion for capturing stories. In working with my clients, I get the privilege of getting to know their personalities and families, capturing some of their most precious moments, and preserving their love stories for the future.

To this day, I carry my camera wherever I go. The ability to capture a photo has given me the opportunity to connect with people across the world and across language barriers. It has allowed me to capture wonderful places, and to freeze memories in time. From weddings to travels to average days with family I always find joy in capturing the story of a moment.

lhwedding.com
instagram.com/latanyaandcoweddings

4 MANAGING YOUR PHOTO LIBRARY

Lesson overview

As your photo library grows, it is increasingly important to organize your files so that they can be found easily. Lightroom Classic offers options for organizing your images before you even click the Import button, and even more once they're in your catalog. You will manage folders and files without leaving the Library module; apply keywords, flags, ratings, and labels; and then group photos in convenient collections, regardless of where they're stored. In this lesson, you'll learn how to:

- Work with a folder structure and understand and use collections.

- Work with keywords, flags, ratings, and labels.

- Tag faces in the People view and organize images by name.

- Edit metadata and use the Painter tool to speed up your workflow.

- Find and filter files.

 This lesson will take about 90 minutes to complete. To get the lesson files used in this chapter, download them from the web page for this book at *peachpit.com/LightroomCIB2024*. For more information, see "Accessing the lesson files and Web Edition" in the "Getting Started" section at the beginning of this book.

Lightroom Classic delivers powerful, versatile tools to help you organize your image library. Use people tags, keywords, flags, labels, ratings, and even GPS location data to sort your images and group them into virtual collections by any association you choose. Make fast, sophisticated searches, based on practically limitless combinations of criteria, that will put the photos you want at your fingertips.

Getting started

Note: This lesson assumes that you already have a basic working familiarity with the Lightroom Classic workspace. If you need more background information, refer to Lightroom Classic Help, or review the previous lessons.

Before you begin, make sure you've set up the LRC2024CIB folder for your lesson files and created the LRC2024CIB Catalog file to manage them, as described in "Accessing the lesson files and Web Edition" and "Creating a catalog file for working with this book" in the "Getting Started" section at the start of this book.

If you haven't already done so, download the lesson04 and lesson04-gps folders from your Account page at peachpit.com to the LRC2024CIB\Lessons folder (see "Accessing the lesson files and Web Edition" in the "Getting Started" section).

1 Start Lightroom Classic.

2 In the Adobe Photoshop Lightroom Classic - Select Catalog dialog box, make sure the file LRC2024CIB Catalog.lrcat is selected under Select A Recent Catalog To Open, and then click Open.

Tip: The first time you enter any of the Lightroom Classic modules, you'll see module tips that will help you get started by identifying the components of the workspace and stepping you through the standard workflow. Dismiss the tips by clicking the Close button. To reactivate the tips for any module, choose [*Module name*] Tips from the Help menu.

3 Lightroom Classic will open in the screen mode and workspace module that were active when you last quit. If necessary, switch to the Library module by clicking Library in the Module Picker at the top of the workspace.

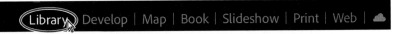

Importing images into the library

The first step is to import the images for this lesson into the Lightroom library.

1 In the Library module, click the Import button below the left panel group.

2 If the Import dialog box appears in compact mode, click the Show More Options button at the lower left of the dialog box to see all of the options in the expanded Import dialog box.

3 Under Source at the left of the expanded Import dialog box, locate and select your LRC2024CIB\Lessons\lesson04 folder. Ensure that Include Subfolders is selected and all 36 images from the lesson04 folder are selected for import.

4 In the import options above the thumbnail previews, select Add so that the imported photos will be added to your catalog without being moved or copied. In the File Handling panel at the right, choose Embedded & Sidecar from the Build Previews menu and ensure that the Don't Import Suspected Duplicates option is selected. In the Apply During Import panel, choose None from both the Develop Settings menu and the Metadata menu, and type **Lesson 04, Collections** in the Keywords text box. Make sure that your import is set up as shown here, and then click Import.

You may get a dialog box asking if you want to enable Address Lookup. You can do so now or when we explore the Map module later in the chapter. The 36 images are imported from the lesson04 folder and now appear in both the Grid view of the Library module and the Filmstrip across the bottom of the workspace.

Folders vs. collections

▶ **Tip:** The Import New Photos option in the Synchronize Folder dialog box (Library > Synchronize Folder) automatically imports any files that have been added to a folder without yet having been added to your image library. Optionally, activate Show Import Dialog Before Importing to choose which of the new files you want to import. Activate the Scan For Metadata Updates option to check for files with metadata modified in another application.

Each time you import an image, Lightroom creates a new catalog entry to record the file's address on your drive—the folder in which it is stored and the volume that contains that folder—in the Folders panel in the left panel group.

To keep a handle on your growing library, you need to store your pictures in folders, and you need those folders to keep some sort of structure. However, folders are an inefficient way of organizing your information, especially when it comes to photography, where you may want access to individual images in a whole bunch of places. To do that, you need collections.

Folders store; they do not organize

Let me give you a quick example. Let's imagine a picture that I think is so amazing, it's one of my best photos and I want to use it for a variety of things. I think this image is a good example of my photography of kids, it captured one of the best moments in our family life, and it is a great picture of my daughter, Sabine. I may want to show it to different people at different times and in different circumstances. My solution? I create an album for each of these moments and place the picture of Sabine in each of the folders.

While that might seem like a good solution, we now have one file living in five separate places. If the photo is 10 MB in size, I would be taking up 50 MB of storage—five times the amount I need—simply to have it easily accessible in every possible photo group I might need it in. From a disk usage standpoint, that's inefficient.

Then what happens if I need to make a change to the file? I would have to remember all of the locations where that file lives and make sure that every change I make is added to the image in each location. That's even more inefficient. Thankfully, Lightroom solves a lot of this with collections.

Using collections to organize images

A collection is a virtual folder that allows you to organize your pictures from any number of separate physical folders, whether on your hard disk, removable drive, or network-attached storage device. A single master image can be included in any number of collections without adding space, which gives you the flexibility to organize all of your images. If we followed the previous example, I can have five different collections in Lightroom—one for each situation—and each collection can have the same image inside of it, but all of those "images" are simply references in the catalog to the same physical file.

This concept is the literal cornerstone of everything you do in Lightroom, and your ability to master this method of organization makes using it so much easier.

There are several types of collections in Lightroom: the Quick Collection, collections, collection sets, and smart collections, listed in what I feel is the order of importance to your workflow.

Any collection can also be part of an output collection—a collection that is created automatically when you save a print layout or a creative project such as a photo book or web gallery, linking a set of images to a particular project template, together with all of your customized settings.

Any collection can also become a publish collection, which automatically keeps track of images that you've shared via an online service or which is synced to Lightroom on your mobile device via Adobe Creative Cloud.

Let's walk through the first four, step by step, as it is vital that you get these under your belt.

The Quick Collection

The Quick Collection is a temporary holding collection, a convenient place to assemble a group of images from different folders. You can access the Quick Collection from the Catalog panel so that you can easily return to work with the same selection of images at any time. Your images will stay in the Quick Collection until you are ready to convert your selection to a permanent collection that will then be listed in the Collections panel.

You can create as many collections and smart collections as you wish, but there is only one Quick Collection; if there is already a selection of images in the Quick Collection, you'll need to clear the Quick Collection or convert it to a standard collection and then clear it before you can use it to assemble a new grouping.

We already created a Quick Collection in Lesson 3, "Exploring the Lightroom Workspace," so let's move on to the two that you will use the most in Lightroom: the collection and the collection set.

> **Tip:** If you are a user of the Apple service iTunes, think of collections as playlists for your pictures. You have one picture, but it can go in multiple playlists.

> **Tip:** You can learn more about publish collections in the bonus lesson in the download files. For how to access those files, see the "Getting Started" section at the beginning of the book.

> **Tip:** If the Thumbnail Badges option is selected in the Library View Options, a photo that is included in a collection of any kind displays the collection badge in the lower right of its thumbnail.

Click the badge to see a menu listing the collections in which the image is included. Select a collection from the menu to switch to that collection.

Creating collections

In the lesson04 folder, there are a series of images that are placed inside subfolders. I think that this example is a tried-and-true way to explain collections in a manner that makes the most sense. As a bonus, you'll get to meet my family!

1　Click the 20230109 folder in the lesson04 folder. Once the images appear in the Grid view, select all of them by pressing Command+A/Ctrl+A.

2　Click the plus sign (+) icon at the upper right of the Collections panel, and choose Create Collection. In the Create Collection dialog, type **Jenn Organizing**, and in the Options area, make sure Include Selected Photos is selected, and then click Create.

 Tip: Once you've grouped a selection of photos as a collection, you can rearrange them in the Grid view or the Filmstrip, changing the order in which they will appear in a presentation or a print layout. Your customized sorting order is saved with the collection.

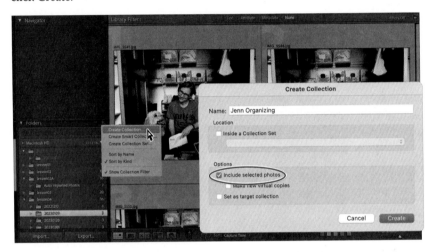

A new collection has been made in the Collections panel with three images in it (if your images are reversed, click the A to Z icon to the left of Sort in the Toolbar below the main work area). The pictures in this collection are digital references to the physical copies on your hard drive.

Let's experiment with the power of collections even further.

3 Create two additional collections, called **Jenn and Dixie** and **Jenn MFP**. Make sure that you place the second file of the previously selected ones (IMG_5546.jpg) in both of the collections you just created.

As a result, we now have three different collections, and each collection has the same file of my wife, Jenn, but they still reference only one physical file. But it gets better.

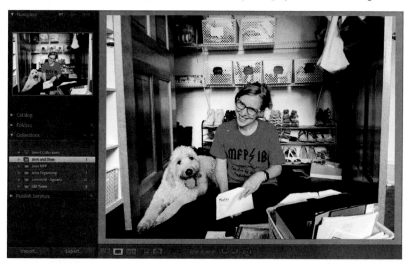

4 Select the Jenn and Dixie collection, and be sure the above picture is selected.

5 In the Quick Develop panel, click the Exposure single arrow on the right once and the double arrow on the left for Highlights twice to bring back detail.

Click each of the collections in the Collections panel, and you'll see that this photo is automatically updated in all three collections the moment you make a change in one of the collections, since they all reference that same, single physical image file.

Smarter file management, smaller file sizes, immediate version control—this is why collections are so important.

Pro tip: Automatic collections from folders

Let's make collections from all of the folders for this lesson.

1 Click the first folder and Shift-click the last one to select all of them. Command-click/Ctrl-click the Jenn Organizing folder (we already made that one). Right-click any one of the selected folders and choose Create Collections From Selected Folders.

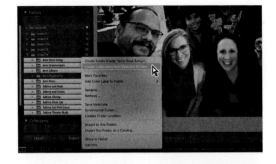

2 In the Collections panel, compare the collection names to the names of the folders that you imported from the lesson04 folder, making sure all match.

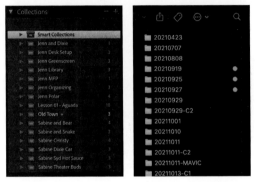

Here, I created folders with names to make it easier for you, but when you're doing this for your archive, I recommend keeping dates for folder names and renaming them in the Collections panel later.

Your turn: Make a new collection

Let's make another new collection, this time one that includes images from multiple folders.

1 Click the Collections panel's plus sign (+) icon again, and create a new collection called **Lightroom Book Highlights**. Make sure Include Selected Photos is unselected. Click Create.

2 Click the lesson04 folder in the Folders panel to see all of the images you've imported. If necessary, make the thumbnails smaller so you can see all of them.

3 Command-click/Ctrl-click any four of the images and drag them into the new collection. The goal here is to make sure that you are selecting images from more than one folder inside the lesson04 folder.

Your new collection now houses images from different folders, yet each one still reflects only a single physical copy on your computer. As your photographic needs grow, you'll find that you need to organize collections like digital albums—to share the best of a series of images in short order.

Working with collection sets

It's easy to see that, as you add more collections, your list in the Collections panel could get a little unwieldy. If you use Lightroom for professional and personal work and have a lot of different collections for each, it will be hard to scroll through them all and see where your work images are versus your family images.

We need to better group and organize our collections. This is where collection sets come in. Collection sets are virtual folders that can hold both collections and other collection sets.

Let's go through some examples with the collections that we have so far. Take a look at the collections we've made so far; we can find some elements that each of them share.

Tip: While it's incredibly useful to have collections created from existing folders, I'm not a fan of having them named exactly the same as my folder names. When I make collections, the names are more descriptive and less technical. So I normally rename the collections to something that makes more sense to me.

There is a series of collections with images of my wife, Jenn. There also is a series of collections with images of my daughter, Sabine. Let's start with Jenn.

1 Click the plus sign (+) icon at the upper right of the Collections panel and choose Create Collection Set.

2 In the Create Collection Set dialog box, for Name, type **Jenn Images**, and make sure Inside A Collection Set is unselected.

3 Click Create, and then drag all of the Jenn collections into the Jenn Images collection set.

You now have all of the Jenn collections organized in one spot.

4 Create another collection set, and this time, for Name, type **Sabine Images**. Place all of the Sabine collections inside of it. When done, your collections should look like the illustration to the right.

5 Looking at the Jenn and Sabine collection sets, what do these two sets have in common? They are family pictures! Let's create one more collection set. In the Create Collection Set dialog box, for Name, type **Family Pictures**. Instead of placing collections in it, drag the two collection sets—Jenn Images and Sabine Images—inside of it.

The great part about this is that you can see all of the family pictures by clicking the Family Pictures collection set, individual people by clicking their individual set, or specific moments by clicking the individual collections. Organizational nirvana!

When I turn to the work I do with people, I have a large collection set called "Model Shoots" that then has a collection set for each individual model I work with. Within the collection set for each model, there are separate collection sets for the individual shoots that I would do with them. This is helpful when you do multiple shoots with a specific person. Inside each shoot collection set, I have individual collections for particular views of my images: All Images, Picked Images, Final Images, and so on.

For my workflow, I like to make a collection set for each individual event, and inside that collection set, I tend to have a common set of collections that I use.

In previous versions of Lightroom, this was a process that required multiple steps, but Adobe has since made this much easier with one change.

Duplicating collection sets

1. Create a collection set called **Dummy Collection Set**. In it, place a series of collections that you will find helpful for your specific workflow. I've included collections for All Images, Picked Images, Rejected Images, and The Final Set. Make sure that this dummy collection set is not inside of any other collection sets.

2. Once you have imported your images for your new shoot, right-click the dummy collection set you just created and select Duplicate Collection Set from the menu.

Tip: The collections that you make inside of the collection set will be listed in alphabetical order. This is why I called the last collection set in the series "The Final Set" instead of "Final Set." If I had not added the article "the," it would have appeared below the All Images collection set. Making sure that I have it at the bottom just works better for me from a workflow perspective.

3 This creates a new collection set called
  "Dummy Collection Set Copy," and
  you'll notice that all of the collections
  that you created in Dummy Collection
  Set also are included in the copy.

4 Right-click the duplicate collection set
  and rename it to the specific name of
  your new shoot.

5 At this point, you can move the renamed
  collection set into any major category
  collection set you have created. Then,
  click Previous Import in the Catalog
  panel and move those images into the
  All Images collection for this shoot. As
  you start to cull the images down to a
  workable set, you can move them into
  the collections that make the most sense
  for you.

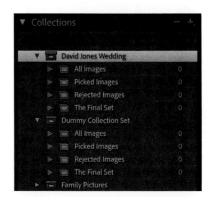

It's important to note that collection sets
can be set up in whatever manner makes
the most sense for you and can vary from
photographer to photographer.

Think of collections and collection sets as
extremely powerful sock drawer organizers.
There are a million ways to set them up, and
each setup will be right for each individual
person. The recommendations I make here
are based on the amount of time I've spent
making pictures, working with Lightroom,
and consulting with other photographers
on how to best set up their sock drawers.
The bigger takeaway is that you need to
have a plan.

Collection sets for organizing your work

Collection sets offer you a way to sort out large areas of your work into sections (as shown above) that are much easier to navigate as your library grows. For example, I have a collection set at the right called "Jobs," where I keep all of my freelance work. In that collection set, I have other collection sets that house individual jobs that I've done. Inside each of my Jobs collection sets, I have individual collections. The David Michel Shoot collection set is a job, but in that job, I have a collection that shows me all of the images, and a collection that shows me the selected images from the shoot.

But what if a subset of my work included baby shoots? I could further break down my Jobs collection set by adding a Baby Shots collection set. In the Baby Shots collection set, I can add collection sets for each individual job (each baby or each client), and inside of those collection sets, I can add collections for different groups of images from that job (All Images, Selects, Final Pictures, and so on).

Smart collections

A smart collection searches the metadata attached to your photos and gathers together all those images in your library that meet a specified set of criteria. Any newly imported photo that matches the criteria you've set up for a smart collection will be added to that collection automatically.

You can create a smart collection by choosing Library > New Smart Collection and entering a descriptive name based on the criteria you add. Then specify the search criteria for your smart collection by choosing options from the menus in the Create Smart Collection dialog box. If you want to search all of your images, deselect the Inside A Collection Set checkbox.

You can add search criteria by clicking the plus sign (+) icon to the right of any rule. Hold down the Option/Alt key and click the plus sign (+) icon to refine a rule. I added a second rule to search for images containing the word *Sabine* in any search-able text and then added a third and a fourth rule to search for images that are flagged and were edited this year.

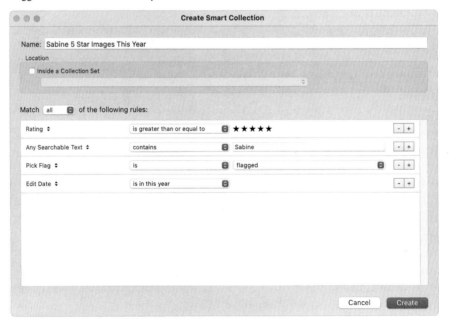

Taking your collections on the road

Lightroom Classic enables you to sync photo collections between your desktop computer and your mobile devices so that you can access, organize, edit, and share your photos anywhere, anytime. Whether you're working in Lightroom on your desktop or on your iPad, iPhone, or Android device, any changes you make to photos in a synced collection will be updated automatically on the other device.

Syncing photos from Lightroom Classic

Lightroom lets you sync from only one catalog. Since we are working on a sample catalog, I won't recommend that you switch to your personal catalog and sync images now. Instead, I'll switch to my personal catalog and demonstrate the process of syncing—it's easy enough to do—so you'll be prepared to share and sync online when you are finished with the book and have switched back to your own catalog.

Note: This exercise assumes that you have already signed in to Lightroom Classic with your Adobe ID. If you have not yet signed in, you'll need to do so before you begin; choose Help > Sign In.

1 Click the cloud icon at the upper right of the workspace to open the activity center, and then click Start Syncing at the bottom left. To change your sync settings, click the gear icon to the right.

2 In the Collections panel, click the empty checkbox at the left of the name of one of your collections to sync it to Lightroom. If the Share Your Synced Collections tip appears, dismiss it for now.

You'll know that your collection is online when you see a Make Public button at the top right of the work area.

By default, when you share it online, your collection is private. If you click the Make Public button, it switches to Make Private, and a URL is generated that you can copy and give to others or click to go to the collection online.

The link that you get from Lightroom Classic is designed to allow recipients to view, like, and comment on your collection. Lightroom also gives you a few options for managing your online collections, both in the mobile app and in a browser.

Viewing synced photos on your mobile device

1   On your mobile device, tap the Lightroom app icon, and then sign in to Lightroom for mobile with your Adobe ID, Facebook, or Google.

The first screen you'll see is the Albums view, which lists the collections you've synced from your desktop, as well as any you create in Lightroom mobile, and also offers some built-in views. First is the All Photos view, where you can browse all of your synced images and all photos taken by your device camera and imported into Lightroom. There is a view that shows you only the images taken in Lightroom, one that shows you the most recently added images, one that shows you the most recently edited photos, and one that shows only photos with faces.

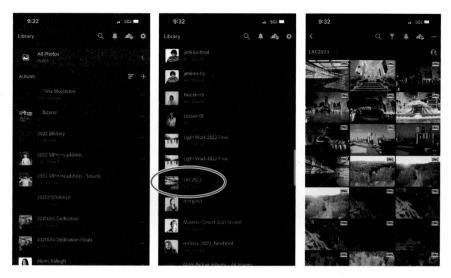

Scroll down to find the album that has been synced online and tap it to see it.

2 One of my favorite features of the mobile app is that you can perform edits on images in collections that you have synced online. Tap an image in the synced collection to see the editing tools in groups along the bottom (with the device vertical) or right side (with the device horizontal) of the screen.

All of the editing tools that you will learn how to use in the Develop module, in the next lesson, are available to you on a mobile device. You can import, sync, and then work on the go in a matter of seconds. Tap a tool group to open it.

Any changes that you make online will automatically sync (if you have an internet connection) with Lightroom Classic. This makes for a powerful editing combination.

Editing on the *lightroom.adobe.com* site

If you don't have access to the mobile app but do have access to a browser, simply go to *lightroom.adobe.com* and sign in. On this site, you'll have access to all of the collections that you shared online, and you can do more than just view the images.

As with the mobile app, the website offers you a suite of controls, similar to what you would use in Lightroom Classic. With all of this flexibility, you are never too far from an edit or a share.

As soon as you complete this book, I encourage you to sign in to the Lightroom website (*lightroom.adobe.com*) and share a couple of your own collections. You'll be surprised at how much you can do.

Colors for collections

Not only can you select colors for images that can be seen in the Library module's Grid view, but the feature also applies to collections and collection sets. This should be another great visual aid to find what you need that much faster.

To assign a color to a collection, right-click the collection or collection set and select Add Color Label To Collection from the menu. You will have the option of selecting Red, Yellow, Green, Blue, or Purple. Once you select a color, it will appear at the far right of the collection's name in the Collections panel.

If you have color-labeled collections nested in a hierarchy of collection sets, you also have an option to filter your collections by a specific color. Click the magnifying glass in the search field at the top of the Collections panel and you will see an option to filter the collections in your list by color labels.

To remove a color from a collection, right-click the collection, select Add Color Label To Collection, and select None from the menu. To create your own label names (like changing Red to In Progress and Blue to Final Images), choose Metadata > Color Label Set > Edit. In the Edit Color Label Set dialog box, click the Collections tab, and then change any label names you want.

Using keyword tags

Perhaps the most direct way to mark your photos so that they're easier to find later is by tagging them with keywords—text metadata attached to the image files to categorize them by subject or association.

For example, the image in the illustration at the right could be tagged with the keywords Jenn, library, and books, and could therefore be located by searching for any one or a combination of those tags. If the Thumbnail Badges option is selected in the Library View Options dialog box, photos with keyword tags are identified by a keywords badge at the lower right of the thumbnail.

You can apply keywords to your photos individually or tag an entire series of images with shared metadata in one operation, thereby linking them by association and making them easier to access among all of the photos that make up your library. Keywords added to images in Lightroom can be read by Adobe applications such as Bridge, Photoshop, and Photoshop Elements, and by other applications that support XMP metadata.

Viewing keyword tags

Because you applied keyword tags to the images for this lesson during the import process, the thumbnails in the Grid view and the Filmstrip are all marked with the keywords badge. Let's review the keywords you already attached to these photos.

1   Make sure that you are still in the Grid view, and then select the lesson04 folder in the Folders panel.

▶ **Tip:** Clicking the keyword badge of an image in Grid view will automatically expand the Keywording panel.

2   Show the right panel group, if necessary, and then expand the Keywording panel. Expand the Keyword Tags text box at the top of the panel. By selecting each thumbnail in the Grid view in turn, you can confirm that all of the images in the lesson04 folder share the keywords "Collections" and "Lesson 04."

3   Select any one of the photos in the lesson04 folder. In the Keyword Tags text box at the top of the Keywording panel, select the text "Lesson 04" and press the Delete/Backspace key on your keyboard to delete it.

4   Click anywhere in the Grid view, and then choose
    Edit > Select All or press Command+A/Ctrl+A
    to select all of the photos in the lesson04 folder.
    In the Keyword Tags text box, the keyword
    "Lesson 04" is now marked with an asterisk to
    indicate that this tag is not shared by every image
    in the selection.

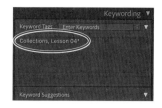

5   Expand the Keyword List panel.

In the Keyword List, a checkmark to the left of
the keyword "Collections" indicates that this tag
is shared by every image in the selection, while
the tag "Lesson 04" is marked with a dash, indicating that it is attached to some, but not all, of the
selected images. The image count to the right of the
Collections tag shows that it is shared by all 36 of the
images for this lesson, while the Lesson 04 tag shows
that it is shared by only 35 of the 36 images.

6   With all 36 images still selected, click the dash in
    front of the Lesson 04 tag to reinstate the deleted
    tag; a checkmark replaces the dash, and the image count for the Lesson 04
    keyword increases to 36.

Tip: You can apply an existing keyword tag to selected images by clicking the tag in the Keyword Suggestions area in the Keywording panel. To remove a tag from a selected photo or photos, either delete the word from the Keyword Tags text box in the Keywording panel or click the checkbox to disable that keyword in the Keyword List panel.

Adding keyword tags

You already added keywords to your images during the process of importing them
into your Lightroom library. Once the images have been added to your Lightroom
library, you can add more keywords by using the Keywording panel.

1   In the Collections panel, click the Sabine and Snake collection, and then click the
    first image to select it.

2   In the Keywording panel, at the bottom of the Keyword Tags area, click where
    it says "Click Here To Add Keywords," and type **Snake, Python**. Make sure to
    separate the new keywords with a comma.

Note: Always use
a comma to separate
keywords; words sepa-
rated by only a space
(Copenhagen Denmark)
or by a period
(Copenhagen.Denmark)
will be treated as a
single keyword.

3 Press Return/Enter when done. The new keywords are listed in alphabetical order in the Keywording panel and in the Keyword List panel.

4 Select the second image in the collection and Command-click/Ctrl-click the third to select both images.

5 In the Keywording panel, click in the text box at the bottom of the Keyword Tags area and type **Pets**. Press Return/Enter.

6 Choose Edit > Select None or press Command+D/Ctrl+D on your keyboard.

7 Add the keywords Hot Sauce to the images in the Sabine Syd Hot Sauce folder.

Working with keyword sets and nesting keywords

Tip: Keyword sets are a convenient way to have the keywords you need at hand as you work on different collections in your library. A single keyword tag may be included in any number of keyword sets. If you don't see the Lightroom presets in the Keyword Set menu, open the Lightroom Preferences and click the Presets tab. In the Lightroom Defaults options, click Restore Keyword Set Presets.

You can use the Keyword Set area in the Keywording panel to work with *keyword sets*—groups of keywords compiled for a particular purpose. You could create a set of keywords for a specific project, another set for a special occasion, and one for your friends and family. Lightroom Classic provides three basic keyword set presets. You can use these sets as they are or as starting points for creating sets of your own.

1 Expand the Keyword Set area in the Keywording panel, if necessary, and then choose Wedding Photography from the Keyword Set menu. You can see that the keywords in the set would be helpful in organizing the shots from a big event. Look at the categories covered by the other Lightroom keyword sets. You can use these as templates for your own keyword sets by editing them to suit your needs and saving your changes as a new preset.

Grouping your keywords in keyword sets is one way to keep your keywords organized. Another handy technique is to nest related tags in a keywords hierarchy.

2 Click the Python keyword in the Keyword List panel, and then drag it onto the Pets keyword. The Pets keyword (the "parent" keyword) expands automatically to show the Python tag (the "child" keyword tag) nested inside it.

3 In the keyword list, drag the Lesson 01, Lesson 03 - Mayaguez, and Lesson 04 keywords onto the Collections keyword. The Collections tag expands to show the nested tags.

4 I want to create a Utah keyword inside of the keyword The Valley that I added to some of the photos in Lesson 2. Click the keyword The Valley in the keyword list; then click the plus sign (+) icon at the upper left of the panel to create a new keyword tag.

5 In the Keyword Name text box in the Create Keyword Tag dialog box, type **Utah**. Make sure the first three options under Keyword Tag Options are selected as shown in the illustration at the right, and then click Create.

- **Include On Export** Includes the keyword tag when your photos are exported.

- **Export Containing Keywords** Includes the parent tag when your photos are exported.

- **Export Synonyms** Includes any synonyms associated with the keyword tag when your photos are exported.

6 In the Folders panel, select the lesson02 folder, set the Sort menu to File Name, and then select the last nine images in the folder. Drag the Utah keyword tag from the Keyword List panel onto any of the selected images in the Grid view.

In the Keyword List, the checkmarks to the left of the Utah and The Valley keyword tags, as well as the image count to the right of each entry, indicate that both keyword tags have been applied to all selected photos.

▶ **Tip:** To transfer lists of keywords between computers or share them with colleagues who are also working in Lightroom, use the Export Keywords and Import Keywords commands, which you'll find in the Metadata menu.

Searching by keyword

Once you've taken the time to organize your images by adding keywords and other metadata, such as ratings, flags, and labels, it is easy to set up sophisticated and detailed filters to find exactly the photo you're looking for.

For now, we'll look at some techniques for finding the photos in your library by searching (or filtering) for keywords alone.

● **Note:** If you find that you cannot have two panels open at the same time in either of the side panel groups, right-click the header of any panel in the group and disable Solo mode in the menu.

1   Choose Library > Show Photos In Subfolders, if it's not already selected. In the left panel group, collapse other panels, if necessary so that you can clearly see the contents of the Catalog and Folders panels. In the Catalog panel, click All Photographs, and then choose Edit > Select None or press Command+D/Ctrl+D.

2   Use the Thumbnails slider in the Toolbar to reduce the size of the thumbnails, so that you'll be able to see as many images as possible in the Grid view. If the Filter bar is not already visible above the Grid view, choose View > Show Filter Bar or press the Backslash key (\).

3   In the right panel group, collapse other panels, if necessary, so that you can see the contents of the expanded Keyword List panel.

4   In the Keyword List panel, move your pointer over the keyword Aguada, and then click the white arrow that appears to the right of the image count.

In the left panel group, All Photographs is now selected in the Catalog panel, if it wasn't already, indicating that your entire catalog was searched for photos with the Aguada tag.

The Metadata filter was activated in the Filter bar at the top of the work area with the Agauda keyword selected in the first column. The Grid view now displays only those images in your library that are tagged with the Aguada keyword tag.

The images in the Grid view are filtered so that only the 11 photos with the tag are still visible. Now you'll use a different technique to search.

5 Click All at the top of the Keyword column and then click Text at the top of the Filter bar. In the Text filter options, choose Any Searchable Field from the first menu and Contains All from the second menu, noting the options in each menu. Then type **Hot Sauce** in the text box at the right and press Return/Enter.

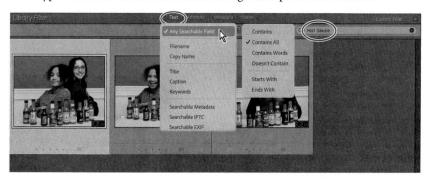

▶ **Tip:** You can use the lock button at the right end of the Filter bar to keep your current filter settings active when you choose a different image source from the Catalog, Folders, or Collections panel.

Only three photos are still visible in the Grid view—the ones you added at the start of the lesson. Of course, the true power of the Library filters comes into play only when you set up more complex filters based on a combination of criteria, but this exercise should have given you at least a glimpse of the possibilities.

6   At the top of the Filter bar, click None to deactivate the filters. In the Folders panel, select the lesson04 folder, and then choose Edit > Select None or press Command+D/Ctrl+D.

Using flags and ratings

The Attribute filters in the Filter bar allow you to search and sort your images according to attributes such as flags and ratings. When you click Attribute in the Library Filter bar, the Filter bar expands to display controls for sorting your images by flag status, edit status, star rating, color label, copy status, or any combination of these attributes.

Flagging images

Assigning flags to sort the good images from the rejects (and from the unflagged so-so images) can be a good way to begin organizing a group of photos. You can flag an image as a pick or a reject, or you can leave it unflagged.

1   Select Attribute at the top of the Filter bar. The Filter bar expands to show the Attribute filter controls.

2   If the Toolbar is not already visible below the Grid view, press the T key. Click the triangle at the right side of the Toolbar and choose Flagging from the menu to show the Flag As Pick and Set As Rejected buttons in the Toolbar.

> **Tip:** In the Grid and Loupe views, you'll find tools for adding ratings, flags, and color labels in the Toolbar. In the Compare and Survey views, you can change any of these attributes using the controls beneath the images. You can also flag, rate, or color label a selected image by using the Set Flag, Set Rating, or Set Color Label commands in the Photo menu.

3   In the Collections panel, select the Sabine Christy collection.

4   In the Grid view, click one of the images from this group of photos. If the Flags option is selected under Cell Icons in the Library View Options dialog box, you'll see a gray (unfilled) flag icon in the upper-left corner of the image cell, indicating

that this photo is not flagged. If you don't see the flag icon, hold the pointer over the image cell or disable the Show Clickable Items On Mouse Over Only option in the Library View Options dialog box. To open the View Options dialog box, choose View > View Options or press Command+J/Ctrl+J.

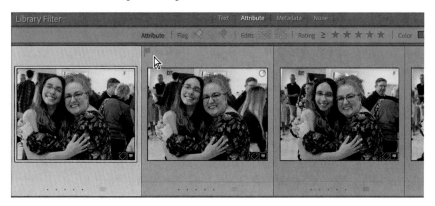

5 To change the flag status to Flagged, you can click either the flag badge in the image cell or the Flag As Pick button in the Toolbar. Note that the photo is now marked with a white flag icon in the upper-left corner of the image cell.

6 Click the white flag button in the Attribute Filter bar. The Grid view displays only the image that you just flagged. The view is now filtered to display only flagged images from the Sabine Christy collection.

> **Tip:** You can use the Library > Refine Photos command to sort your photos quickly on the basis of their flagging status. Choose Library > Refine Photos, and then click Refine in the Refine Photos dialog box; any unflagged photos are flagged as rejects, and the picks are reset to unflagged status.

Lightroom Classic offers a variety of ways to flag a photo. To flag a photo as a pick, choose Photo > Set Flag > Flagged or press the P key on your keyboard. Click the flag icon at the upper-left corner of the image cell to toggle between Unflagged and Pick status. To flag an image as a reject, choose Photo > Set Flag > Rejected, press the X key, or Option-click/Alt-click the flag icon in the upper-left corner of the image cell. To remove a flag from an image, choose Photo > Set Flag > Unflagged or press the U key. To set any flag status for an image, right-click the flag icon in the upper-left corner of the image cell and choose Flagged, Unflagged, or Rejected from the menu.

7   With the white flag still selected in the Attribute Filter bar, click the gray flag button (the flag in the center). The Grid view now displays any photos flagged as picks and all unflagged photos, so once again we see all of the images in the Sabine Christy collection.

8   In the Filter bar, click None to disable the Attribute filters.

Assigning ratings

A quick and easy way to sort your images as you review and evaluate them is to assign each photo a rating on a scale from one to five stars.

1   Click the Sabine Syd Hot Sauce collection, and in the Grid view, make sure the Toolbar's Sort menu is set to Capture Time, and then click the second photo to select it.

2   Press the 3 key on your keyboard and the words "Set Rating To 3" will appear onscreen briefly. The photo is now marked with three stars at the bottom of its image cell.

● **Note:** If you don't see the star rating in the image cell, choose View > View Options and make sure Rating And Label is chosen in the Bottom Label or Top Label menu in the Compact Cell Extras display options or the Show Rating Footer option is selected in the Expanded Cell Extras.

3   Click the triangle at the right of the Toolbar and choose Rating in the menu, if necessary. The stars in the Toolbar reflect the rating you just applied to the selected image. If you have multiple images selected with different ratings, the Toolbar will reflect the rating of the first image selected.

▶ **Tip:** You can also assign ratings in the Metadata panel, by choosing a rating from the Photo > Set Rating menu or by choosing a rating from the Set Rating submenu when you right-click a photo's thumbnail.

4   It's easy to change the rating for a selected image: Simply press another key between 1 and 5 to apply a new rating or press the 0 key to remove the rating altogether. For this image, press the 0 key.

Working with color labels

Color labeling can be a very versatile tool for organizing your workflow. Unlike flags and ratings, color labels have no predefined meanings; you can attach your own meaning to each color and customize separate label sets for specific tasks.

While setting up a print job, you might assign the red label to images you wish to proof, the blue label to those that need retouching, and the green label to mark images as approved. For another project, you might use the different colors to indicate levels of urgency.

Applying color labels

You can use the colored buttons in the Toolbar to assign color labels to your images. If you don't see the color label buttons, click the triangle at the right of the Toolbar and choose Color Label from the menu. You can also click the color label icon displayed in a photo's image cell (a small gray rectangle, for an unlabeled image) and choose from the menu. Alternatively, choose Photo > Set Color Label and choose from the menu; you'll notice that four of the five color labels have keyboard shortcuts.

To see—and set—color labels in the Grid view image cells, choose View > View Options or right-click any of the thumbnails and choose View Options from the menu to open the Library View Options dialog box. On the Grid View tab, select Show Grid Extras. In the Compact Cell Extras options, you can choose Label or Rating And Label from either the Bottom Label or Top Label menu. In the Expanded Cell Extras options, select the Include Color Label option.

Editing color labels and using color label sets

You can rename the color labels to suit your own purposes and create separate label sets tailored to different parts of your workflow. The Lightroom default options in the Photo > Set Color Label menu are Red, Yellow, Green, Blue, Purple, and None. You can change the color label set by choosing Metadata > Color Label Set and then choosing either the Bridge or Lightroom default set or the Review Status set.

The Review Status label set gives you an idea of how you might assign your own label names to help you keep organized. The options in the Review Status set are To Delete, Color Correction Needed, Good To Use, Retouching Needed, To Print, and None. You can use this label set as it is or as a starting point for creating your own sets. To open the Edit Color Label Set dialog box, choose Metadata > Color Label Set > Edit. Choose a preset to start from, make sure you're on the Images tab, enter your own name for each color, and then choose Save Current Settings As New Preset from the Preset menu.

Searching by color label

In the Filter bar, click Attribute to see the Attribute filter controls. You can limit your search to a single color label by clicking just one button or select more than one button. To deselect a color label button, simply click it again. You can use the color label search buttons together with other Attribute filters or to refine a Text or Metadata search. The Attribute filters, including the color label filters, are also available in the bar above the thumbnails in the Filmstrip (if you don't see them, click Filter to the left of the menu).

Adding metadata

You can leverage the metadata information attached to the image files to help you organize and manage your photo library. Much of the metadata, such as capture date, exposure time, focal length, and other camera settings, is generated by your camera, but you can also add your own metadata to make it easier to search and sort your catalog. In fact, you did just that when you applied keywords, ratings, and color labels to your images. In addition, Lightroom supports the information standards evolved by the International Press Telecommunications Council (IPTC), which includes entries for descriptions, keywords, categories, credits, and origins.

You can use the Metadata panel in the right panel group to inspect or edit the metadata attached to a selected image.

Note: At the bottom of the Metadata panel, on the Metadata Set menu's Default setting, there is a Customize button. Clicking it allows you to select which fields you show on that setting.

1   In the Sabine Syd Hot Sauce collection, select the first image in the grid view.

2   Expand the Metadata panel. If necessary, collapse the other panels in the right panel group or hide the Filmstrip so that you can see as much of the Metadata panel as possible. Choose Default from the Metadata Set menu in the header of the Metadata panel.

Even the default metadata set exposes a great deal of information about the image, and clicking the Customize button allows you to add information from a large list of other fields. Although most of this metadata was generated by the camera, some of it can be very useful in sorting your photos—you could filter images by capture date, search for shots taken with a particular lens, or easily separate photos taken on different cameras. However, the default set displays only a subset of an image's metadata.

3   Choose EXIF And IPTC from the Metadata Set menu. Scroll down in the Metadata panel to get an idea of the kinds of information that can be applied to an image.

4   For the purposes of this exercise, choose Quick Describe from the Metadata Set menu.

In the Quick Describe metadata set, the Metadata panel shows the filename, copy name (for a virtual copy), folder, rating, and some EXIF and IPTC metadata. You can use the panel to add a title and caption to a photo, attach a copyright notice, provide details about the photographer and the location where the photo was shot, and change the star rating.

5 In the Metadata panel, click the third dot to the right of Rating to assign the image a rating of three stars, and then type **Sabine and Syd complete the Hot Ones hot sauce challenge.** in the Caption text box and press Return/Enter.

6 Command-click/Ctrl-click either of the two similar photos to add it to the selection. Click Selected Photos near the top of the Metadata panel and you can see that the folder name, dimensions, and camera model are shared by both files, but items not shared by both images now show the entry <mixed>. Changes made to any of the items in the Metadata panel, even those with mixed values, will affect both of the selected images.

▶ **Tip:** If you need to add a longer caption to your files (which is very important for photo-journalists and people making images for sports), select the Large Caption Metadata Set. This will give you a large window for the caption, making it easier to write in.

Storage of metadata

File information is stored using the Extensible Metadata Platform (XMP) standard. XMP is built on XML. In the case of camera raw files that have a proprietary file format, XMP isn't written into the original files. To avoid file corruption, XMP metadata is stored in a separate file called a sidecar file. For all other file formats supported by Lightroom (JPEG, TIFF, PSD, and DNG), XMP metadata is written into the files in the location specified for that data.

XMP facilitates the exchange of metadata between Adobe applications and across publishing workflows. For example, you can save metadata from one file as a template, and then import the metadata into other files. Metadata that is stored in other formats, such as EXIF, IPTC (IIM), and TIFF, is synchronized and described with XMP so that it can be more easily viewed and managed. To find out more about metadata, please refer to Lightroom Classic Help.

—From Lightroom Classic Help

Tagging faces in the People view

Undoubtedly, your growing photo library will include many photos of your family, friends, and colleagues. Lightroom Classic makes it quick and easy to tag the people who mean the most to you, taking much of the work out of sorting and organizing what probably amounts to a large portion of your catalog, and making it even easier to retrieve exactly the photos you're looking for.

Face recognition automatically finds the people in your photos and makes it simple for you to tag them. And the more faces you tag, the more Lightroom Classic learns to recognize the people you've named, automatically tagging their faces whenever they appear in new photos.

There are no lesson images provided for this exercise, so the first thing you need to do is import some of your own photos.

▶ **Tip:** If any of the photos you import have embedded GPS information, the Enable Address Lookup dialog box will open. Click Enable.

1 Use either the Import button or the drag-and-drop method you learned in Lesson 2 to import a selection of photos featuring the faces of people you know. Make sure you have a mix of single-person images and groups of various sizes, with plenty of overlap—and at least a few strangers' faces.

By default, face recognition is disabled, so we need to have Lightroom analyze our photos and build an index of those images that include faces.

2 In the Catalog panel, change the image source from Previous Import to All Photographs so that Lightroom Classic will index the entire catalog. Press Command+D/Ctrl+D or choose Edit > Select None.

3 Press T to show the toolbar, if necessary, and click the People button.

4 Lightroom displays a message screen welcoming you to the People view. Click Start Finding Faces In Entire Catalog. A progress bar appears at the upper left of the workspace, and the Activity Center menu opens with a tip showing you where you can turn face recognition off and on. Wait for the indexing process to complete before moving on.

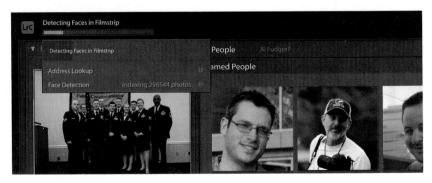

The work area is now in People view mode. Lightroom Classic stacks similar faces for tagging, with an image count for each stack. The default sorting order is alphabetical, but as none of the faces are yet tagged, they are arranged by stack size. At this point, all of the faces are listed in the Unnamed People category.

5   Click the stack badge on a people stack to expand it. Command-click/Ctrl-click all of the photos in the stack that belong together; then click the question mark below a selected thumbnail, type the person's name, and press Return/Enter.

Lightroom moves the selected photos into the Named People category, and the image counts in both category headers are updated.

6   Repeat the process for two or more unnamed stacks. Already, Lightroom is learning, suggesting more photos that may belong with those you've named. Move the pointer over a suggested name to confirm or dismiss the suggestion.

7   Continue until you've named at least five or six people and tagged several photos for each; then double-click one of the faces in the Named People stack to enter the Single Person view. In this view, the upper division is now labeled as the Confirmed category, showing all of the photos tagged with the selected name. Below, the Similar category displays only the suggested matches for this face.

8 Add as many photos as you can to the group in the Single Person view; then when you're done, click "< People" above the Confirmed header to return to the People view.

▶ **Tip:** You can quickly isolate your People tags in the Keyword List panel by expanding the filter options at the top of the list of keywords and clicking People.

9 Repeat the process for all named people, alternating between the People and Single Person views, until the only untagged photos are people you don't know or image fragments incorrectly identified as faces. Dismiss any incorrect suggestions on the leftover photos, and then remove them from the Unnamed People list by clicking the X icon that appears with the question mark in the label.

10 Click the Grid view button in the toolbar, and then double-click a photo with multiple people to see it enlarged in the Loupe view. Click the Draw Face Region button in the toolbar to see the People tags attached to the image. When you find a face that has not been identified by face recognition, you can use the Draw Face Region tool to drag a box around it, and then enter a name.

11 Inspect the Keyword List panel to see your new People tags listed with your other keywords. You can use the Keyword List panel or the Text and Metadata filters to search for People tags, just as you would for any other keyword.

Using the Painter tool

Of all of the tools Lightroom Classic provides to help you organize your growing image library, the Painter tool is the most flexible. By simply dragging across your images in the Grid view with the Painter tool, you can "spray on" keywords, metadata, labels, ratings, and flags—and even apply developing settings, rotate your photos, or add them to a target collection.

When you pick up the Painter tool from its well in the Toolbar, the Paint menu appears beside the empty tool well. From the Paint menu, you can choose which settings or attributes you want to apply to your images. Once you've made your choice, the appropriate controls appear to the right of the Paint menu.

▶ **Tip:** In Keywords mode, the Painter tool can apply entire keyword sets or any selection from your favorite set. With the Painter tool in Keywords mode, press the Shift key to activate the eyedropper and access the Keyword Set picker.

In this exercise, you'll use the Painter tool to mark images with a color label.

1   In the Library module, click the Import button below the left panel group.

2   Under Source at the left of the Import dialog box, navigate to the folder LRC2024CIB\Lessons\lesson04-gps. Make sure that all of the images in the folder are selected for import. Set the import options at the top to Add, type **Lesson 04, Jade Mountain** in the Keywords text box, and then click Import.

3   Click the lesson04-gps folder in the Folders panel, switch to the Grid view, and make sure that none of the images is selected. If you don't see the Painter tool in the Toolbar, choose Painter from the tools menu at the right side of the Toolbar.

4   Click the Painter tool to pick it up from its well in the Toolbar, choose Label from the Paint menu beside it, and click the red color label button.

5   The Painter tool is now "loaded." Move the pointer over any of the thumbnails in the Grid view and a red spray can icon appears.

6   Click the thumbnail in the Grid view and the Painter tool applies the red label. Whether you see the color as a tint in the image cell depends on your Library View Options settings and on whether the image is currently selected (our example is not). If you don't see the red color label marker (circled in the illustration at the right), choose View > Grid View Style > Show Extras.

7   Move the pointer back over the same thumbnail; then hold down the Option/Alt key and the cursor changes from the Painter tool spray can to an eraser. Click the thumbnail with the eraser cursor and the red color label is removed.

8   Release the Option/Alt key and click the image once more, but this time drag the spray can across several photos to apply the red color tag to multiple images with one stroke. Hold down the Option/Alt key again, and remove the label from all but one of the photos.

9   Click Done at the right side of the Toolbar, or click the Painter tool's empty well, to drop the Painter tool back on the Toolbar.

Finding and filtering files

Now that you're familiar with the different techniques for categorizing and marking your photos, it's time to see some results. Next you'll look at how easy it is to search and sort your images once they've been prepared in this way. You can now filter your images by rating or label, or search for specific keywords, GPS locations, and other metadata. There are numerous ways to find the images you need, but one of the most convenient is to use the Filter bar across the top of the Grid view.

Using the Filter bar to find photos

1   If you don't see the Filter bar above the Grid view, press the backslash key (\) or choose View > Show Filter Bar. In the Folders panel, select the lesson04 folder. If you don't see all 36 photos, choose Library > Show Photos In Subfolders.

The Filter bar picker contains three filter types: Text, Attribute, and Metadata; choose any of these and the Filter bar will expand to display the settings and controls you'll use to set up a filtered search. You can either use the different filters separately or combine them for a more sophisticated search.

Use the Text filter to search any text attached to your images, including filenames, keywords, captions, and the EXIF and IPTC metadata. The Attribute filter searches your photos by flag status, star rating, color label, or copy status. The Metadata filter enables you to set up to eight columns of criteria to refine your search; choose to add or remove a column from the menu at the right end of the column headers.

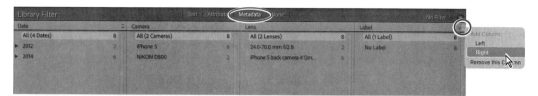

2   If the Text or Metadata filters are active, click None to disable them. Click Attribute to activate the Attribute filters. If any of the flag filters are still active from the earlier exercise, click the highlighted flags in the Filter bar to disable them, or choose Library > Filter By Flag > Reset This Filter.

3   In the Rating controls, click the third star to search for any image with a rating of three stars or higher. The Grid view only displays images that have a three-, four-, or five-star rating.

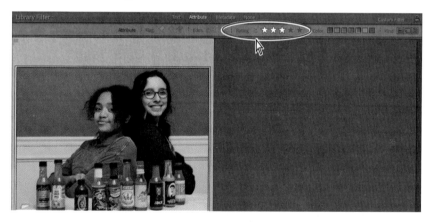

4   There are many options for refining your search. Click All Photographs in the Catalog panel, and then click Text in the header of the Filter bar to add an additional filter. In the Text filter bar, open the first menu to see the search target options. You can narrow the search to Filename, Copy Name, Title, Caption, searchable IPTC and EXIF metadata, or Any Searchable Field, but for this exercise you can choose Keywords as the search target. Click the second menu and choose Contain All.

5 In the search text box, type **Aguada**. Your narrowed search returns one image in the Grid view.

6 In the Rating controls, click the third star to disable the current Rating filter or choose Library > Filter By Rating > Reset This Filter. Click Attribute in the header of the Filter bar to close the Attribute filter controls.

7 In the Text filter bar, clear the previous search by clicking the X icon at the right of the text box, and then type **Jade Mountain**.

The Grid view now displays eight images in the lesson04-gps folder.

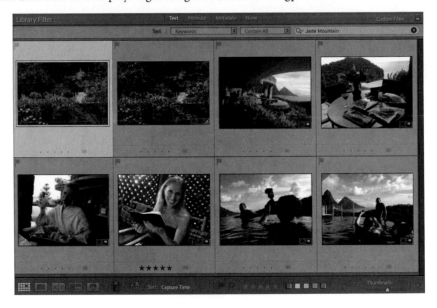

Using the filters in the Filmstrip

The Attribute filter controls are also available in the header of the Filmstrip. As in the Filter bar, the Filter menu lists the different attributes you can filter by and offers you the option to save your filter settings as a custom preset, which is then added to the menu at the right of the Filter bar.

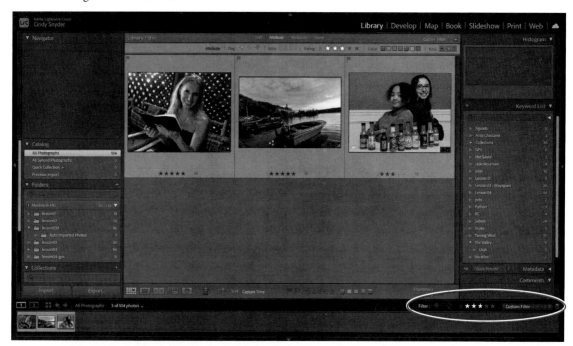

The Default Columns preset opens the four default columns of the Metadata search options—Date, Camera, Lens, and Label—in the Filter bar.

Choose Filters Off to turn off all filters and collapse the Filter bar. Choose Flagged to display only photos with a Pick flag.

Choose Rated to display any photos that match the current star rating criteria. Click a different star to change the star rating and the symbol before the stars to choose whether to see photos with three stars or more, three stars or less, or exactly three stars. Choose Unrated to see all of the photos without a star rating.

Here, I filtered to images that have a rating of three stars or higher. This returned a result of three images.

To disable all filters and display all of the images you've imported, choose Filters Off from the Filter menu or click the switch at the far right of the Filmstrip's header.

▶ **Tip:** If you don't see any filter presets in the Filter menu, open Lightroom Preferences and click Restore Library Filter Presets under Lightroom Defaults on the Presets tab.

Hardware suggestion: Monogram Creative Console

When trying to work on the iterative culling process, I find that I am the most successful when I make sure that I do not touch anything on the computer other than the buttons I need for Pick, Reject, Previous, and Next.

Many photographers bemoan the process and the time it takes them to "edit" a shoot, but it's not really the editing of the shoot, but the amount of time wasted in culling that is causing the problem.

I found this company called Monogram (the company was redesigned; it was previously called Palette Gear) that produces a series of analog controls that you can plug into your computer and assign commands to from a variety of applications. While there are a ton of different applications that it can be used with (I'm using them in InDesign to write this book!), I think the strongest case can be made for their simplest kit: two buttons and one dial, and that's it.

Assign one of the buttons to Pick and the second to Reject, and the dial moves you between the pictures.

This hardware is not required for this process, but I found it enough of a help to make a video about it for those who want to learn how to incorporate it into their workflow. You can find it at *https://rcweb.co/paletteRC*.

Review questions

1 When do you use a collection, and when do you use a collection set?

2 What is a smart collection?

3 What are keyword tags?

4 What are the three modes in the Filter bar?

5 How can you access your collections when you're away from your computer?

Review answers

1 Use a collection when you want to group a number of images that reside in different folders, put the same image in more than one group, or arrange your photos in a custom order. Use a collection set to further organize your images by putting multiple collections or collection sets in the same group.

2 A smart collection can be configured to search the library for images that meet specified criteria. Smart collections stay up to date by automatically adding any newly imported photos that meet the criteria you've specified.

3 Keyword tags are text added to the metadata of an image to describe its content or classify it in one way or another. Shared keywords link images by subject, date, or some other association. Keywords help to locate, identify, and sort photos in the catalog. Like other metadata, keyword tags are stored either in the photo file or (in the case of proprietary camera raw files) in XMP sidecar files. Keywords applied in Lightroom Classic can be read by Adobe applications, such as Bridge, Photoshop, or Photoshop Elements, and by other applications that support XMP metadata.

4 The Filter bar offers three filter groups: Text, Attribute, and Metadata filters. Using combinations of these filters, you can search the image library for metadata or text; filter searches by flag, copy status, rating, or label; and specify a broad range of customizable metadata search criteria.

5 In Lightroom Classic, choose the collection(s) you want to be able to access when you're away from your computer and turn on syncing for that collection(s). This allows you to access your synced collections in Lightroom mobile on your phone or tablet, or on *lightroom.adobe.com* on any computer. It also allows you to share a collection with a client or friends on that site.

PHOTOGRAPHY SHOWCASE
JOE CONZO

"Photography saved my life."

Photography. A word you didn't hear too much where I grew up. Growing up in the South Bronx, you had few choices: sports, gangs, or drugs. My mother raised five kids on her own and wasn't about to let us succumb to the latter, and sports really didn't come naturally for me. You see, I was that chubby kid with the huge Angela Davis afro, and having a camera set me apart from everyone in my neighborhood. My camera allowed me to document my surroundings and preserve a time that is long gone. Film was expensive for a kid like me, so each shot was planned or at least had some planning. Film allowed me to experiment with expressing my imagination. I tried to imitate Pablo Picasso and his light writing on film. Documenting the struggles of the South Bronx became important to me because of the role my family had as community activists. The kids I grew up with would end up creating a genre of music that has surpassed rock and roll, and I was there with my camera to document the birth of hip-hop.

Fast-forward 40+ years and photography has become my love and passion. It has brought me around the world documenting, exhibiting, and sharing. I tell some of the youth today that this kid from the South Bronx has been to Bulgaria—yep, Bulgaria! Never would I have imagined that my archives would be stored and displayed at Cornell University. I tell people that my images sit on the same shelf as the Gettysburg Address! How cool is that??!! I'm always pushing myself with the changing world of photography today. So much has changed, but I try to stay true to the way I started out: respect your subject, document your life, and have fun!

joeconzo.com
instagram.com/joeconzo

5 DEVELOPING BASICS

Lesson overview

Lightroom delivers an extensive suite of powerful, yet easy-to-use, developing tools to help you make the most of your photos with a minimum of effort, whether they're incorrectly exposed, shot at an angle, poorly composed, or even spoiled by extraneous objects.

This lesson introduces you to a range of basic editing options in the Develop module, from automatic adjustments and develop presets to cropping, straightening, and finishing tools. Along the way, you'll pick up a little background knowledge in digital imaging as you become familiar with some basic techniques. You'll learn how to:

- Crop your images for the best effect.

- Use the histogram and properly set your white balance.

- Perform basic edits in the Develop module.

- Apply artistic color profiles to your images.

- Effectively use sharpening and noise reduction.

- Create versions of images using virtual copies and snapshots.

 This lesson will take about 2½ hours to complete. To get the lesson files used in this chapter, download them from the web page for this book at *peachpit.com/LightroomCIB2024*. For more information, see "Accessing the lesson files and Web Edition" in the "Getting Started" section at the beginning of this book.

Now that you've imported your photos and organized your catalog, you can jump right in and begin editing them with a range of options from one-click automatic adjustments to specialized retouching tools. You can experiment with any of these, secure in the knowledge that, thanks to Lightroom's non-destructive editing, the modifications you make while you're learning won't alter your master files.

Getting started

● **Note:** This lesson assumes that you already have a basic working familiarity with the Lightroom Classic workspace. If you need more background information, refer to Lightroom Classic Help, or review the previous lessons in this book.

Before you begin, make sure you've set up the LRC2024CIB folder for your lesson files and created the LRC2024CIB Catalog file to manage them, as described in "Accessing the lesson files and Web Edition" and "Creating a catalog file for working with this book" in the "Getting Started" section at the start of this book.

If you haven't already done so, download the lesson05 folder from your Account page at *peachpit.com* to the LRC2024CIB\Lessons folder, as detailed in "Accessing the lesson files and Web Edition" in the "Getting Started" section.

1 Start Lightroom Classic.

2 In the Select Catalog dialog box, make sure the file LRC2024CIB Catalog.lrcat is selected under Select A Recent Catalog To Open, and then click Open.

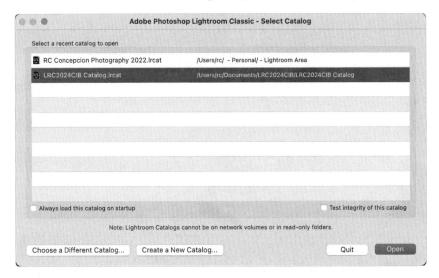

● **Note:** If you can't see the Module Picker, choose Window > Panels > Show Module Picker, or press the F5 key. If you're working on macOS, you may need to press the fn key together with the F5 key, or change the function key behavior in the system preferences.

3 Lightroom Classic will open in the screen mode and workspace module that were active when you last quit. If necessary, switch to the Library module by clicking Library in the Module Picker at the top of the workspace.

Importing images into the library

The first step is to import the images for this lesson into the Lightroom library.

1 In the Library module, click the Import button below the left panel group.

2 If the Import dialog box appears in compact mode, click the Show More Options button at the lower left of the dialog box to see all of the options in the expanded Import dialog box.

3 Under Source at the left of the expanded Import dialog box, locate and select your LRC2024CIB\Lessons\lesson05 folder. Ensure that all 17 images in the lesson05 folder are selected (checked) for import.

4 In the import options above the thumbnail previews, select Add so that the imported photos will be added to your catalog without being moved or copied. Under File Handling at the right of the expanded Import dialog box, choose Embedded & Sidecar from the Build Previews menu and leave the Don't Import Suspected Duplicates option selected. Under Apply During Import, choose None from both the Develop Settings menu and the Metadata menu, and type **Lesson 05, Develop** in the Keywords text box. Make sure that your import is set up as shown here, and then click Import.

The 17 images are imported and now appear in both the Library module's Grid view and the Filmstrip across the bottom of the Lightroom workspace.

The Develop module

▶ **Tip:** The first time you enter any of the Lightroom Classic modules, you'll see tips that will help you get started by identifying the components of the workspace and stepping you through the workflow. Dismiss the tips by clicking the Close button. To reactivate the tips for any module, choose [*Module name*] Tips from the Help menu.

Although the Library module's Quick Develop panel offers access to many basic image editing options, you'll work in the Develop module to make more detailed adjustments and modifications to your photos. The Develop module is a comprehensive editing environment, presenting all of the tools you'll need to correct and enhance your images in a single workspace. The controls are simple enough for a beginner to use and yet have the depth and power required by the advanced user.

The Develop module offers three viewing modes: the Loupe view, where you can focus on a single image; the Reference view, where you can compare your image to a reference image; and the Before/After view, which has several layout options that make it easy to compare the original and edited versions of a photo. The Toolbar across the bottom of the work area presents buttons for switching between the views and a slightly different suite of controls for each viewing mode.

The left panel group contains the Navigator panel, which can be collapsed but not hidden, and any combination of the Presets, Snapshots, History, and Collections panels, which can be shown or hidden to suit the way you prefer to work.

At the top of the left panel group, the Navigator panel helps you find your way around a zoomed image, lets you preview the effects of Develop module presets before you apply them, and lets you review past stages in an image's developing history. At the right of the Navigator panel's header is a zoom picker for setting the magnification level in the working views.

At the top of the right panel group is the Histogram panel. Immediately below the histogram is an array of tools for cropping, removing image flaws, applying local adjustments through masking, and painting develop settings directly onto an image selectively. Clicking any of these tools expands a tool options panel with controls and settings for that tool.

Below these editing tools is the Basic panel, your starting point for color correction and tonal adjustments. In many cases, this may be the only panel you need to achieve the result you want. The remaining panels offer specialized tools for various image enhancement tasks.

For example, you can use the Tone Curve panel to fine-tune the distribution of the tonal range and increase midtone contrast. Use the controls in the Detail panel to sharpen an image and reduce noise.

It's not intended that you use every tool on every photo. In many circumstances, you may make only a few slight adjustments to an image; however, when you wish to polish a special photo—or if you need to work with shots captured at less than ideal camera settings—the Develop module gives you all of the control you need.

Tip: The tools and controls in the Develop module's right panel group are arranged from top to bottom in the order in which they would ordinarily be used, a layout that guides you intuitively through the editing workflow, although you can change that (see "Reorganizing the Develop module" next).

Reorganizing the Develop module

If you find that you use the panels in the Develop module in a different order or just want them arranged differently, right-click any panel's header in the right panel group and choose Customize Develop Panel. You'll be presented with a dialog box with the names of all of the panels in the group. Drag the panel names to rearrange the order of the panels. The checkboxes toggle each panel's visibility. Clicking the Save button will prompt you to restart Lightroom. After the restart, your panels will be organized as you set them, showing only the ones you need in the order you prefer.

To get back to the original arrangement, go back into the Customize Develop Panel dialog box, click Default Order at the bottom left, click Save, and then restart Lightroom to see the change.

Creating a collection from a previous import

Now that you've learned how to create collections inside Lightroom in Lesson 4, "Managing Your Photo Library," it's a good idea to get into a workflow habit of making collections for images that we will be working on in Lightroom.

1 After importing images into the Library, all of the images reside in the Previous Import group in the Catalog panel. Press Command+A/Ctrl+A to select all of the images in the group.

2 Click the plus sign (+) icon at the upper right of the Collections panel and make a collection called **Develop Module Practice**, making sure the Include Selected Photos option is selected.

● **Note:** If you do not see the Toolbar at the bottom of the panel, press the letter T to show it.

3 The images are automatically added to the Develop Module Practice collection. Now you can drag them around to reorganize them to your liking or choose File Name from the Sort menu in the Toolbar at the bottom of the work area to see them by filename.

Now that we have ourselves organized, let's start tackling the Develop module by working on some of the most popular tools from the top down.

Cropping and rotating images

The Crop Overlay tool makes it simple to improve your composition, crop away unwanted edge detail, and even straighten your image.

1 Select the raw image of the baby chicks (lesson05 - 017) in the Grid view or Filmstrip and press the D key to switch to the Develop module.

2 Hide the left panel group to enlarge the work area; you'll find keyboard shortcuts for showing and hiding any or all of the panels listed beside the commands in the Window > Panels menu. If you're not already in the Loupe view, press the D key or click the Loupe view button in the Toolbar. If you don't see the Toolbar, press the T key.

3 Click the Crop Overlay tool button just below the Histogram panel or press the R key. A crop overlay rectangle appears on the image in the Loupe view, and an options panel for the Crop Overlay tool opens above the Basic panel.

4 Drag the top corners inward and the area outside of the crop overlay will darken, giving you a better idea what the crop will look like. Drag the image to reposition the crop. Move your pointer outside the corners of the overlay, and it turns into a curved double-headed arrow, allowing you to drag clockwise or counterclockwise to rotate the image.

5 The crop overlay includes a set of compositional aids you can use to make better crop adjustments to your images. The default overlay is the Thirds (Rule Of Thirds), shown above. Press the O key to cycle between the overlays. The Golden Spiral overlay is shown in the illustration at the right.

Changing crop overlays

● **Note:** The following crop overlays are available in Lightroom Classic: Grid, Thirds, Fifths, Diagonal, Center, Triangle, Golden Ratio, Golden Spiral, and Aspect Ratios.

These crop overlays are meant to be guidelines or suggestions for aligning and cropping your image. In the example to the right, I am using the Aspect Ratio overlay. This guide allows me to see the different cropping ratios available to me and how each would change the composition.

● **Note:** If you press Shift+O, you can change the orientation of the overlays.

You may not need all of the guides that are available, however. Here's how you can limit the amount you see. Choose Tools > Crop Guide Overlay > Choose Overlays To Cycle. In the resulting dialog box, you can deselect any of the guides that you do not find necessary. Click OK, and the next time you use the Crop Guide Overlays menu, you will see only the ones that you have selected.

Using the Straighten tool

▶ **Tip:** Whether you use the Straighten tool or rotate the photo manually, Lightroom will automatically trim the angled edges of the rotated photo when you commit the crop by clicking the Crop Overlay tool or double-clicking the image in the Loupe view. Lightroom will find the largest crop possible with the specified aspect ratio. Changing or unlocking the aspect ratio can minimize the amount of the photo that is trimmed away.

In the Crop Overlay tool's options panel is the Straighten tool. Its icon looks like a level, and you can use it to adjust your images if they are askew.

1 Switch to lesson05 - 010 and click the tool in the panel and your pointer turns into a crosshair and a level.

2 Move over the picture and drag along something that should be horizontally level or Shift-drag along something that should be vertically straight. In this case, I am using the wall in the foreground. Drag a line that runs along your straight edge, and when you let go, the picture will level itself along that guide. You can also drag the Angle slider until it looks right to you; for this picture, I rotated it 2.02 degrees.

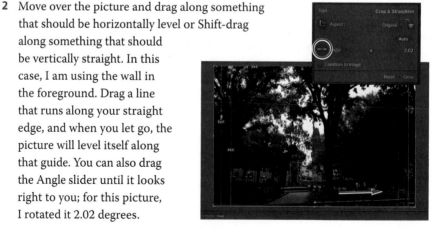

Cropping to specific dimensions

Photographers often want to lock their picture's crop to the specific ratio it was shot at (in this example, the aspect ratio of a DSLR sensor, 3:2). There are times, however, when you may want to change your cropping ratio, perhaps creating a square crop for Instagram, a wider Facebook cover post, or a 16:9 wide shot.

With the Crop Overlay tool active, click to the right of Aspect, and you'll see a menu of commonly used photo sizes, such as 1x1 (square crop), 4x5 (great for making 8x10 images), and 16x9. For this example, choose the 16x9 crop to give the image a little more of a cinematic feel. The crop overlay automatically resizes and now is constrained by the 16x9 crop.

Seeing your crop better

Let's switch back to lesson05-0017. One last piece of advice: When you are making a crop, make sure that you get rid of the Lightroom interface while you are making judgments on the crop. The best way to do this is to press Shift+Tab on the keyboard. This will hide the panels, Module Picker, and Filmstrip, giving you the most real estate for your picture.

Once the panels are hidden, press the L key twice. The first press of the L key will switch Lightroom to Lights Dim mode, dimming the interface by 80%. The second time you press the L key the lights turn off entirely (Lights Out mode). This gets rid of all of the distractions around the edges and lets you focus on only the elements you want in the picture as you move the crop around.

▶ **Tip:** Thanks to non-destructive editing, you can return at any time and adjust your crop—or the angle of the photo—by simply reactivating the Crop Overlay tool. The crop becomes "live"—the trimmed portions of the image become visible once more, and you can rotate the photo or resize and reposition the cropping rectangle as you wish.

Press Return/Enter to complete your crop, then press the L key to turn the lights back on, and press Shift+Tab to bring back the panels.

What are camera profiles?

When shooting in JPEG mode, the camera applies color, contrast, and sharpening to your image files. When you shoot in raw mode, your camera captures all of the raw data at the point of capture but builds a small JPEG preview as well. This JPEG preview—with all of the color, contrast, and sharpening—is what you see in the LCD on the back of the camera.

When you import this image into Lightroom, Lightroom initially shows you that JPEG preview as a thumbnail. Behind the scenes, it starts to render the raw data into pixels you can view and work with onscreen (a process known as *demosaicing*). To do this, Lightroom looks at the image's metadata—white balance and everything buried in your camera's color menu—and interprets it as best it can.

Because Lightroom can't interpret some proprietary camera settings, the preview almost never looks like the JPEG that you saw on the back of your camera. This is why your thumbnails shift in color shortly after (or during) the import process.

This shift frustrated many photographers before Lightroom's developers added camera profiles (presets that attempt to mimic the settings included in a camera's JPEGs). While not 100 percent accurate, they let you get closer to what you saw on the back of your camera. They used to be located in the Camera Calibration panel.

As more photographers started using them, some created profiles for artistic effects. Adobe realized that users wanted to add profiles first—for both color fidelity and artistic expression—and moved them to the top of the Basic panel.

Profiles in Lightroom

Lightroom Classic offers photographers a variety of camera profiles in three categories to use in their workflow:

- **Adobe Raw profiles** These profiles are not camera-dependent and aim to give users of any camera a more unified look and feel for their images.

- **Camera Matching profiles** These profiles mimic the profiles built into your camera and vary by camera manufacturer.

- **Creative profiles** These profiles are built for artistic expression and leverage Lightroom's ability to include 3D LUTs for even more coloring effects.

Now that we know what these tools can do, let's spend some time exploring how to use them to make our work really stand out. Let's continue to use the baby chicks image that we just cropped. If you switched modules, press the D key to make sure you are in the Develop module. To make it easier for you to see the changes we are making, close the left-side panels (if they aren't already) and the Filmstrip by clicking the gray triangles in the middle of each side.

> **Tip:** Color lookup tables (LUTs) are tables that remap or transform color in an image. Originally used in the video space to attempt to make footage from different video sources look similar, LUTs gained popularity as Photoshop users began using them to colorize their images as an effect. These effects are sometimes known as *cinematic color grading.*

At the top of the Basic panel (directly below the Auto, B&W, and HDR buttons) is the Profile area. On the left is the Profile menu, a quick way to access some of the Adobe Raw profiles that mimic your camera settings (these appear only when working on a raw file). You also can add your favorite profiles from the Profile Browser to this menu for easier access.

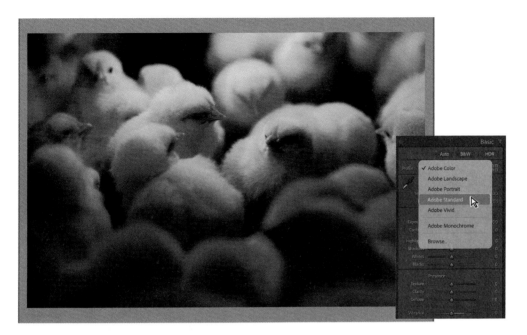

On the right is the Profile Browser icon (it looks like four squares), where you can access a variety of profiles, including the Adobe Raw Profiles. Josh Haftel, principal product manager for Adobe, wrote a blog post explaining these color profiles:

> *Adobe Color* is the new standard baseline for a color image, providing a neutral tone similar to what you captured in-camera.
>
> *Adobe Monochrome* has been carefully tuned to be a great starting point for any black-and-white photograph, resulting in better tonal separation and contrast than photos that started off in Adobe Standard and were converted into black and white.
>
> *Adobe Portrait* is optimized for all skin tones, providing more control and better reproduction of skin tones. With less contrast and saturation applied to skin tones throughout the photo, you get more control and precision for critical portraiture.
>
> *Adobe Landscape*, as the name implies, was designed for landscape photos, with more vibrant skies and foliage tones.
>
> *Adobe Vivid* provides a punchy, saturated starting point.

While I believe that Adobe has done a great job with the Adobe Raw profiles, many photographers will want to go directly to the Camera Matching profiles, the profiles that are specific to your camera make and are based on the ones you can choose on your camera. To do this, click the Profile Browser icon.

● **Note:** If you've made an image with a camera preset, like Monochrome, you'll notice that Lightroom now applies the Monochrome image by default. Many users have gotten used to having their black-and-white images shot in raw automatically convert back to color. In this version, this will not be the case.

Using the Profile Browser

The Profile Browser gives you access to all of the profiles Adobe created. We already discussed the Adobe Raw profiles at the top of the Profile Browser. The Camera Matching profiles include any profiles that are specific to your camera make, so the number of profiles available will vary by camera type.

At the bottom of the Profile Browser are the creative profiles, separated by category: Artistic, B&W, Modern, and Vintage. If you expand any of them, you'll see a series of thumbnails showing what each profile will look like on your photo.

I encourage you to experiment with all of the profiles. While the Camera Matching profiles might offer you a one-click solution to get closer to what you saw on the back of your camera, the creative profiles might spark a new interpretation of your image.

My other favorite part? The creative profiles have an Amount slider, allowing you to dial in the effect to your liking. Once you choose a profile and an Amount setting, click the Close button at the upper right of the browser to return to the Basic panel.

The profiles that have been created also include black-and-white presets that can really enhance your photo and serve as a great starting point for creating compelling black-and-white images. We'll talk about how to create your own black-and-white images in Lesson 6.

For the purposes of this image, select the Vintage01 preset and click the Close button. The result is a softer look with more compressed midtones.

Setting your picture's white balance

White balance refers to the color of light in a photo. Different kinds of light—fluorescent or tungsten bulbs, overcast skies, and so on—create different color casts in your photo. White balance adjustment is done by adjusting the temperature and tint to bring the color back to what you intended. Click the lesson05 - 003 file; then click As Shot next to WB near the top of the Basic panel and experiment with the different white balance menu choices.

If you shoot in a raw format, you have more choices in the menu—the ones you typically find in your camera (they're not available with a JPEG). Choose the one that most closely matches the lighting you shot in. You can also make your own adjustments with the Temp and Tint sliders.

If you don't like the results, in the Basic panel, click the White Balance Selector (it looks like an eyedropper) or press W on your keyboard. Move your cursor over your image, and click an area that *should* be neutral in color, such as a light or medium gray (you can use the Loupe that appears to help you find a neutral color).

▶ **Tip:** On raw images, you can use the WB menu to access white balance presets, although it's usually quicker to set it manually using the White Balance Selector. Your camera's white balance is baked into JPEGs, so this menu has fewer options for them.

In this example of a bunch of bananas in Puerto Rico, I used the back wall to sample for color. In one click, I was able to get the picture to look a lot more natural. This tool doesn't have to be a one-step solution, but it can certainly shave some time off the process.

About white balance

To correctly display the full range of color information recorded in an image file, it's critical to balance the distribution of color in the photo—that is, to correct the photo's *white balance*.

This is achieved by shifting the image's *white point*, the neutral point around which the colors in the image are distributed on the two axes of temperature (blue to red, visualized in the illustration at the right as a curved axis) and tint (green to magenta).

An image's white point reflects the lighting conditions in which the photo was captured. Different types of artificial lighting have different white points; they produce light that is dominated by one color or deficient in another. Weather conditions also have an effect on the white balance.

The higher the red component in the lighting, the warmer the colors in the photo will appear; the higher the blue component, the cooler the image, so movement along this axis defines the photo's color *temperature*, while the term *tint* refers to shifts in the direction of green or magenta.

The sensors in a digital camera record the amount of red, green, and blue light that is reflected from an object. Under pure white lighting, an object that is a color-neutral gray, black, or white reflects all color components of the light source equally.

If the light source is not pure white but has a predominant green component, for example (typical of fluorescent lighting), a higher amount of green will be reflected. Unless the composition of the light source is known—and the *white balance* or *white point* is corrected accordingly—even objects that should appear color-neutral will have a green color cast.

When shooting in auto white balance mode, your camera attempts to estimate the composition of the light source from the color information measured by the sensors. Although modern cameras are doing better at automatically analyzing lighting and setting the white balance to meet conditions, the technology is not infallible; it's preferable—if your camera supports it—to use your camera to measure the white point of the light source before shooting. This is usually done by photographing a white or neutral, light gray object in the same lighting conditions as the intended subject.

Together with the color information collected by the camera sensors, raw images also contain "As Shot" white balance information, a record of the white point determined automatically by the camera at the moment of capture. Lightroom can use this information to correctly interpret the recorded color data for a given light source. The recorded white point information is used as a calibration point in reference to which the colors in the image will be shifted to correct the white balance.

You can use the White Balance Selector tool, located in the upper-left corner of the Basic panel, to correct the white balance in your photo. Click to sample an area in your photo that you know should appear onscreen as a light neutral gray; Lightroom will use the sampled information to determine the point around which the image can be calibrated and set the image's white balance accordingly.

As you move the White Balance Selector tool across the image, you will see a magnified view of the pixels under the eyedropper cursor and RGB values for the central target pixel. To avoid too radical a color shift, try to click a pixel where the red, green, and blue values are as close as possible. Do not use white or a very light color (such as a spectral highlight) as the neutral target; in a very bright pixel, one or more of the color components might already have been clipped.

Color temperature is defined with reference to a concept known as *blackbody radiation* theory. When heated, a blackbody will first start glowing red, then orange, yellow, white, and finally blue-white. A color's temperature is the temperature—in kelvin (K)—to which a blackbody must be heated to emit that particular color. Zero K corresponds to −273.15°C or −459.67°F, and an increment of one unit kelvin is equivalent to an increment of one degree Celsius.

What we generally refer to as a warm color (with a higher red component) actually has a lower color temperature (in kelvin) than what we would call a cool color (with a higher blue component). The color temperature of a visually warm scene lit by candlelight is about 1500 K. In bright daylight, you would measure around 5500 K, and light from an overcast sky results in a color temperature in the photo of about 6000 to 7000 K.

The Temperature slider adjusts the color temperature (in kelvin) of the designated white point, from low at the left side of the range to high on the right side. Moving the Temp slider to the left reduces the color temperature of the white point. In consequence, the colors in the image are interpreted as having a higher color temperature relative to the adjusted white point and are shifted toward blue. The colors displayed in the track of the Temp slider control indicate the effect a change in that direction will have on the image. Moving the slider to the left will increase the blue in the image; moving the slider to the right will make the image look more yellow and red.

The Tint slider works in the same way. For example, to remove a green cast in an image, you would move the Tint slider to the right, away from the green displayed inside the slider control. This increases the green component in the white point so the colors in the image are interpreted as less green relative to the adjusted white point.

Adjusting the Temp and Tint sliders corresponds to shifting the white point within the color gamut.

Setting exposure and contrast

Exposure is determined by how much light your camera's sensor captures and is measured in f-stops (indicating how much light your camera's lens lets in). In fact, the slider simulates stops on a camera: a setting of +1.00 is like exposing one stop over the metered exposure in-camera. In Lightroom, the Exposure slider affects midtone brightness (in portraits, that's skin tones). Drag to the right to increase brightness, or drag to the left to decrease brightness (you can see this in the slider itself—white is to the right and black is to the left).

1 Select the lesson05 - 009 image and move the Exposure slider to the right to +1.70. This immediately brightens the image.

2 If you move your pointer over the middle of the histogram at the top of the right-side panels, the area affected by the Exposure slider is highlighted in light gray, and the word *Exposure* appears below the lower-left corner of the histogram.

Before the change, the range of information lived toward the left side of the histogram (shown above left). With the exposure adjustment, all of that has moved toward the right (shown above right).

▶ **Tip:** To have Lightroom perform an auto adjustment for a single slider, no matter where it appears in the adjustment panels, Shift-double-click it. This is especially helpful when setting contrast if you opt to set exposure and contrast manually rather than using the Auto button. Contrast can be tough to get right (you can easily mess up your highlights and shadows).

Contrast adjusts the difference in brightness between the darkest and lightest tones in your picture. When you drag this slider to the right (increasing contrast), you "stretch out" the histogram's data, creating darker blacks and brighter whites. It's like parting (or joining) the middle of the histogram.

If you drag this slider to the left (decreasing contrast), you scrunch the histogram's data inward, shortening the distance between the darkest (pure black) and lightest (pure white) endpoints, making the photo's tones look flat or muddy.

3 Experiment with adjusting the contrast of the image and see the results. In this image, I moved the Exposure to +1.70 and the Contrast slider to +46, which makes the picture stand out a bit more.

4 Press the Y key for a side-by-side comparison between the before and after of the image. This will give you a great idea of just how far you have taken the file. This is one of the greatest benefits of making images in a raw format.

Adjusting shadows and highlights

The Highlights and Shadows sliders let you recover detail in areas that may be clipped. Clipping occurs when areas in the picture are too dark or too light. If an area is too dark (sometimes referred to as *blocked*), there is not enough data in the shadows to show detail—it's too black, too muddy, and no good. If there is an area that is clipped in the highlights (sometimes referred to as *blown out*), it is so bright that there is no detail in it.

▶ **Tip:** You can turn clipping warnings on and off by pressing J on your keyboard.

As a general rule, you want both your shadows and highlights to have as much detail as possible without affecting the rest of the image. I made this image by underexposing it to keep from blowing out the highlights, but I still lost some detail in the bottom of the picture. Let's see if Shadows can help us here.

1 Open lesson05 - 008. Click the shadows clipping warning at the upper left of the histogram, which turns the clipped shadows in your image blue. Blown-out highlights appear in red and show when you move over or turn on the highlights clipping warning at the upper right of the histogram.

Experiment with this by adjusting the Exposure up and down to see the warnings; then set the Exposure to +0.75 and turn the shadows clipping warning off.

2   Drag the Shadows slider to the right to see how much information you get back in the lower part of the buildings, the people, and the street. I am using a value of +81.

3   Open lesson05 - 006. Drag the Exposure slider to −1.10 to darken the image. The image is still a little bright, so drag the Highlight slider to −100. Not only does it bring detail into the buildings, but also gives us a little more color in the sky that we did not originally see.

4   Finish this image by moving the Shadows in the image to +52, decreasing the Exposure further to −1.35, and increasing the Contrast to +41. Finally, change the temperature to +5600.

When you use the Shadows and Highlights sliders, the important thing is to notice what they *aren't* doing. When you adjust the Shadows slider, it doesn't affect the highlights. When you drag the Highlights slider, it doesn't mess with the shadows. This is pretty powerful stuff.

While there are plenty of times when Lightroom requires you to make elaborate modifications to your images, I cannot stress how many times I've relied on these four sliders—Exposure, Contrast, Shadows, and Highlights—to do a lot of my heavy lifting. Most of the time, they're all I need.

Adjusting whites and blacks

If we understand that a histogram is a representation of pixel data across the range of tones in a picture, then it's a good idea for us to establish what those limits are within that range.

The whites and blacks are the brightest and the darkest parts of the picture. Setting their values sets the "limits" of your tonal range. In many (but not all) pictures, making sure that all of your pixel information is within those white and black limits can yield great photos.

I look at it this way: Imagine seeing a bunch of kids playing in only half of a yard. The key to happiness is to spread the kids (pixels) all around the yard (your image's tonal range). The problem with setting the limits (the brightest and darkest parts of the image) is that it can be difficult to see exactly where they are.

1   Open lesson05 - 002 in the Develop module. Hold down the Option/Alt key and click the Whites slider, and the image turns almost black. As you drag the Whites slider to the right, you'll see some color changes. What you're looking for is the first large area that turns white. White tells you that portion of the picture is clipping, so that is the brightest you can make the whites without losing information. If other colors appear before you see white, Lightroom is letting you know that they are predominantly bright in the image.

If you see a bright color appear when you are adjusting your white point, this is known as a *color cast*. In the image there is a little blue that appears in the bottom of the picture, but I am okay with that. You may see other colors as you drag, but what you're looking for is white.

What is a histogram?

When you start looking at your images in Lightroom, you may get into (occasionally heated) discussions about the histograms of your photos. In photography, you may hear that you need to keep the histogram "as a curve" or, worse, hear about the "perfect" histogram (supposedly the one illustrated at the right). It's essential for you to understand what it is that you are looking at when you look at a histogram, but it's even more important for you to understand that this tool is intended to be just that—a tool, not a goal.

This is extremely oversimplified, but think of a histogram as kind of a chart. On the left side of the histogram are pixels of 0% luminance. On the right are pixels of 100% luminance. The white area is showing you color values from 0 to 255, each of them from darkest to lightest.

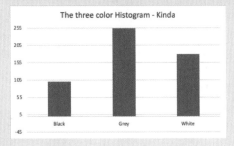

Imagine if you had only three luminance values in your picture. Your histogram would (kind of) look like the top chart here (and would probably not be from the camera you want to buy in 2022).

Now, imagine if your histogram had only 12 tones. A sample readout of these 12 luminance values might look like the bottom chart here. It's starting to get a little crowded in that bar chart.

The histogram is just a whole mess of bars in a bar chart. There are so many of those bars that they are literally butting up to one another. But the concept is still the same. Going from left to right are the luminance values (the *x* axis), and from top to bottom is how bright each luminance value is (the *y* axis), from 0 to 255.

When you see color in a histogram, think of the same bar chart, but with a new bar chart for each color behind that original chart. Each color chart (say, for blue) measures the amount of that color's (blue's) pixels, from super-dark (blue) on the left to super-bright (blue) on the right.

It's the same for yellow, and the same for red. All they are is bar charts, informing you how much data you have in the picture. The more important question is: what were you aiming to get?

The Histogram Hall of Fame

I used to believe that we were all in search of the perfect bell curve in a histogram until a conversation that I had with famed portrait photographer Gregory Heisler at Syracuse University. Professor Heisler explained that intention would prove to be infinitely more important than what the readout of the histogram said.

In our conversation, he offered a series of pictures that he often uses as a foundation for the "Histogram Hall of Fame." These histograms would often be rejected as problematic, until you realize that the photographer intended them to be this way. They were made like this for a reason.

Because of copyright law, I can't show you what the original images look like, but I'll leave you with a test. Here, we have the histograms of five pictures. Take a look at those pictures online, and compare them with the histograms below (the URLs should take you right to them).

What you should watch out for when using the histogram is whether you are clipping a portion of tone and how best to remedy that. We will cover that in this lesson.

Igor Stravinsky, by Arnold Newman
rcweb.co/histogram1

Moonrise, Hernandez, New Mexico, by Ansel Adams
rcweb.co/histogram2

Seascapes, by Hiroshi Sugimoto
rcweb.co/histogram3

American West Portraits, by Richard Avedon
rcweb.co/histogram4

The Tetons and the Snake River, by Ansel Adams
rcweb.co/histogram5

Tip: Hold down the Shift key and double-click the Whites or Blacks slider, and Lightroom makes the change automatically.

2 Once you're done with the whites, Option-click/Alt-click the Blacks slider and drag it to the left. This time, the image turns white, and what you're looking for is the first spot of black. This tells you how far you can drag the Blacks slider. If you see other colors, they are predominantly dark.

3 To complete this picture, we'll apply an Exposure setting of –0.30, Highlights of –100, and a Shadows setting of –21. The Whites are set to +65 and the Blacks to –23. The Temp is set to 6425. These settings add brightness to the final image yet retain its detail and take some of the blue out of it. I also made a 16 x 9 crop of the image.

This leads us to a question: Does this mean that the "Whites and Blacks first" method is preferable to working with Exposure and Contrast? Not necessarily. You could have achieved a similar result by starting with Exposure and Contrast and then adjusting Shadows and Highlights to your liking. In learning how to develop pictures, it's important that you understand how the technology works, but also that you allow yourself the opportunity to find your own way of getting to the solution that you feel is best.

Clarity, vibrance, and saturation

Once you've dialed in your picture's tonality, you can move on to making some of the final Basic panel adjustments to the shot. Clarity, vibrance, and saturation round out the basic editing of a picture. Let's switch to a different image for this: lesson05 - 014.

1   Make the following adjustments to this image: set the Temp to 5000, Tint to +10, Exposure to −0.20, Contrast to +17, Shadows to +10, and Whites to +27.

Setting the picture's contrast affects the shadows and highlights, and the whites and blacks. The one part that doesn't get a lot of attention is the midtones, and sometimes, adding a little punch in the midtones is very helpful.

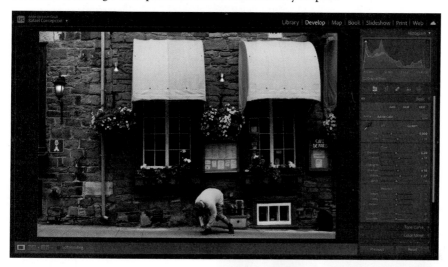

2   Set the Clarity slider to +32.

The Clarity slider controls midtone contrast. It's great for adding a bit of a gritty element to your pictures—things like metals, textures, brick walls, and hair all can do with a little bit of a clarity boost. For the brick background, it worked well.

Keep in mind, though, when you're using the Clarity slider, that out-of-focus areas in a picture generally don't look good with clarity applied to them. Use it sparingly, or use the effect attached to a mask. To add detail, increase the Texture to +30.

Taking detail further: The Texture slider

In May 2019, the Lightroom team released a new feature that I find myself using more and more: the Texture slider.

Originally developed as a function to help portrait retouching for skin smoothing, the Texture slider can be considered a subtler way to add details—or frequency—to an image in a specific area.

Think of it this way: Images are composed of high, medium, and low frequencies. When you add adjustments like sharpening to a picture, you are invariably affecting the edges of things in that picture. These are the high frequency areas of a picture. Adjust it too much, and you'll see those enhancements creep into midtone and shadow areas of an image.

The Texture slider allows you to add this detail into the medium frequencies of the picture but does not affect the lower frequencies.

While clarity does a good job of enhancing the midtone contrast, it tends to affect more regions of the picture. Texture looks a little like clarity when added to an image, but you'll notice that you get all of the benefit of the details but none of the negative effects of excessive clarity.

The image to the right has had clarity applied to the extreme. Notice the change in the wall behind the car and the dark halo along the top of the car.

The picture at the bottom has texture applied to the extreme. The wall does not seem to be affected as much, but a lot more detail has been added to the picture.

In the end, I find myself using a combination of both the Clarity and Texture sliders to get the amount of detail I want in my images, and I would encourage you to experiment with them to see how much detail you can get into your pictures.

While adding detail in the frequencies is something that you may find yourself doing, you'll also find that many use these techniques to separate the frequencies and smooth out the higher frequencies. In Photoshop retouching, it's a technique called *frequency separation*.

In frequency separation, you separate the high (detail) frequencies from low (color and tone) frequencies so that you can soften up some of the blemish details and still keep some skin texture. Previously, this was something that required you to create separate layers in Photoshop for manipulation. Now, you can get the same effect in Lightroom Classic with one slider.

The photo above is of my wife, Jenn. Now, I have to say she is beautiful and does not need to have this effect applied to her, as I believe she is perfect, but she gamely allowed me to use this photo to educate. On the left, you have the original image; on the right, you have a negative Texture setting applied. Notice that her skin seems softer but still has a good amount of color and texture. You can take this effect even further by applying it locally with the Masking Brush tool. We'll cover the Masking Brush in the next lesson.

The Texture slider is the brainchild of Max Wendt, lead engineer of the Texture project at Adobe, and he has a wonderful blog post on the Adobe Blog site that goes into even more detail on how you can really unlock the slider's potential. Be sure to check out his blog post at *https://rcweb.co/lrtexture*.

The Saturation and Vibrance sliders both deal with the application of color to a picture, but they work a little differently. Let's experiment with the lizard again (lesson05 - 002).

3 Drag the Saturation slider all the way to the right to +100. This intensifies all of the colors in your image evenly, as shown in the illustration at the right.

Saturation doesn't take into account whether a color is overrepresented. It's an easy way to make a photo look too colorful and unrealistic.

Vibrance should really be called "Smart Saturation." Drag the Vibrance slider to the right, and any underrepresented colors are intensified more. Any colors that are overrepresented are not adjusted as much. If there are any skin tones in the picture, Vibrance tries not to affect them at all.

4 Reset Saturation to 0 and raise the Vibrance to +40. Notice that only certain parts of the image are affected. Most importantly, the yellow is barely touched.

As a general rule, I usually start by making any color adjustments I need as Vibrance adjustments and then move on to Saturation only if necessary. Here I will leave the Vibrance at +40 and the Saturation at 0. With the color and tone taken care of, we need to finish the picture by adding a little detail to it.

Adding detail to your images

When you shoot in JPEG mode, the camera adds color, contrast, and sharpening to the final image. Photographers are quick to make the tonal adjustments we just discussed, but many skip sharpening their images. By default, Lightroom adds a small amount of detail to raw files, but it is never really enough for input sharpening.

In the Detail panel, there is a Sharpening area with four sliders: Amount, Radius, Detail, and Masking. Above those sliders is a 100% preview of the picture (click the little triangle at the upper right of the panel to show/hide it). This preview doesn't give you a good idea how much sharpening is being applied.

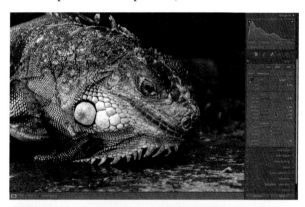

1   Click the larger image in the center preview area once to zoom in to 100%. Drag around the picture to find an area where you can better see the sharpening you're applying, so you can make better sharpening decisions.

2   The Amount slider is pretty straightforward: it dictates how much sharpening you want to apply to the picture. Let's drag it to 96. Hold down the Option/Alt key as you drag to see a black-and-white preview, which may help you see the sharpening better.

The Radius slider lets you change how far from the center of the pixel you want to apply that sharpening. It's hard to see this by just dragging the Radius slider, so here's a trick.

3   Hold down the Option/Alt key as you drag the slider. Drag it to the left, and your image turns gray; drag it to the right, and you start seeing more edge information. The visible edge information is the area that is sharpened. Anything that's gray won't be sharpened. Let's drag it to 2.2 here.

Once you have the Radius set, move on to the Detail slider. The Detail slider brings out more texture or detail in a picture as you drag it to the right. However, if you move it too far, or all of the way to the right, it will start introducing a little bit of noise. You'll want to watch out for that.

4 Hold down the Option/Alt key and drag the Detail slider to +51.

If you want to limit how the sharpening is applied, use the Masking slider. It creates a black-and-white mask, where the black areas won't be sharpened and the white areas will be sharpened, confining your sharpening to only the edges.

5 Hold down the Option/Alt key and drag the Masking slider to the right to determine where you want the sharpening to occur. As soon as you release the Option/ Alt key, you'll see a much sharper picture without the noise you might get from sharpening everything evenly. Let's move the masking to +72 as shown in the illustration at right.

To see a before/after of your sharpening, click the power switch at the far left of the Detail panel's header to turn the sharpening off. Click it again to turn the sharpening back on, and now you can see whether you've added enough.

New: Denoise, AI-enhanced noise reduction

Noise in a picture appears for one of two reasons: you used a camera with a really high ISO setting (you shot in low light) or you added a lot of sharpening to your photo. As camera sensors have improved, they perform better at higher ISOs with less noise in the image, but you still need to remove some noise from older images
or images on specific cameras. To illustrate this, I went back in time and found an image that I shot of a zombie in Guanajuato, Mexico. This image was made in a tunnel at a whopping 12,800 ISO!

1   Select lesson05 - 011 and apply an Exposure of +1.5 to it.

2   It may be hard to see the noise in the image at the Fit zoom percentage of Loupe view. Click the image to zoom in to 100% and you'll see how much noise there really is in the image.

3   In the Detail panel, you'll notice that there are two options for noise reduction: artificial-intelligence (AI)-based Denoise and Manual Noise Reduction. If the image that you selected is a raw file, you will have the option to use Denoise. If you click Denoise on a raster image (JPG, PNG, or TIFF), you will get an error message letting you know that you cannot use it. For this image, click Denoise.

4   An Enhanced Preview dialog box appears, showing you a preview with the default amount of denoise applied. Dragging the slider to the right changes the enhanced preview. Clicking and holding the enhanced preview will show you what the image looked like before. Enter a value of 68% and click the Enhance button.

Once you click the Enhance button, Lightroom will render a copy of the raw image as a DNG file with the Denoise settings you chose. Printed in a book, it's hard to see just how well it performs, so I would recommend you see the image at full screen to really appreciate it.

5   In this example, I applied a rather aggressive Denoise to really get the most out of it. In doing so, I lost some of the sharpness in the image. Thankfully, I can use the same Detail panel to bring some of that back. Under Sharpening, set the Amount to 100, the Radius to 1.5, the Detail to 42, and the Masking to 39.

The resulting file, while somewhat frightening, has a great amount of detail and a lot less noise thanks to the new Denoise feature. AI for the win! Below is a before and after of the noise reduction.

Manual Noise Reduction

If you prefer to do it without AI, the Manual Noise Reduction area has two different types of noise you can affect. The first of these is luminance noise, which is that grainy look.

1 Switch back to the lizard photo and drag the Luminance slider to the right—the noise starts to disappear. You'll use this slider for 90% of the noise you want to remove.

2 If you feel you have lost too much detail after dragging the Luminance slider, grab the Detail slider below it and drag it to the right. If you want to add contrast back after these adjustments, drag that slider to the right a bit. Increasing the Detail and Contrast sliders reduces some of the effect of the luminance noise reduction because they tend to counterbalance each other, so be careful.

3 Set the Luminance Noise Reduction slider to 50, the Detail slider to 50, and the Contrast slider to 0. Click the Detail panel's power switch to turn your adjustments off and back on to see your results.

Color, Detail, and Smoothness are used when you see noise that comes in different colors: red, green, or blue dots (this problem is prevalent with some cameras and tends to appear in shadows). To get rid of that kind of noise, you'll drag the Color slider to the right until those dots are desaturated and then add a bit of detail back in and balance it with a little smoothness.

Noise reduction brings back some smoothness to a file with a high ISO, but it's also something you have to do if you excessively sharpen a picture. The more you sharpen a picture, the more noise gets introduced, especially if you use the Detail slider. So every time you go into the Detail panel's Sharpening area and create a lot of sharpening, add a little bit of noise reduction to counterbalance the effect.

Lens corrections and transformations

All lenses exhibit some trademark problem: distortion, dark edges (vignetting), or the appearance of chromatic aberrations (colored pixels that appear along the edges of objects). To correct these problems, we have the Lens Corrections and Transform panels. Select lesson05 - 009 again and make the following changes in the Basic panel: under Tone, set the Exposure to +1.70, the Contrast to +46, the Whites to +25, and the Blacks to −6. Then, under Presence, set Texture to +36, Clarity to +6, Vibrance to +32, and Saturation to +6.

1   Expand the Lens Corrections panel. In the panel's Profile tab, select Enable Profile Corrections to have Lightroom read the image's embedded EXIF data to determine what make and model of lens you used. It then chooses a built-in profile and automatically adjusts the picture, often yielding a better-looking file. If it can't find your lens, choose the closest one from the Make and Model menus.

There are times, when the problem with your image has little to do with your lens and more to do with your position when you made the picture. In this photo, though, I was shooting at a wide angle to capture the entire space. This is where the Transform panel can help. To see if the image is crooked, click a Transform panel slider and a grid appears over the image.

The buttons in the Upright area of the panel automatically tilt and skew your image in an attempt to fix it. You have the following four options:

*   **Auto**   Balances level, vertical, and horizontal perspective corrections, and keeps the aspect ratio as much as possible.

- **Level** Perspective corrections are weighted toward horizontal details.

- **Vertical** Perspective corrections are weighted toward vertical details and level corrections.

- **Full** Combination of full Level, Vertical, and Auto perspective corrections.

2 Click each of the transformation options to see if any of the results help what you are trying to do.

If none of the options fully solves your problem, try the Guided option to really move things along. Guided transformation allows you to draw up to four lines on the picture, tracing along the edges of areas that should be straight. As you draw the lines, the image adjusts itself to what it believes is a straight picture.

3 Click the Guided Upright tool and draw a vertical line on the left edge of the counter and one on the right side of the sign on the right and then a horizontal line along the top of the counter.

Once the transformation is complete, use the Transform sliders to make any final tweaks. If the image ends up with a lot of white background in the bottom corners that needs to be cropped, you can use the Crop Overlay tool (R). You can also select the Constrain Crop option to have Lightroom automatically remove the white areas. Press Return/Enter.

4 Add some finishing adjustments using the Basic panel as you like, and the transformation is quite noticeable.

Using virtual copies for variations

Lightroom does a great job of keeping your library organized by keeping the number of duplicate images down to zero. One image can be referenced in multiple collections, and making a change in the file in one collection automatically cascades that change to the file in all other collections.

What if you want a copy of the file to try out a different look without changing the original? This is where another powerful feature comes in handy: the virtual copy.

1 Press the letter G to go to the Grid view, and keep the same image selected.

2 Click the plus sign (+) icon at the right of the Collections panel's header and make a new collection called **Virtual Copies**. Make sure you include the selected photo.

● **Note:** You can create virtual copies by pressing Command+' (apostrophe)/Ctrl+' on the keyboard.

3 Right-click the image and select Create Virtual Copy from the menu.

4 Make an additional virtual copy so you have a total of three files here.

These new files are virtual copies of the original image. You can make changes to each of the copies in the Develop module and they will be treated as separate images with separate changes.

While they look like separate images—full copies not tied to the original image—they actually refer to the same physical copy of the image. That's the virtual part. You can create multiple virtual copies of a photo to try out different edits without taking up much additional space on your hard drive. You can make better judgments about which edits you prefer by having these virtual copies side by side.

5 Highlight all three images and press the letter N on your keyboard to enter Survey mode to compare your changes. When finished, press the G key to get back to the Grid view.

Using snapshots for variations

To save different edits to a photo without making separate copies of the image for comparison, snapshots are a great option.

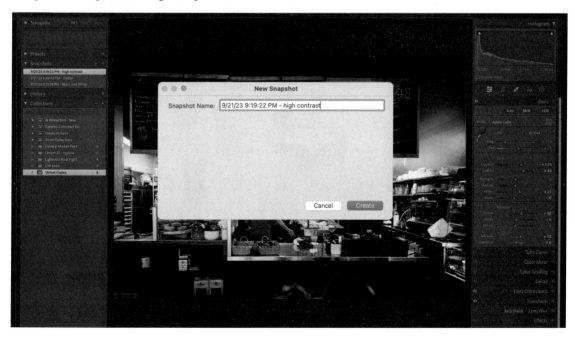

1   In the Develop module, edit the image to a point you want to save, and then click the plus sign (+) icon at the right of the Snapshots panel's header. A dialog box will appear with the date and time that you are creating the snapshot in the Snapshot Name text box. You can either keep that date and time or rename the snapshot (maybe to a brief description of the photo at that stage) and click Create.

2   Continue editing your picture, and when you are ready to save another change, click the plus sign (+) icon again to save a new snapshot. This is a great way to save variations and keep tabs on your progress, although I prefer the side-by-side nature of working with virtual copies.

Review questions

1 How can you customize the panels in the Develop module's right panel group?

2 What is the meaning of the term *white balance*?

3 How can you straighten a crooked photo?

4 How do you get Lightroom to perform an automatic adjustment for a setting in the Basic panel?

5 How do you get Lightroom to perform an automatic lens correction?

Review answers

1 You can rearrange the Develop module's right panel group and turn off those panels' visibility by right-clicking any panel's header in the group and choosing Customize Develop Panel. In the resulting dialog box, you can drag the panel names to rearrange the order of the panels and turn their visibility on or off with the checkboxes. You will see the changes once you save and restart Lightroom.

2 An image's white balance reflects the light source when the picture was taken. Different types of artificial lighting and weather conditions can produce light that is dominated by one color or deficient in another, resulting in images with a color cast.

3 You can straighten a tilted image by dragging to rotate the cropping rectangle or using the Straighten tool, which lets you mark a horizontal or vertical element in a tilted photo as a reference around which Lightroom then straightens the image.

4 Holding the Shift key while double-clicking any slider in the Basic panel will cause Lightroom to automatically adjust that setting.

5 In the Profile tab of the Lens Corrections panel, select the Enable Profile Corrections option. If Lightroom cannot locate your lens make and model, select the closest match using the Lens Profile menus.

PHOTOGRAPHY SHOWCASE
BINUK VARGHESE

"Photography is the universal language of this era."

I am a travel photographer based in Dubai, but hailing from Kerala, India. My passion is traveling around the globe, experiencing its unique cultures and scenic beauty. One of the best things about being a travel photographer is connecting with people and learning about their habitats and lifestyles.

My recent project *Life in Frames* includes some of my personal favorite portraits of people taken on my journeys. Each portrait depicts a different character and silently echoes their story. I try to reflect real life and its emotions through my photographs, exploring the unexplored and sharing the unseen. I push myself to capture that moment of magic, that glimpse of time that gives an insightful perspective or that is visually sublime. As you can see through my photographs, I love to keep things simple in life.

Photography is the universal language of this era, and my work tells a variety of tales in this language. My photographs reexamine and redefine the moments I capture. Photography has become the oxygen of my life, which helps me keep moving forward.

I use Lightroom extensively for cataloging my files and maintaining a library of images, enabling me to deliver my work faster.

I intend to continue nurturing, encouraging, cajoling, appreciating, and celebrating photo stories.

instagram.com/binuk.varghese/

6 ADVANCED EDITING

Lesson overview

The Develop module offers a series of sliders that can quicky change your images, bringing out their best. But not all problems can be solved with global sliders. Some images have localized problems that need correcting. Often, the difference between a good photo and a great photo lies in you paying attention to those little details. This lesson builds upon what you've learned in the Develop module and pushes your toolbox even further. In this lesson, you'll learn how to:

- Use the new masking AI to speed up editing.
- Use lens blur to change your depth of field.
- Use the Healing tool to fix sensor spots and problem areas.
- Use the Brush tool to adjust specific image areas.
- Use People masking to even out lighting across a group and bring out the best in each person.
- Experiment with range masking for adjusting light and color.

 This lesson will take about 3½ hours to complete. To get the lesson files used in this chapter, download them from the web page for this book at *peachpit.com/LightroomCIB2024*. For more information, see "Accessing the lesson files and Web Edition" in the "Getting Started" section at the beginning of this book.

Fine-tune and polish your photographs with precise, easy-to-use tools, and then take your developing a step beyond just correcting your images; use the Develop module tools and controls creatively to customize your own special effects, and then save them as custom develop presets.

Getting started

Note: This lesson assumes that you already have a basic working familiarity with the Lightroom Classic workspace. If you need more background information, refer to Lightroom Classic Help, or review the previous lessons.

Before you begin, make sure you've set up the LRC2024CIB folder for your lesson files and downloaded the lesson06 folder from your Account page at peachpit.com to the LRC2024CIB\Lessons folder, as described in "Accessing the lesson files and Web Edition" in the "Getting Started" section at the start of this book. Also, be sure you have created the LRC2024CIB Catalog file to manage the lesson files, as detailed in "Creating a catalog file for working with this book," also in the "Getting Started" section of this book.

1 Start Lightroom Classic.

2 In the Select Catalog dialog box, make sure that LRC2024CIB Catalog.lrcat is selected, and then click Open.

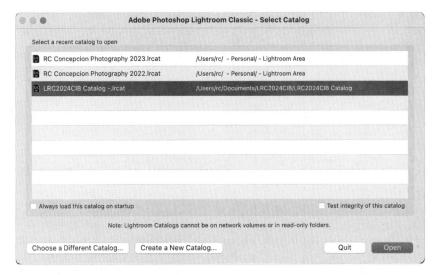

Note: If you can't see the Module Picker, choose Window > Panels > Show Module Picker, or press the F5 key. If you're working on macOS, you may need to press the fn key together with the F5 key or change the function key behavior in the system preferences.

3 Lightroom Classic will open in the screen mode and workspace module that were active when you last quit. If necessary, switch to the Library module by clicking Library in the Module Picker at the top of the workspace.

Importing images into the library and creating collections

The first step is to import the images for this lesson into the Lightroom library.

1 In the Library module, click the Import button below the left panel group.

2 If the Import dialog box appears in compact mode, click the Show More Options button at the lower left of the dialog box to see all of the options in the expanded Import dialog box.

3 Under Source at the left of the expanded Import dialog box, locate and select your LRC2024CIB\Lessons\lesson06 folder. Ensure that all 17 photos in the lesson06 folder are selected for import.

4 In the import options above the thumbnail previews, select Add so that the imported photos will be added to your catalog without being moved or copied. Under File Handling at the right of the expanded Import dialog box, choose Embedded & Sidecar from the Build Previews menu and leave the Don't Import Suspected Duplicates option selected. Under Apply During Import, choose None from both the Develop Settings menu and the Metadata menu and type **Lesson 06** in the Keywords text box. Make sure that your import is set up as shown here, and then click Import.

The 17 photos are imported from the lesson06 folder and now appear in both the Grid view of the Library module and in the Filmstrip across the bottom of the Lightroom workspace.

While we're in the Library module, let's create three collections from these photos: Selective Edits, Synchronize Edits, and HDR and Panorama.

Note: If you do not see the picture numbers at the top left of the grid cells, cycle through your view options by pressing the letter J.

Tip: The first time you enter any of the Lightroom Classic modules, you'll see tips that will help you get started by identifying the components of the workspace and stepping you through the workflow. Dismiss the tips by clicking the Close button. To reactivate the tips for any module, choose [*Module name*] Tips from the Help menu.

5   Make sure Previous Import is selected in the Catalog panel and the Sort menu is set to Capture Time. Select the first nine pictures (click the first one and Shift-click the last one). Click the plus sign icon in the upper right of the Collections panel and create a collection called **Selective Edits**. Make sure the Include Selected Photos option is selected.

6   Click Previous Import in the Catalog panel. Press Command+D/Ctrl+D to deselect all of the images, and make sure your Sort menu below the image grid is set to Capture Time. Select the next eight pictures (they should be labeled 10 through 17). Again, click the plus sign icon in the upper right of the Collections panel and create a collection called **Select People**. Make sure Include Selected Photos is selected.

7   Click Previous Import in the Catalog panel. Press Command+D/Ctrl+D to deselect all of the images and make sure the Sort menu is still set to Capture Time. Now select the last seven pictures (they should be labeled 11 through 17). Create a collection called **Synchronize Edits**. Make sure the Include Selected Photos option is selected.

8   Click Previous Import in the Catalog panel one more time. Press Command+D/Ctrl+D to deselect all of the images. Select the two images labeled 8 and 9. Create a collection called **Sky and Ground**. Make sure the Include Selected Photos option is selected.

9   To keep all of the collections we are using in Lesson 6 together, click the plus sign icon at the upper right of the Collections panel and create a new collection set. In the Create Collection Set dialog box, let's call it **Lesson 06 Practice**.

10 Command-click/Ctrl-click the four collections you made in the previous steps and drag them into the Lesson 06 Practice collection set. This organization will allow us to work on the images we want and declutter our library view.

11 Select each one of the collections in turn and make sure that they each have the images sorted by filename.

A major change to Lightroom: AI-based selections and masking

Lightroom Classic 2024 has undergone one of the more substantial changes in recent memory with the inclusion of new artificial intelligence (AI)– and machine learning–based tools to speed up your workflow. In 2022, the Masking tool replaced several tools in the tool strip below the Histogram panel. Clicking it opens the Add New Mask options, which include several older tools as well as a couple of newer tools, and now some additions to those newer tools.

The Brush replaced the Adjustment Brush, while the Linear Gradient and Radial Gradient replaced the Graduated Filter and Radial Filter. Range masking (Color Range, Luminance Range, and Depth Range) also moved under Add New Mask.

We had masks for Subject and Sky and now have added Background and Objects masks. All use AI and machine learning to make a precise mask around whatever you choose. Clicking Select People lets you not only choose which person or people to select but also refines your selection further by choosing exactly which part of a person to select. These AI features completely redefine how editing is done in Lightroom Classic, making it even easier and faster.

In this chapter, we will start with the AI-based tools that will make your selections so much easier. The goal is to become familiar with the ways you can leverage all the new features to make your work easier.

Using the Select Sky, Subject, and Background masks

One of the biggest benefits of using AI and machine learning in your work is the amount of time that can be saved. What would normally require you to make precise selections (and corrections to those selections) can be done with a couple of keystrokes and the inverting of a selection. In this picture of my friend's daughter, we have a sky that is really overexposed. Because of the overall coolness of the picture, I also want to warm up the subject a little. Finally, I would like to bring down the brightest highlights in the image and give the sky a little more drama.

1 Select the lesson06 - 008 image in the Sky and Ground collection and switch to the Develop module.

2 Click the Masking tool, and click the Sky option at the top of the Add New Mask panel to select the sky behind the subject.

3 Once the sky is selected, a light red overlay will appear over the selection, and it will appear as Mask 1 in the Masks panel. The area in white on the mask is the area that will be affected by the changes you make in the Select Sky options panel that opens below the tool strip.

With the sky selected, let's make the following changes to bring back the sky in the picture: drag the Exposure slider to –0.8, set the Contrast to 58, set the Highlights to –87, set the Shadows to –65, set the Whites to –14, and decrease the Tint to –10.

▶ **Tip:** Press O on your keyboard to turn on the mask overlay in red. Press the same key to turn it off (or select Show Overlay at the bottom of the Masks panel). To change the mask color, press Shift+O on your keyboard (this is helpful when the mask color also appears in large areas of your photo).

4   Once the change has been made, click the Create New Mask button at the top of the Masks panel and choose Select Subject at the top of the menu. A red overlay will appear over the little hut.

5   With this mask set, let's warm up the structure and bring back some detail in the inside of it. To do this adjust the Temp to 26 and the Shadows to 29. This will counteract the large amount of blue falling on the area because of the late cloudy day, and add a little bit of detail. Together, they will make the hut stand out a bit more.

● **Note:** If you don't see the tool options below the mask in the Masks panel, you can click the active mask to show that mask's tool selection(s) and click again to hide it.

6   I want to add a little bit more contrast to the image, but not on the inside of the building. To do that, let's create another new mask, but this time, choose Select Background. This will quickly select everything that the AI believes is the background part of the image. Thankfully it works as we want it to here.

7 We'll add a Contrast of 16 to this part of the image. In this specific example, adding contrast to the wood that we brought out by lightening the shadows earlier would have been counterproductive.

8 While making masks with AI is really easy, it is also really easy to get confused about which mask is affecting what element. To stay organized, double-click the words "Mask 1" and in the Rename dialog box, type in **Sky Adjustment** and click OK. Double-click the name of each of the other two masks and rename them **House and Person** and **Contrast Adjust**.

Pressing the letter Y on the keyboard will show you a before and after view of the image, showcasing just how much you are able to get out of this individual raw file.

A couple of things to keep in mind before you think AI is the magic solution for all your needs. First, the amount of image information that you will be able to recover will vary from camera to camera—with older or different cameras your results may vary. In the end, Lightroom's AI allows you to take the tedium out of making these complex selections. What is in the file and what you choose to do with it is entirely up to you.

New: Lens Blur

▶ **Tip:** If your pictures have depth information stored in them (for example, a picture that has been taken in Portrait mode on the iPhone), you can allow Lightroom to use the photo's built-in depth information, or you can opt to use Lightroom's AI-based blur.

One of the most sought after skills in photography is the manipulation of depth of field. This is achieved when using lenses that have wider openings to let more light in, allowing a shallower focus. The wider the opening—known as *aperture*—the more you can bring a subject into focus while blurring the background. Unfortunately, this has a financial cost as the lenses required to do it are usually more expensive. Over the last few years, we have seen this effect added to images everywhere, from mobile phones to Zoom backgrounds.

As AI gets better and better, the technology has been added to Lightroom as an early access feature. While not yet at its full capacity, the Lightroom team has given us a feature that does a pretty good job of simulating these effects on images—no matter what aperture they were shot at—using AI.

This shouldn't be seen as a replacement for the results you can get by using a lens with a wider aperture. Think of it as an extremely powerful creative tool that will get exponentially better in time—another tool to your creative toolbox.

Let's explore this feature with a picture of my wife and daughter taken in Quebec City, Canada.

1   Select lesson06 - 001 in the Selective Edits collections. You'll notice that the image is quite dark. Not to worry! This is a raw file, so we can get more detail out of it. Adjust the Exposure to +1.50, the Highlights to −20, the Shadows to +78, and the Whites to +52. Crop it as you see here.

2   Select the Apply option in the Lens Blur panel and Lightroom uses AI to detect what it believes is the subject of the picture. From there, Lightroom creates a depth map of each area of the photo to determine where to apply the blur and how much in each area.

3 These defined areas can be seen in the ramp at the bottom of the panel, but you can also visualize them in the photo by selecting the Visualize Depth option at below the ramp. The in-focus area is in yellow.

4 Drag the edges of the Focal Range area (the light gray box on the ramp; its handles appear when you move your pointer over it), make it narrower, and you'll see that the blur is refined to include or exclude specific areas. Clicking inside Focal Range area and dragging to the right changes what is blurred.

To the right of Focal Range is a person icon. Clicking it tells the Lightroom AI to select a person. Clicking the next icon lets you define the subject by clicking it directly. Let's keep this automated by clicking the person icon.

5 While Lightroom has done a great job with this blur, there are areas that could be better. We can refine these with a brush by expanding the Refine section. Use the Focus button to bring back some of the blurred out areas by Sabine and Jenn's hair indicated here. If you bring too much into focus, you can always hold down the Option/ Alt key and remove a portion of what you brushed in (your Focus

brush turns to a Blur brush).
Once completed, you can add
additional brushes to this mask
by clicking the + sign to the
right of the Blur button.

6   Create a brush-based blur by clicking the Blur button and painting over the
    person in pink on the left side of the picture as well as the hand on the right side
    of the picture. Once complete, click the + sign and make any final adjustments
    you feel are necessary.

7   Press Y to switch to Before/After mode to see the changes that you've made to
    this picture.

New: AI Based Noise Reduction

While Lightroom has long had very capable Luminance noise reduction, Adobe has taken it a great step further in leveraging AI to automatically detect and remove noise in pictures. In the hut example that we used earlier in this chapter, we had to increase the ISO to 1600 to compensate for a dark and gloomy day. As a result, there is some noise in the shadow areas of the picture.

◆ **Warning:**
Photographers tend to obsess over how much noise there can be in a picture. In this example, we are looking at an area that may be about 5% of the total picture—much less than I would normally consider when applying noise reduction. The truth is that noise can actually bring some character into a picture, so don't overdo it.

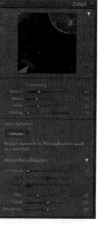

1 At the top of the Noise Reduction section of the Detail panel, click Denoise. When the Enhance Preview dialog box opens, you can drag the Denoise Amount slider to adjust the amount of noise reduction you want in the image. Clicking and holding the image in the preview will show you what the before image looked like.

2 Click the Enhance button, and Lightroom generates a new DNG raw file with the noise reduction applied. In this example, I applied more reduction than I normally would so you could see the difference in the printed book.

Using the Select People mask

The Select People mask in Adobe Lightroom Classic uses AI to quickly scan your image and identify individuals in it. Once each person has been identified, the AI goes deeper, making selections of commonly edited individual features and providing a mask for each feature to make quick work of editing your pictures.

Making single-person selections

1   Select the lesson06 - 003 photo in the Selective Edits collection and switch to the Develop module by pressing the letter D on your keyboard. I would like to quickly bring out some detail in the subject's hair and maybe add even more sparkle to her eyes.

2   Click the Masking tool at the far right of the tool strip, and the mask options will open. In a few moments, the Lightroom AI performs a scan of the picture and determines that there is a person in it. The People area, at the bottom of the mask options, populates with a Person 1 circular thumbnail, showing you the person it has identified. If you hover over the person thumbnail, a red overlay will show you a preview of the selection. Click the Person 1 thumbnail.

3 The Person 1 mask now shows you individual features that you can select. Hover over each possible selection to see a preview of what that mask looks like on the image. If you select a mask option, its red overlay remains on. You can then preview what several mask options look like together. For this image, let's bring up some detail in the hair and lighten the whites of the eyes—the sclera. You also have the

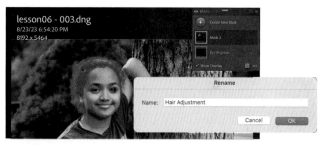

option to merge both selections into one mask or keep them separate. Let's create two separate masks by selecting Eye Sclera, Hair, and Create 2 Separate Masks and then clicking Create Mask.

4 Double-click each of the mask names and in the Rename dialog box, type in a descriptive name for each one. In this case, let's call Mask 1 **Eye Brighten** and call Mask 2 **Hair Adjustment**.

5 For this picture, very minor adjustments are needed. To show the detail in the hair, select the Hair Adjustment mask in the Masks panels, and then drag Contrast to 38 and Blacks to −7 in the tool options. For some additional eye sparkle, select the Eye Brighten mask and raise Exposure to 0.40 and Whites to 4.

Making multiple-person selections

With the single-person mask tackled quickly, let's leverage Lightroom's ability to select multiple people to finish a picture of some of my students here at Newhouse.

In terms of what I want to do here, there are minor adjustments from left to right:

- I'd like to increase contrast and saturation in the clothing of person 1.
- I'd like to open the shadows up in the clothing of person 2.
- I'd like to bring attention to person 3 by brightening her up a little bit.
- I'd like to drop the exposure on the face of person 4 to match the group.

Let's tackle these one at a time.

1 Select the lesson06-0017 image from the Select People collection, and press the letter D to switch to the Develop module.

2 Click the Masking tool in the tool strip, and Lightroom automatically creates individual thumbnails for everyone in the group. Hover your pointer over each thumbnail to see its mask. What's most impressive is that Lightroom can detect individuals who are not facing the camera straight on. Person 1 and person 2 are at an angle, and you cannot see their faces completely; Lightroom, however, doesn't have a problem with it.

3 Click the person 4 thumbnail. Options will appear for each of that person's features that you can edit. You also have the option to select Entire Person. Select Facial Skin and then click Create Mask.

4 With the mask created, decrease the Highlights to −42 and the Temperature to −9. This will bring back some detail in the face and match the color a little better with the rest of the group. Let's name this mask Person 4's Face Adjust so we can keep the masks straight.

5 Moving on to person 2, click the Create New Mask icon at the top of the Masks panel and choose Select People from the menu to start the next adjustment.

6 Click the person 2 thumbnail, and you'll see the multiple features you can choose to edit for that person, as well as the entire person. Let's select the Clothes option and create a mask with that.

7   For this mask, let's increase the
    Shadows to 37 and the
    Saturation to 26. Label this
    mask **Person 2 Hoodie**.

8   Create a new mask for person 1
    that highlights their clothes.
    Increase the Contrast to 75
    and the Saturation to 32, and
    then decrease the Highlights to
    −26 and Blacks to −8. Name
    this selection **Person 1 Clothes**.

Inverting AI selections

For person 3, we want to draw a little more attention to the center of the picture.
To do this, we'll create a little bit of a vignette effect. Rather than having a circular vignette, we can slightly underexpose all of the other elements in the picture,
bringing more attention to the center. We can do that with a mask that darkens the
picture but excludes person 3.

1   Click the Create New Mask icon and choose the Select People. Once all of the
    people are identified, click the Person 3 thumbnail, and select the entire person.
    Finally, click the Create Mask button.

2 At the upper right of the mask options panel you will see an Invert option, which flips the selection so that everything but person 3 is selected. Once the option is selected, the red overlay appears on the rest of the picture. Change the Exposure setting to –0.30. Name this mask **Vignette**.

Combining people into a single selection

With all of the changes to the image, the faces for person 1, 2, and 4 are a little darker than I'd like. We can change this with a slight Exposure change that only affects the facial skin of person 1, person 2, and person 4.

1 Create a new Select People mask and choose Person 1. With Person 1 selected, click the Add People button to the right, and select the additional people you would like to include for this adjustment.

2 This will show the additional people in another window. Click the checkbox for each of the people you want to include and click Continue.

Once the people are selected, click the Facial skin checkbox and a red overlay will appear showing where the adjustment will be made. Make sure that you do not have Create 3 Separate Masks selected and click the Create Mask button.

▶ Tip: If you want to get the Masks panel off your image preview, grab its top bar and drag the panel below the tool strip in the panel area on the right. Once you see a blue bar below the tool strip, release the mouse and the Masks panel will dock above the right-side panels. Grab it and drag it over the image preview until you see a blue frame; then drop it to return it to its original position in the top right.

3 Make a slight adjustment to the facial skin by increasing the Exposure to 0.08 and set the Temp to 3.

4 Once you're finished, press the letter Y to see a before and after view of the image.

The goal of this is not to alter the original image drastically. What we are looking for is to make sure that the portrait highlights the students as well as we can while making sure that we don't spend a lot of time doing so. For quick edits like this one, the Lightroom AI features are a godsend.

Using the Select Object mask

Adobe has taken its AI technology and turbocharged selective masking in Lightroom with a Select Object feature. With this tool, you can paint over an object or create a rectangular selection around it and the AI will detect what you want to edit. Once it's selected, you can create specific adjustments to that object. Let's enhance this picture by adjusting the yellows, the menu board, and the window frames.

1 Select the lesson06 - 002 photo from the Selective Edits collection and press the letter D to go into the Develop module. To start, let's adjust the Exposure to –0.45 to bring back some darker yellow color in the picture.

2 Click the Masking tool, and then below Add New Mask, choose Objects. A new mask is created in the Masks panel, and you'll see two Mode icons at the top of the Select Objects options.

3 The icon on the left allows you to create a selection using a brush. The icon on the right allows you to create a mask by drawing a rectangular selection around the object you want to select. Click this second icon and we will use it to make a quick selection around the menu board.

4 Create a rectangular selection around the menu board by dragging from a spot above and to the left of it to down below and to the right of it. Lightroom uses the selection as a basis for making a smarter AI-based selection and highlights the board with no problem. Set the Exposure to 0.50 in the mask options.

5 Let's use an even more powerful tool here with the Brush. Create a new mask and choose Objects. In the mask options panel, select the Brush option and set the size to 12.

6 Paint over the window frame on the right, as shown in the illustration at the right. Lightroom automatically selects the entire green window frame and window box, making a precise selection. Set the Exposure to 0.50, the Contrast to 27, the Whites to 27, and the Saturation to 58.

7 Let's make one more mask for this image by creating a new mask and choosing Select Background. Apply a Contrast setting of 30 to this mask.

Adding and Removing Masks

In the previous example, I assumed that Lightroom would see the big yellow awnings and the subject in the picture as the subject and select the areas around those elements as the background. Thankfully, it worked out well for me here. (If it sees one of the awnings as background, you can use this next trick to subtract it.)

I bring this up because I believe that, thanks to AI, we are at a spot where we can redefine how we approach working with our images. Normally, selections like this would take a much longer amount of time. Now complex selections can be done in seconds but they require us to think more about what we are asking of the edit.

This becomes even more apparent when you dive in to how to add and remove areas from these AI masks. Once you create a mask in Lightroom, you cannot go back and modify the original mask you created by painting directly on it. A good way to see this is to look at the mask at the top when you click a mask in the Masks panel to expand it. The top mask, with the black and white areas, is the aggregated result of the individual steps beneath it.

Note: If you have used Photoshop previously and are familiar with the concept of layer masks, masking in Lightroom may feel a little bit different. Spending a little time learning how to make the selections you need, however, will pay great dividends later. Trust me. :)

To modify this top mask, you have to use an Add or Subtract option. I recommend you spend a little time thinking through how this process works and how you can use the concept of adding and subtracting to get what you need. I can guarantee you will see great benefits to this later in the book.

Let's start with a simple example. What if we want to take the effect that we created on the window frame on the right and add it to the window frame on the left?

1   Select the mask for the right window (Mask 2) and click the Add button that appears at the bottom of the expanded mask. From the menu, choose Objects and set it to Brush with a size of 12.

2 Use the paintbrush to make a U-shaped brushstroke over the green window frame and window box of the left window. The Lightroom AI makes a precise selection and adds this area to the existing selection. The use of AI in this brush-based selection really saves time here.

3 I would like to remove the adjustments that I made to the background from the two windows in the picture. Select Mask 3, then click the Subtract button and choose Objects from the menu. This time, for Mode, click the Rectangular Select option.

4 Draw a rectangular selection around the window on the left and it will automatically be removed from Mask 3.

5 Click the Mask 3 layer again and repeat the Subtract process, but make a selection around the window on the right to remove it from Mask 3.

Notice that the Mask 3 has changed, showing you the areas that are subtracted in black and the areas that have the effect applied in white. It's a good idea to reach each of the masks from a bottom-up approach. The AI Background selection was made first. From there, you can see that there is a subtract icon to the left of each of the Object masks, letting you know those masks are being removed from the original.

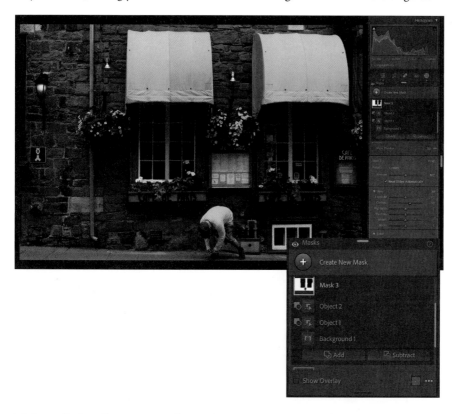

Using Color Range and Luminance Range selections

Two other great tools in Lightroom Classic to isolate regions of an image are the Color Range and Luminance Range selections. These bitmap-based masks allow you to quickly create changes in color and tone.

1 With the lesson06 - 002 image selected, click the Masking tool in the tool strip below the Histogram panel, and then click the Create New Mask icon and choose Color Range from the menu.

2 A new mask is created in the Masks panel, and new Color Range options appear below the tool strip, with a prompt for us to sample a color in our image.

3 Move the pointer over the image and it becomes an eyedropper. Click the yellow awning on the right. A color overlay appears on the awnings and the man's shirt, showing you the area that you will be modifying. If you want to add any other colors to the selection, simply Shift-click another part of the image. This color will be replaced with the red overlay, letting you know that it was added to the selection.

4 Let's make the colors pop a little more by increasing the Contrast to 72 and the Whites to 24.

5 Let's add a little more texture to some of the brick and sidewalk areas in the picture. To do this, click the Create New Mask icon again and choose Luminance Range from the menu. As with the Color Range mask, your pointer becomes an eyedropper. Click the sidewalk in the lower left of the picture. A red overlay appears, showing you the area in the picture that is included in the mask, which is the entire image here. In the Luminance Range options is a ramp that allows you to adjust the brightness areas that are being included.

6 Drag the Luminance Range sliders to the values shown in the illustration below right and you will limit the selection to mostly the bricks on the wall and the sidewalk at the bottom of the image.

7 With the Luminance Range mask adjusted, increase the Texture to 72 and the Clarity to 17 to get more detail in the brick and sidewalk.

8 Once it's complete, press the letter Y to see a before and after view that shows how much you improved this image with these two tools.

Removing distractions with the Healing tool

Tip: Sometimes, when shooting with Fujifilm cameras in a raw format, the RAF file will keep the crop proportions that you set in-camera. If you want to reset these to see the full picture, press the letter R to access the Crop Overlay tool. Then, right-click the image, choose Reset Crop from the menu, and press the Return/Enter key.

Lightroom's Healing tool does a nice job of removing smaller distractions such as sensor dust spots, objects with lots of open space around them (say, power lines), blemishes, and so on. It also can be used to perform some quick photo retouching of your subjects.

This tool works in both Heal and Clone modes, which lets you determine whether you want an automatic blending of surrounding pixels or a straight copy and paste, respectively. The tool can also be powered by Content-Aware technology with Content-Aware Remove.

Removing sensor spots and syncing changes

In this exercise, you'll use the Healing tool to get rid of sensor spots from the top of the hut picture we worked on earlier.

1 In the Develop module's Collections panel, click the Selective Edits collection (if it's not already active) and select the lesson06 - 008 photo from the Filmstrip.

2 If the Masking tool is still active (you still see the Masks panel), click it in the tool strip to close the mask options. Click the top of the picture, above the left side of the hut, to zoom in to the tree area on the left side.

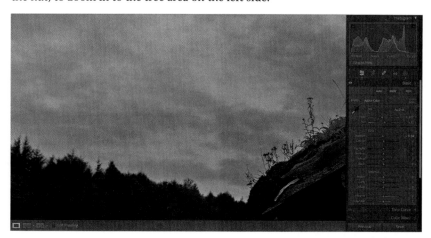

3 Click the Healing tool in the tool strip (it's the third tool from the left). In the tool options panel that appears, click Heal so that Lightroom blends the change with the surrounding pixels. Set the Size slider to 53, the Feather to 0, and the Opacity to 100.

4 In the Toolbar beneath the image preview, select Visualize Spots. Lightroom inverts the image in black and white, making it like a negative so the outlines of its content are visible. Any sensor spots in the photo appear as white circles or grayish dots. Drag the Visualize Spots slider to the right to increase sensitivity and see more spots; drag to the left if you see too many spots.

Note: If you don't see a Toolbar beneath your image in the preview area, press T on your keyboard to summon it.

The Visualize Spots feature is critical for revealing spots caused by dust on your lens, sensor, or scanner. Although these tiny imperfections may not be noticeable onscreen, they often show up when you print the photo. You can see some easily in this photo.

5 Zoom in to the photo by clicking 100% in the Navigator panel at the upper left. Hold down the spacebar on your keyboard, and drag to reposition the photo so you can see one of the spots.

▶ **Tip:** When a local adjustment tool is active, you can zoom in by pressing the spacebar on your keyboard as you click the photo; then continue to hold down the spacebar as you drag the image to move around. When a local adjustment tool isn't active, simply clicking the photo zooms in/out.

6 Move your cursor over one of the spots, resize it so it's slightly bigger than the spot itself, and then click the spot to remove it.

Lightroom copies content from a nearby area in the photo and uses it to remove the spot. You see two circles: One marks the area you clicked (the destination), and another marks the area Lightroom used to remove the spot (the source), with an arrow that points to where the spot used to be.

● **Note:** If the Tool Overlay menu in the Toolbar beneath the photo is set to Auto, the circles disappear when you mouse away from the photo. To change this behavior, click the Tool Overlay menu and choose Always, Never, or Selected (to see only the selected fix).

▶ **Tip:** To thoroughly inspect a photo for spots (if, say, you'll print it or submit it to a stock photography service), press the Home key on your keyboard to start at the upper-left corner of the photo. Press the Page Down key on the keyboard to page through the photo from top to bottom in a column-like pattern.

7 If you don't like the results, you can try changing the area Lightroom used for the fix or you can try changing the tool size. To do that, click the destination circle to select the spot and then:

- Press the Forward Slash (/) key on your keyboard to have Lightroom pick a different source area. Keep tapping the key until the removal looks good.

- Manually change the source area by moving your cursor over the source circle and, when your cursor turns into a tiny hand, dragging the circle to another location in the photo.

- To resize the destination or the source, move your cursor over either circle, and when your cursor changes to a double-sided arrow, drag outward to increase or inward to decrease the size of the circles. Alternatively, you can drag the Size slider in the Healing options panel.

Of course, you can always start over by removing the fix. To do that, select the destination circle and then press the Delete/Backspace key on your keyboard.

8 Spacebar-drag to reposition the photo, and repeat these instructions to remove all of the spots.

9 Turn off Visualize Spots in the Toolbar to return to regular view, and see if all of the spots are gone.

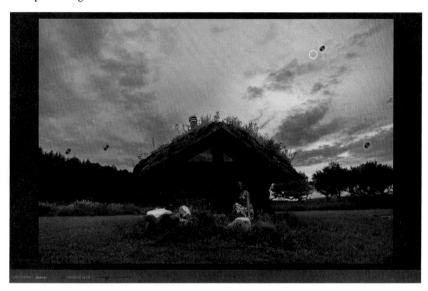

You can remove spots in either view, or you can switch back and forth between views as you work by turning Visualize Spots on and off.

Using Content-Aware Remove on your image

Now let's take a look at how you can use the Content-Aware Remove tool to remove slightly larger objects by dragging over them. I couldn't think of a better way to showcase this than to finish the yellow awnings picture.

1 Select the lesson06 - 002 photo in the Filmstrip. We're going to remove the dark red sign on the left. Click the image to go to a 100% view.

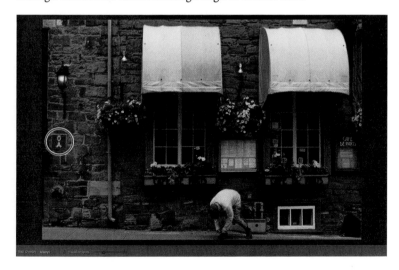

2 Click the Healing tool and click the Content-Aware Remove icon. Set the brush Size to 76 and the Opacity to 100.

3 Start at the top of the sign and drag down toward the bottom of the sign. Keep painting until you cover the entire sign and a bit of the area around it. You can see the white outline of the area I painted in the illustration at right.

4 As good as the Content-Aware Remove tool is, there will be spots that won't automatically look good. To fix this, press the forward slash (/) key and Lightroom will redo the repair.

5 I am going to use the same technique to eliminate the light and the power line on the left side of the picture.

6 Spacebar-drag to move to the center of the picture and remove the light and power line from between the two awnings.

7 You can use the [and] keys to increase the size of the brush on the fly to remove objects. In this instance I made the brush size 60 and painted a tight selection around the bookbag at the lower right of the picture.

8 Cycle through new samples of Content-Aware Remove by pressing the / key. Remember that this is random, so you may have to do this several times in order for it to look closer to what you'd like.

9 If you are not happy with the results of the fill that Lightroom performed, hold down the Command/Ctrl key and drag out a rectangular selection. Lightroom will then use that area to resample the selection and fill it in.

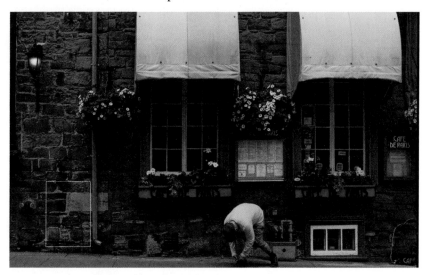

The combination of masks for removal and retouching saves a lot of time when editing images right from within Lightroom. I encourage you to use the other images in this lesson to see how much can be edited using this AI-based technology.

Putting it all together in one image

Now that we have learned to remove some background elements and perform light retouching, we can finish off this portrait by leveraging the different masks we experimented with earlier in the chapter. This will give you a good idea of how to use these tools to quickly get to your final result.

1 Select the lesson06 - 007 image in the Filmstrip. Then, increase the Exposure to +1.00 and decrease the Highlights to −25 to brighten your photo without blowing out the Highlights.

2 Click the Masking tool, and in the People area, click the Person 1 thumbnail. Then select the Facial Skin and Body Skin options and leave Create 2 Separate Masks unselected. Click Create Mask.

3 Reduce the Highlights to −26 and reduce the Texture to −66. This produces a skin smoothing technique that still keeps some details in the features.

4 Click the Create New Mask button and choose Select Background. Once the mask is created, reduce the Exposure of the background to −0.95.

5 Notice the tree trunk that is partially hidden by leaves on the left of the photo. To remove this, click the Healing tool in the toolstrip below the histogram. For Mode, select the Content-Aware Remove option and set the Size to 79 and the Opacity to 100. Drag over the trunk, as shown at right.

6 To direct the focus to our subject, let's add some blur to the background. In the Lens Blur panel, select the Apply option. Once Lightroom calculates the amount of blur, drag the left side of the white box on the Focus Range ramp to 17 and the right side to 49.

7 In the Detail panel, under Noise Reduction, click the Denoise button. In the Enhance Preview dialog box, select Denoise and drag the Amount slider to 32. Drag the preview around to see how this affects areas in the image or click the preview for a before view. Click Enhance.

8 Press Shift+Tab to hide the panels and show the image with no distractions. Press the \ (backslash) key to move between before and after versions of the image.

Easy organization and powerful editing in Lightroom mobile

As a Creative Cloud subscriber, you can take advantage of the mobile version of Lightroom. In an earlier lesson, you created a collection that you can view online. But you can also create collections of images that you have captured on your mobile device and bring those images back into your desktop version of Lightroom Classic.

Additionally, all of the masking features that we've covered in this chapter are available to you inside the mobile app. When you choose to use a specific feature, Lightroom will prompt you to download the associated features from the cloud. Once the download is complete, you will be able to use these features just as you would on your desktop, but on your mobile device.

The mobile version of Lightroom does a great job of providing tips and tricks on how to use the interface, as well as built-in tutorials, community features, and a host of other tools that are not available to you in Lightroom Classic. I recommend that you think of Lightroom mobile as a great companion to the work that you are doing in Lightroom Classic.

Hardware suggestion: Digital tablets

I've always found that using brush-based tools with a mouse is a little harder than it needs to be. To that end, I've always invested in a digital tablet.

Having a surface and a tool that let you mimic the actions of a pen or pencil on paper is more efficient when doing detail work, like painting in your adjustments.

The Wacom Intuos tablet on my desk has been with me for years—inside my bookbag and thrown almost everywhere—and it's still ticking. They make a great product.

There are two versions of the Intuos and three sizes. For my students, I recommend the smallest size to make it easier when traveling. The Pro versus regular question is largely based on your own needs.

Whichever you choose, it will last and will make your job so much faster.

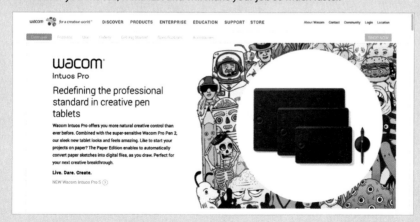

Review questions

1 Can you combine different masks while editing a single image in Lightroom Classic?

2 What Masking tool would best select a specific brightness in an image?

3 How do you add to or remove part of a mask's effect?

4 What is the difference between the Healing tool's Heal, Clone, and Content-Aware Remove modes?

5 How many different options are available using the Select Object tool?

6 You have a subject on a bright background. What tool is the best choice to quickly make the background darker?

7 When masking a person, which Select People options should you select to lower the highlights on the person's skin?

8 How do you delete an existing mask?

Review answers

1 Yes, you can create AI-based masks and add or subtract other masks quickly in the Masks panel. You can even add vector-based Brush masks to existing masks.

2 The Luminance Range Masking tool is responsible for selecting luminance (brightness) values in an image. This range can be further defined with the Luminance Range ramp.

3 Once you have created a mask, if you need to add to it or remove a portion of the effect, click the Add or Subtract button in the Masks panel, and then choose whichever tool in the menu that you want to use to remove that area.

4 When using the Healing tool, Heal gives you an automatic blending of surrounding pixels, while Clone gives you a straight copy and paste. Content-Aware Remove uses AI to replace parts of a picture with what Lightroom thinks should be there.

5 There are two options available for the Select Object tool. You can use a brush or draw out a rectangular selection.

6 The AI mask for Select Background will quickly select the background of any image, allowing you to adjust the exposure or highlights to darken it.

7 To affect only a person's skin, you should select Facial Skin and Body Skin in the Select People options for that person.

8 To delete a mask, right-click the mask and select Delete *mask name*; click the mask in the Masks panel and press the Delete/Backspace key on your keyboard; or click the mask in the Masks panel, click the three dots to the right of the name, and choose Delete *mask name*.

PHOTOGRAPHY SHOWCASE
SARA LANDO

"...you'll have to invest some time in finding your voice..."

My personal work explores identity, the boundaries between what is real and what is imagined, and the way memory deteriorates and is reshaped over time. I am interested in the moments when the traditional relationship between us and the world around us is unraveled and replaced by a new definition of what we are or what we could be.

I work using photography, illustration, collage, and digital manipulation. The techniques I use derive from a playful curiosity and direct interaction with the object. I am fascinated by the fragmentation and degradation of the image, and the concept of creation as a consequence of the physical and digital destruction of a photograph.

To me, photography is a medium, not dissimilar from writing, that allows me to be honest without needing to be univocal. It is a language. To most of us, it's a foreign language we are learning how to speak. Even if you are fluent in shutter speed and aperture, even if you know everything about bouncing flash and own the best camera on the market, if you don't have something to say, then you're pretty screwed.

I have been taking pictures for the last 20 years, and I think the single most important advice I could give is that, at some point, you'll have to invest some time in finding your voice, in making sure you're not actually wasting time narrating someone else's story.

I've been using Photoshop since you could only go back a few steps in the history. At first it was a crutch to help me fix my mistakes, but over the years it became a tool that helped me to add subtlety.

saralando.com
instagram.com/holeinthefabric

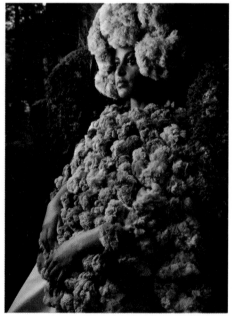

7 LOCALIZED EDITS & TIME SAVERS IN LIGHTROOM

Lesson overview

While the Lightroom AI-based tools make quick work of your photo projects, you'll find that combining these tools with the existing tools in the Develop module makes a powerful combination to get even better images. This workflow also makes it easier to replicate the changes you make to your images in no time at all. By the time you finish this chapter, you will be able to:

- Use linear and radial gradient masks to narrow your adjustments.

- Use the Masking Brush tool to adjust specific image areas.

- Use Point Color to make color changes with precision.

- Create compelling black-and-white images.

- Experiment with color grading effects.

- Develop and view panoramic and HDR images with ease.

- Synchronize your changes to multiple images and use presets.

 This lesson will take about 2 hours to complete. To get the lesson files used in this chapter, download them from the web page for this book at *peachpit.com/LightroomCIB2024*. For more information, see "Accessing the lesson files and Web Edition" in the "Getting Started" section at the beginning of this book.

Fine-tune and polish your photographs with precise,
easy-to-use tools, and then take your developing
a step beyond just correcting your images; use the
Develop module tools and controls creatively to customize your own special effects and then save them
as custom develop presets.

Getting started

Note: This lesson assumes that you already have a basic working familiarity with the Lightroom Classic workspace. If you need more background information, refer to Lightroom Classic Help, or review the previous lessons.

Before you begin, make sure you've set up the LRC2024CIB folder for your lesson files and downloaded the lesson07 folder from your Account page at *peachpit.com* to the LRC2024CIB\Lessons folder, as described in "Accessing the lesson files and Web Edition" in the "Getting Started" section at the start of this book. Also, be sure you have created the LRC2024CIB Catalog file to manage the lesson files, as detailed in "Creating a catalog file for working with this book," also in the "Getting Started" section of this book.

1   Start Lightroom Classic.

2   In the Select Catalog dialog box, make sure that LRC2024CIB Catalog.lrcat is selected, and then click Open.

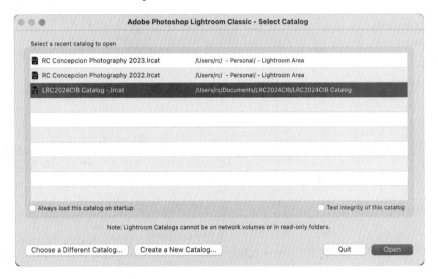

Note: If you can't see the Module Picker, choose Window > Panels > Show Module Picker, or press the F5 key. If you're working on macOS, you may need to press the fn key together with the F5 key or change the function key behavior in the system preferences.

3   Lightroom Classic will open in the screen mode and workspace module that were active when you last quit. If necessary, switch to the Library module by clicking Library in the Module Picker at the top of the workspace.

Importing images into the library and creating collections

The first step is to import the images for this lesson into the Lightroom library.

1   In the Library module, click the Import button below the left panel group.

2 If the Import dialog box appears in compact mode, click the Show More Options button at the lower left of the dialog box to see all of the options in the expanded Import dialog box.

3 Under Source at the left of the expanded Import dialog box, locate and select your LRC2024CIB\Lessons\lesson07 folder. Ensure that all 35 photos in the lesson07 folder are selected for import.

4 In the import options above the thumbnail previews, select Add so that the imported photos will be added to your catalog without being moved or copied. Under File Handling at the right of the expanded Import dialog box, choose Embedded & Sidecar from the Build Previews menu and leave the Don't Import Suspected Duplicates option selected. Under Apply During Import, choose None from both the Develop Settings menu and the Metadata menu and type **Lesson 07, Timesavers** in the Keywords text box. Make sure that your import is set up as shown here, and then click Import.

The 35 photos are imported from the lesson07 folder and now appear in both the Grid view of the Library module and in the Filmstrip across the bottom of the Lightroom workspace.

While we're in the Library module, let's create three collections from these photos: Selective Tools, Timesavers, and HDR and Panorama.

5 Make sure Previous Import is selected in the Catalog panel and the Sort menu is set to File Name. Select the first 15 photos (click the first one and Shift-click the last one). Click the plus sign icon in the upper right of the Collections panel and create a collection called **Selective Tools**. Make sure to include the selected photos.

6 Click Previous Import again. Press Command+D/Ctrl+D to deselect all of the images, and with your Sort menu set to File Name, select the first four photos. Again, click the plus sign icon in the upper right of the Collections panel and create a collection called **Timesavers**. Make sure Include Selected Photos is selected.

7 Click Previous Import, deselect all of the images. Now select pictures 16 through 35. Create a collection called **HDR and Panorama**. Make sure the Include Selected Photos option is selected.

8 Click Previous Import in the Catalog panel one more time. Deselect all of the images, and then select images 7 through 13. Once they are selected, drag them into the HDR and Panorama collection. Press Command+D/Ctrl+D to deselect all of the images.

9 To keep all of the collections we are using in Lesson 7 together, click the plus sign icon at the upper right of the Collections panel and create a new collection set. In the Create Collection Set dialog box, let's call it **Lesson 07 Practice**.

10 Command-click/Ctrl-click the three collections you made previously and drag them into the Lesson 07 Practice collection set. This organization will allow us to work on the images we want and declutter our library view.

11 Select each of the collections in turn and make sure that they all have their images sorted by filename.

Using the Linear Gradient mask

The Linear Gradient mask lets you apply adjustments to part of a picture in a linear direction. The effect uses sliders that are similar to the ones in the Basic panel but that let you fade out the effect in the direction you drag. In this exercise, you'll apply two Linear Gradient tool adjustments to a single photo.

1 Click the Selective Tools collection in the Collections panel. Select the lesson07 - 005 image and press the D key to switch to the Develop module. The sky is a little dull in this image, and the image is a bit underexposed. We want to add some contrast to it, fading the effect as it reaches the horizon.

This will draw the viewer's attention toward the middle of the picture. We also want to lighten the foreground a little (at the bottom) without lightening the top part of the picture.

We're going to add two different gradients to the picture—one to emphasize the top half and one to lighten the bottom and enhance the color in the water.

⏵ Tip: By default, the Masks panel first appears over your image, to the left of the Histogram panel. You can drag it just below the tool strip, releasing the mouse button when you see a blue line, to dock it above your tool options.

2 Select the Masking tool in the tool strip above the Basic panel (the tool on the right) and then choose Linear Gradient, or press M on your keyboard. You'll see the Linear Gradient options panel appear below the tool strip.

The sliders for all of the local adjustment tools are sticky, so it's important to remember to reset them. To reset an individual slider to its default value, double-click its label or the slider itself. To reset all of the sliders to 0, double-click the Preset label at the upper left of the panel or hold down the Option/Alt key, and when the Preset label changes to Reset, click it.

⏵ Tip: Press Tab to move down through the settings in the options panel and manually enter a number. If you'd like to move up through those fields, press Shift+Tab.

3 Reset all of the sliders in the Linear Gradient options panel; then drag the Exposure slider to the right to 0.26, Contrast to 57, Highlights to –100, Shadows to 100, Whites to 45, and Blacks to –10. Setting one or more sliders before you use the tool loads it with those settings so they're applied as soon as you drag on the photo. You can adjust them after the fact.

4 To apply the filter, Shift-drag from just below the center of the trees down a short distance so the adjustment covers the sky and the trees just above the lake (holding down the Shift key keeps the gradient straight).

Lightroom adds a linear gradient mask over the area where you dragged. This gradient mask controls where the adjustment is visible. Drag the pin in the middle of the gradient to reposition the mask. When the pin is selected, it's a black square, and you can adjust the gradient's sliders; when it's not selected, it's pentagonal, and the sliders no longer affect it. To delete a gradient, click its pin and press Delete/Backspace.

The filter's three white lines represent the strength of the adjustment from the direction you dragged: 100%, fading to 50%, and then down to 0%. You can contract or expand the filter's gradient by dragging the top or bottom lines toward or away from the center line. To rotate the gradient, move your cursor over the white dot just

below the bottom line, and when your cursor turns into a curved arrow, drag it clockwise or counterclockwise.

5 Normally, to create our second gradient, we would click the Create New Mask button and repeat the steps from the first one, but there's an easier way for this one. To add our second linear gradient, hover your cursor over Mask 1 in the Masks panel. Click the three little dots that appear to the right and choose Duplicate And Invert Mask from the menu. Lightroom automatically creates the second mask for you.

6 Double-click Preset to reset all of the sliders if needed, and then drag the Temp slider to 12. Next, drag Exposure to 0.34, Contrast to −36, Highlights to 62, Shadows to 23, Whites to 100, and Blacks to −33. This will bring out the tree reflections in the water better.

7 Click the eye icon at the right of each mask in the Masks panel to turn them off and on to see how each one affects the image. Round out the picture by clicking the Edit tool in the tool strip below the histogram and adding an Exposure of +0.35 and a Vibrance of +30 to the entire picture.

▶ **Tip:** Press O on your keyboard to turn on the gradient mask overlay in red. Press the same key to turn it off (or select Show Overlay at the bottom of the Masks panel). To change the mask color, press Shift+O on your keyboard (this is helpful when the mask color also appears in large areas of your photo).

▶ **Tip:** Lightroom automatically hides the pins when you move your mouse away from the preview area. To change this, use the Show Edit Pins menu in the Toolbar below the photo. (If you don't see the Toolbar below your photo, press T on your keyboard.)

▶ **Tip:** You can create overlapping linear gradients too!

There are some other things we may want to do with this picture, but this is a good start. Let's talk about how to use the Radial Gradient tool.

Using the Radial Gradient mask

You can use the Radial Gradient mask to apply the same adjustments as the Linear Gradient tool, but in a circular pattern instead of a linear gradient. The Radial Gradient tool is handy for spotlighting a specific area of your photo by brightening, darkening, blurring, or shifting the color of a background, or for creating an edge vignette that you can move around (say, to draw attention to a subject that is off-center).

In this exercise, you'll learn how to add a radial gradient that draws your attention to a non-circular area. This area will be off-center (common in photography).

1 In the Selective Tools collection, click the lesson07 - 001 image in the Filmstrip, a photo of my nephew building his first arcade machine. A post-crop vignette might look good here, darkening the edges of the image. If we want his hands to be the center of the attention, though, the darkening needs to happen slightly off-center.

2 Click the Masking tool in the tool strip above the Basic panel (it's the tool at the right) and choose Radial Gradient, or press Shift+M on your keyboard. The Radial Gradient options panel appears beneath the tool strip.

3   Double-click Preset at the upper left of the panel to reset all the sliders to 0.

4   At the top of the tool options, set the Feather to 44. This ensures a gradual, soft transition at the outside edge of your gradient.

5   Click the field to the right of the Exposure slider to highlight it, and enter **−0.79**.

▶ **Tip:** There is a checkbox near the top of the Masking tool's options (above the Tone area) that allows you to reset all of your slider changes in those options automatically. This is a big time-saver.

6   Position your pointer near the center of his hands, and then drag diagonally downward and to the right (the filter is created from the center out).

The adjustments you made immediately darken the area inside the oval. While this is a good start, we want to reshape it to better fit the hand area.

7   You can reposition and resize the gradient to your liking using the following techniques:

   •   Reposition the gradient by clicking inside its boundary, and when your pointer changes to a hand, dragging it to a different place.

   •   Resize the gradient by moving your pointer over one of the round anchor points on the gradient's outline. When your pointer changes to a double-headed arrow, drag toward or away from the gradient's center to resize it. Do this to adjacent anchor points to reshape the gradient.

   •   Rotate the filter by moving your cursor outside the filter's outline. When your pointer changes to a curved arrow, drag to rotate the filter.

8   Adjust the Feather of the gradient to 32 to limit the area of transition.

9   This mask is set to darken the hands, but we want to do the exact opposite here. To achieve that, select the Invert option above the Feather slider.

10 The result is a bit of a spotlight on the hands, which draws the eye to what you want the viewer to focus on. However, I want to brighten up his head to connect him more to the picture. So, click the Create New Mask button at the top of the Masks panel and create a new radial mask. Drag out an oval from the center of his head until it covers the area. Once you've released the mouse button, grab the edges of the oval to reshape it as necessary.

11 Adjust the radial mask to brighten up the head and add a little more detail by choosing Dodge (Lighten) from the Preset menu near the top of the tool's options and applying the following adjustments:

- Exposure: 1.03

- Contrast: 10

- Highlights: −30

- Whites: 10

12 I want to warm up a portion of his hands in the picture. To do this, click the Mask icon and select Color Range. With the eyedropper, select his skin just above the red pencil cap.

13 To limit the effect to the smallest area possible, refine the edge to 1. Set the Temp in the Color area to +23 to warm up the hands.

14 Press Y on your keyboard to switch to the Before and After view and see the differences that three quick adjustments can make.

Using the Masking Brush tool

While the linear and radial gradients allow you to make specific adjustments to an image, they do not have the fine control that is sometimes needed. Ideally, you'd pin-point every adjustment in the Basic and Detail panels to the specific areas that need them. This is where the Masking Brush makes quick work of adjustments.

▶ **Tip:** You can change the size of the Brush tool or Erase tool by using the [and] keys on your keyboard.

1 Select the lesson07 - 006 image to do some localized corrections on the trees and marsh. Press D to return to Loupe view.

2 Click the Masking tool in the tool strip and choose Brush, or press the letter K. Type in **0.15** for Exposure, **42** for Contrast, **95** for Whites, and **92** for Saturation. Set the brush's Size to 7, Feather to 100, and Flow to 71, and then paint over the trees in the background.

A brush-shaped pin is dropped on the picture where you painted. Move your pointer over the pin, and an overlay appears, showing you what the adjustment affects. With your pointer over the pin, press Shift+O to cycle through the overlay colors.

A few things to remember about the Masking Brush:

- The Size of the brush is indicated by the smaller solid circle in the center.

- The Feather of the brush creates a soft-edged transition between the area you're working on and the surrounding pixels. The distance between the inner and outer circle represents the feather amount.

- Flow controls the rate at which the effect is painted on the image.

- Density controls the transparency of the effect.

- Auto Mask confines the brush stroke you made to areas of similar color.

- Holding down the Option/Alt key allows you to access the Erase brush temporarily, so you can remove the effect from any areas you accidentally painted over.

3 Create a new Brush Mask and set your brush size to 18. Set the Exposure to −0.72, the Contrast to 45, and Highlights to −39. Use this brush to bring in some color and detail into the grass along the water.

4 To round out the picture, create a Select Sky mask and add the following adjustments:

- Exposure: −0.37

- Contrast: 88

- Highlights: −23

- Whites: 63

- Saturation: 28

5 This step may not be necessary, but I want to keep the attention on the trees in the distance, and the tree on the left takes away from that. To counter this, switch to the Crop tool (R) and bring in the crop selection to the area as shown here. You can also rotate the image slightly to straighten the horizon out a little.

6 Press the backslash (\) key to switch between the before and after views or the Y key to see the side-by-side Before and After view. There's a lot in these files just waiting for you to coax it out!

The Color Mixer panel

The Color Mixer panel has two ways for you to creatively explore color: the Mixer and the new Point Color. While the Mixer allows you to make creative changes to Hue, Saturation, and Luminance very quickly, the newly introduced Point Color gives you incredibly precise control over specific colors in the image.

Another thing to keep in mind here: the HSL/Color, Tone Curve, and B&W panels all operate with a similar set of tools, making it easy to learn how to use all three panels by learning one of them. Let's start by exploring how to manipulate the HSL/Color panel.

Working with HSL adjustments

Inside the HSL/Color panel, there are a series of sliders that allow you to change colors by dragging them to the left or right. While the sliders offer you a very detailed way to adjust color, to me, the Targeted Adjustment tool gives you even more control.

1   Select the lesson07 - 014 file in the Selective Tools collection, and press D to switch to the Develop module, if you're not already there. To start, set the Exposure to +0.20, the Contrast to +42, the Whites to +38, and the Blacks to −11.

2   At the top of the Color Mixer panel, click Mixer, then choose HSL from the Adjust menu, and then click Hue. Click the Targeted Adjustment tool just above the color sliders to select it (it looks like a small bullseye that has arrows on top and bottom when you hover your pointer over it).

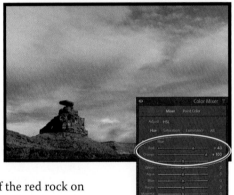

To use the tool, click any portion of the red rock on the left with it. Drag up or down and Lightroom will determine which colors are under the tool and adjust the sliders of only those colors, adjusting their hue (here, you can see that the reds and oranges turned more green). As you drag, the sliders in the Hue panel automatically change to adjust the color. This is much easier than guessing which colors are in the area you want to affect. Double-click each slider to reset it.

3   Click Saturation below the Adjust menu and use the Targeted Adjustment tool to drag up and down on any colors in a specific area and desaturate them (drag down) or oversaturate them (drag up). Note that the changes are not confined to the area you drag, but to the colors where you drag. If those colors appear elsewhere in the photo, they will be affected there too.

4 Click the Luminance tab and use the Targeted Adjustment tool to drag up and down on the colors in a specific area to make them brighter (drag up) or darker (drag down). In this instance, I dragged downward on the rock to affect the orange Luminance. Once you've experimented, double-click each of the sliders to return them to their original positions.

New: Using Point Color adjustments

While mixing color can yield great results, Lightroom has taken things to a new level with the introduction to Point Color. Now you can isolate a specific color in an image and adjust how that color is manipulated with great control. We'll use the Point Color technology to isolate specific colors and make adjustments to them in our fall image.

Selecting a point color

1 Select lesson07 - 006 from the Selective Tools collection and click Point Color at the top of the Color Mixer panel.

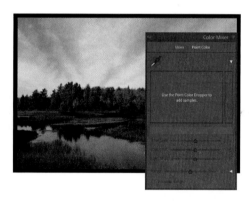

2 Use the eyedropper in the Point Color options to select a portion of the green trees. You'll see a zoom selection appear allowing you to see what you are selecting a little clearer. In the color field, you will see the color that you are hovering over.

3 Once you click on the tree area, a swatch will appear to the right of the dropper, and the color field will change, showing you a small dot that is the color you selected. The larger dot represents the change you are trying to make. Below the color field, there are sliders that allow you to shift the Hue, Saturation, and Luminance as

well. You can move the large dots on the color field and the ramp to the right up and down to change the saturation and luminance, respectively. Move the large dot in the color field to the left and right to change the Hue. If you would like a result similar to mine, shift the Hue to 62, the Saturation to −55, and the Luminance to 15.

Adjusting a color range

1 You can isolate the colors you want to change by adjusting the Range slider. Moving it to the left will decrease the number of colors you are changing, while moving it to the right will increase the number of colors. Selecting the Visualize Range option will make the image grayscale and show you only the colors you are trying to change in the image— a great tool to see your work!

2 Expand the Range slider area and you have even more control over how an area of color is selected. Hue, Saturation, and Luminance have a range of color that is going to be changed (noted by the rectangle) and how much the color is fading by the slider knobs at each end of the ramp. Adjusting the rectangle will limit the amount of hue, saturation, or luminance in the image, while adjusting the slider knobs will adjust the fade range of each of the colors. The

color field offers a great way for you to see the exact color that is being changed, but I encourage you to use the Visualize Range option at the bottom. While it may be hard for you to see the exact color that is being manipulated in the printed version of this book (I've highlighted the sections that are being changed), it will make quick work of making these adjustments.

Adding a second color

1   Get the eyedropper again in the Point Color panel and select orange trees in the center of the image. To follow along with this tutorial, try to select the color that is shown here in the zoom field.

2 With a second color swatch added to the right of the eyedropper, you can make adjustments to the hue, saturation, and luminance of this area. For this example, I made a Hue shift of −70, but your results may vary based on the experimentation you do and the exact spot you click.

Using Point Color with a Mask

Having the option to change specific colors makes editing inside of Lightroom extremely powerful. However, combining Point Color with an existing mask will make this feature even more useful.

1 Click the Create New mask button and make a gradient from just below the middle of the image up to the edge of the river, below the trees.

2 In the mask options, you'll see that you also have Point Color as an option here. Grab the eyedropper and sample the brownish grass along the water. Once selected, shift the Hue to a green color. For this example, I used a Hue of 67, but yours may vary.

3 To give the grass a little more texture, in the Tone options, I added a Contrast setting of +41. This darkens the edges of the grass and rounds out the picture.

4 To best see how far you've come along with this image, press the Y key to enter the Before/After view in Lightroom.

Working with the Tone Curve panel

If you want to add a little more contrast on top of what you have added in the Basic panel, you can use the Tone Curve panel. Expand the Tone Curve panel to see the tone curve and the sliders that let you adjust the curve (if you don't see the sliders, click the Parametric Curve button to the right of the Targeted Adjustment tool at the top left of the panel).

This curve represents changes made to the tonal scale of your picture. The horizontal axis shows the original tonal (input) values, with black on the left and moving progressively brighter to the right. The slider below the horizontal axis lets you adjust the tonal regions (shadows, darks, lights, and highlights).

The vertical axis represents the changed tonal (output) values, with black on the bottom and progressing to white at the top.

Tip: To switch from the Parametric Curve controls (a curve that has limits for how much you can push it) to the Point Curve (a curve that lets you do whatever you want to it), use the Adjust buttons at the right of the Targeted Adjustment tool. The first shows the Parametric Curve controls, the second shows the Point Curve controls, and the others show the Red channel, Green channel, and Blue channel controls, respectively.

If a point on the curve moves up, it becomes a lighter tone; if it moves down, it becomes darker. A straight, 45°-angle line indicates no change to the tonal scale.

While this gives you an understanding of how to adjust tonal regions in your picture, I find it much more intuitive to use the same Targeted Adjustment tool we used in the Color Mixer panel to make adjustments to the picture.

1   Click the Targeted Adjustment tool in the Tone Curve panel and hover over the picture. Notice that as you hover over an area of the picture, the corresponding area in the tone curve is highlighted.

2   Drag downward to make that area of the picture darker; drag upward to make that tonal region brighter. Keep an eye on how dragging up or down affects your tone curve.

You can do a lot of creative experimentation with the Tone Curve panel, but your ability to add contrast and detail to an image using the Targeted Adjustment tool cannot be overstated.

Creative color and black-and-white effects

According to famed environmental portrait photographer Gregory Heisler, black-and-white imagery "allows you to see the structure of the image in a way that color cannot." While we often see photographs in black and white as nostalgic, the lack of color in the image allows the viewer to focus on stronger components of the picture—composition, structure, gesture, and so on.

Creating virtual copies for image treatments

Just as we did back in Lesson 5, we can create virtual copies to experiment with color and black-and-white effects without taking up more hard drive space.

1 With the lesson07 - 006 image still selected, click the plus sign in the Collections panel's header and choose Create Collection. In the Name field, enter **Color Adjustments** and make sure that Include Selected Photos is selected, as is Inside a Collection Set with Lesson 07 Practice chosen.

2 Press G to switch to the Grid view. Right-click the image and choose Create Virtual Copy two times. This will give you three images in the filmstrip or Grid view. We will use the second one to create a black-and-white image.

Converting a color photo to black and white

1 Click the second photo in the Color Adjustments collection and press D to switch to the Develop module.

2 Click B&W in the upper right of the Basic panel. The image undergoes a basic black-and-white conversion and the Color Mixer panel changes into the B&W panel.

3 Expand the B&W panel to reveal a series of sliders representing different colors in your image. Dragging any of the sliders to the right will make any color in that range lighter; dragging to the left will make that range of colors darker. I dragged Green here.

4 The biggest problem that we run into here is that we are attempting to adjust color sliders in an image that's now black and white. Click the Targeted Adjustment tool and move to a part of your photo you'd like to adjust, and then drag upward to brighten the colors underneath the tool or drag downward to darken them.

Color grading

A few years ago, Lightroom replaced Split Toning with color wheels for controlling shadows, midtones, and highlights in an interface that many users were waiting for!

For each tone, you have a wheel. Dragging the center point or outside knob in a circular motion around the wheel changes the overall hue. Dragging the center point inward or outward changes the saturation. Finally, the bottom slider changes the brightness.

1 Select the lesson07 - 014 image in the Selective Tools collection and expand the Color Grading panel. At the top of the panel, click the black dot to the right of the word *Adjust* to switch to the Shadows wheel, and then drag the center point down and to the left, for a Hue of 215 with a Saturation of 62.

2 Move to the Midtones wheel (click the gray Adjust dot), and drag the center point to the left for a Hue of 167 and a Saturation of 14. The Blending slider sets how each of the ranges will mix with one another. Here, I set it to 50.

3 Click the Highlights (white) dot, and drag the center point down and to the right to a Hue of 310 and a Saturation of 36. I encourage you to experiment with coloring images further using these wheels.

The Effects panel

The Effects panel in Lightroom allows you to add grain and post-crop vignetting to your images. Post-crop vignetting is a great feature when you want to add focus to the center of the picture, but it requires a lot of care or you risk your image looking kitschy.

Switch to the lesson07 - 001 image we worked on earlier and expand the Effects panel. We'll start with the Post-Crop Vignetting sliders at the top of the panel.

Post-crop vignetting is an effect that evolved from the undesirable darkening in the corners of images taken using specific lenses. People started to like this effect of "burning the edges in," as it drew attention to the center of the picture.

Lightroom introduced a Vignetting slider in the original release of the program that was supposed to be used to correct the effect, not add it. Photographers, however, began using it to apply a vignetting effect, but when they cropped their pictures, the vignette effect disappeared.

Lightroom has since moved the Vignetting sliders (to remove vignetting) into the Lens Corrections panel and added Post-Crop Vignetting (which retains the size and centeredness of the vignetting even if you crop the image) to the Effects panel. There are three Style menu choices available under Post-Crop Vignetting:

*   Highlight Priority can bring back some blown-out highlights, but it can lead to color shifts in darkened areas of a photo. It's good for images with bright areas, such as clipped specular highlights.

- Color Priority minimizes color shifts in darkened areas of a photo, but it cannot perform highlight recovery.

- Paint Overlay mixes the cropped image values with black or white pixels and can result in a flat appearance.

There are five sliders available to you under Post-Crop Vignetting:

- *Amount* darkens the edges of the picture as you drag to the left and lightens as you drag to the right.

- *Midpoint* adjusts how tight to the corners the effect is created. A low number moves it away from the corners, toward the center; a higher number moves it closer to the corners.

- *Roundness* adjusts whether the effect looks like an oval or a circle. Drag to the left and it becomes more of an oval; drag to the right and you get a circle.

- *Feather* adjusts how soft the effect's transition appears. Drag to the right and the effect appears softer; drag to the left for a hard transition.

- *Highlights* is available only when Highlight Priority or Color Priority is chosen in the menu. This slider controls the degree of highlight contrast that is preserved.

Grain is a little more straightforward. You can control the amount of grain added to your image, how big the individual grains are, and how jagged they are. The grain looks pretty realistic and can add extra punch to images, especially if you're working in black and white.

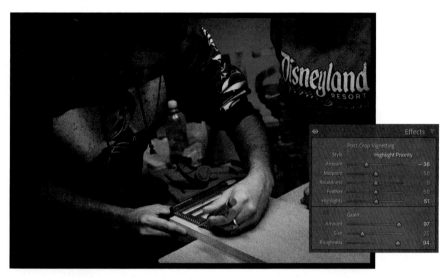

I am not a fan of post-crop vignetting, as I would rather have the greater control of the Masking tool's Brush and Radial Gradient. Let's reset all of the post-crop vignetting by double-clicking the sliders for each of the values, from the bottom up. Feel free to add these effects if you believe they add something to your images.

Making panoramas

Panoramic images can give people a feeling of complete immersion in a picture. But taking panoramic pictures used to require specialized lenses that were wide enough to fit the scene you wanted to capture. Lightroom has made such incredible strides in making panoramic images out of regular-sized images that it borders on magic. Simply take a series of pictures, and let Lightroom take care of the rest.

There are a couple of key things that Lightroom does when making panoramic images that really make it stand out. First, Lightroom includes a Boundary Warp slider that all but negates the need to crop the resulting panorama due to the spherical distortion necessary to align so many images. Previously, you had to rely on Photoshop to use Content-Aware Fill to avoid cropping, but now more of that can be done in Lightroom.

▶ **Tip:** When capturing images for a panorama, try to overlap each shot with the preceding one by about 30 percent. Set your camera to both manual focus and manual exposure so that those parameters don't change automatically as the camera moves from shot to shot. If possible, use a tripod.

Second, the resulting file in Lightroom is also a raw file (specifically, a DNG), allowing you to work in the Develop module with a much greater range than you were able to previously. Third, the panorama merge supports a headless mode.

Lightroom also lets you create HDR panoramas, making the task of creating individual HDR files and then merging them into a panorama a thing of the past.

Finally, Lightroom Classic allows you to fill the edges of a picture, offering you a complete look without warping the image.

Merging to a panorama in Lightroom Classic

In this exercise, you'll stitch five photos together. Happily, it doesn't matter what order the photos are in because Lightroom intelligently analyzes the photos to see how they logically fit together. You can wait to adjust tone and color until after you've merged the images.

1   Press G to switch to Grid view, and in the HDR and Panorama collection, Command-click/Ctrl-click the lesson07 - 020, lesson07 - 025, and lesson07 - 030 images to select them.

2   Right-click one of the thumbnails and choose Photo Merge > Panorama or press Control+M/Ctrl+M. One of the first things that is apparent is the speed at which the panorama is built. Lightroom uses the embedded JPEG images to create your preview. There's nothing more frustrating than waiting a while to see if the panorama is good only to find out it's a bust.

3   The options in the Panorama Merge Preview dialog box control the layout method Lightroom uses to align the individual images. It's worth taking each method for a spin, although if your pano is really wide, Adobe suggests using Cylindrical. If it is a 360-degree or multirow pano (you took two rows of photos), try Spherical. If it has a lot of lines in it (say, an architectural shot), try Perspective.

In this case, Spherical works well; however, there are white areas all around the image that need to be cropped out or filled in.

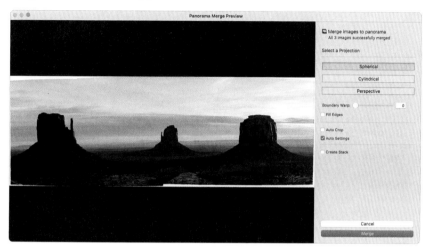

4 Drag the Boundary Warp slider to the right until the white areas disappear to see how it looks. This slider corrects the image distortion so well that you may never need to crop or fill in the edges of your panorama again. Reset it to 0 for now. If you decide that you want to crop out the edges, select the Auto Crop option.

5 Deselect Auto Crop and select Fill Edges and all of the edges are filled, giving you an even more natural look. Once complete, click Merge to close the dialog box. Lightroom merges all five images, and the result is a seamlessly blended panorama. If you left the Auto Settings option selected in the Panorama Merge Preview dialog box, Lightroom will try to develop your image. Select the panorama in the Filmstrip (it has the word *pano* in its name) to see how it did.

◆ **Warning:** If the panorama doesn't immediately appear in the Library module's Grid view or the Filmstrip, give it a few seconds. The same goes for merging to HDR.

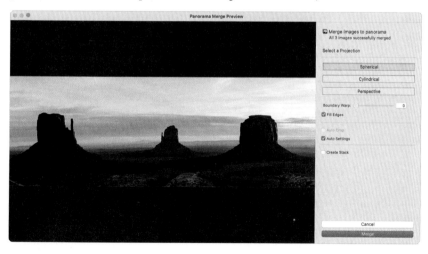

6 Use the panels in the Develop module as well as the color range techniques we've discussed in this lesson to tweak the tone and color. The merged file is a DNG, so you have all of the tonal benefits of a raw file.

Headless mode for panoramas

Since panoramas can take some time to perform their final merge, I tend to use headless mode to speed things up a bit. Hold down the Shift key as you select Photo Merge > Panorama, and the file will skip the Panorama Merge Preview dialog box and render the file in the background.

Making HDR images

Very few images exploit the full range of possible brightness tones, from the lightest lights to the darkest darks. Often, you'll have more info on one end of the histogram than the other, meaning that either the highlights *or* the shadows are well exposed and full of detail, but not both. That's because digital cameras have a limited dynamic range; they can collect only so much data in a single shot. If you have a scene with both light and dark areas, you have to choose which area to expose correctly. In other words, you can't expose for both areas in the same photo.

▶ **Tip:** The term *tone mapping* means to take the existing tones in your image and alter them so they reflect a broader dynamic range.

To create photos that take advantage of the full range of tones from light to dark, you need to do one of the following:

- Shoot in raw format and tone map the photo in Lightroom. As long as you capture good detail in the highlights—check the histogram on the back of your camera to make sure you do—you may be able to pull out an incredible amount of detail using the sliders in the Basic panel.

- Shoot multiple versions of the same shot at different exposure values (EVs), and then merge them into a high dynamic range (HDR) image. You can do this manually by taking three to four photos with, say, a single f-stop difference between them, or you can have your camera do it automatically by turning on its bracketing feature.

Bracketing lets you tell the camera how many shots to take (use a minimum of three, though more is better) and how much of an exposure difference you want between each one (pick one or two EV stops if you have the choice). For example, for three shots, you'd have one at normal exposure, one that's one or two stops lighter than normal, and another that's one or two stops darker than normal.

In the last couple of releases, Lightroom has taken great leaps forward in the ease of creating HDR images. While both Lightroom and Photoshop can merge to HDR, it's easier to do it in Lightroom because you can quickly switch to the Basic panel to tone map the merged result.

Let's cover how to create an HDR image in Lightroom and how to speed up the process when we need to work with more than one set of images. You will be shocked to see how simple it actually is.

Merging to HDR in Lightroom Classic

In this exercise, you'll use Lightroom to merge five exposures of a butte, taken in the morning, into a single image that you'll then tone map.

1   Select the lesson07 - 031 through lesson07 - 035 images by clicking the first image and Shift-clicking the last image.

2   Right-click one of the thumbnails and choose Photo Merge > HDR or press Control+H/Ctrl+H.

As with the panorama, the overall speed with which Lightroom creates an HDR preview of your images is fast. I've merged really large image files to HDR and been amazed at how fast the preview renders.

3 The HDR Merge Preview dialog box gives you a quick series of options to help you along with the process, as follows:

- Auto Align automatically corrects any movement in between the capture of the images—perhaps you moved the tripod slightly as you made the images.

▶ **Tip:** An HDR image can be tone mapped to look realistic or surrealistic. The realistic approach brings out detail but leaves the image looking natural. The surrealistic look emphasizes local contrast and detail and is either very saturated or undersaturated (for a grungy style). There's no right or wrong here; it's purely subjective. If you are interested in exploring how to make realistic and surrealistic HDR images, you can check out my book *The HDR Book*, second edition.

- Auto Settings applies Develop module settings you normally see in the Basic panel, so you get a good result right out of the gate. It's okay to leave it on, since you can always change any settings when the merge is complete.

- Deghosting compensates for anything inside the frame that moved. Imagine there was a strong wind and the trees moved when you made the picture, or people walked through the frame. Deghosting gives you a choice of intensities to remove the movement. Select this setting on a case-by-case basis.

- If you have selected a Deghost Amount, you can select the Show Deghost Overlay option to see where changes will be made.

- Finally, you have the option to create a stack of all of the component images and the resulting HDR. Stacks are outside the realm of this book, so let's leave this unselected.

Once you click Merge, the HDR processing happens in the background—another benefit of doing this in Lightroom. In older versions, merging HDR images in Lightroom meant that you were locked out of doing any work until the HDR image was complete. Now, you can go back into Lightroom and continue to work until the HDR is finished.

One of the other powerful features of HDR in Lightroom is that the resulting HDR file that is created is still a raw file (a DNG, specifically). This means you can change temperature and tint, and perform Develop adjustments with much greater range than if the image were turned into pixel data. Dragging the Exposure slider from one side to the other shows just how much tone you have available to you in the resulting image.

When Lightroom finishes merging your HDR, it will appear next to the images you merged. Click it in the Filmstrip (it has *HDR* in its name), and press D to go to the Develop module, if necessary. Expand the Basic panel so you can see, and make changes to the settings Lightroom applied. I adjusted all of the Basic panel's Tone settings. Finally, let's flag this image with a red color by pressing the number 6.

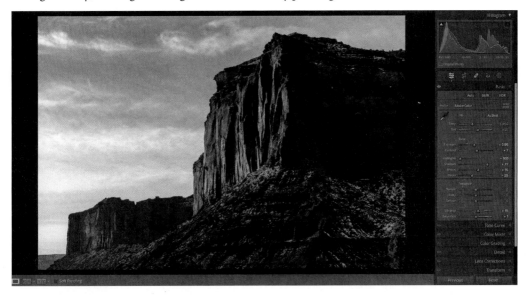

Headless mode for HDR

Another great feature that has been added to HDR in Lightroom is headless mode. There are plenty of times when you do not need to see the HDR Merge Preview dialog box to make any decisions—you just want Lightroom to get to work. Hold down the Shift key when you choose Photo Merge > HDR, and Lightroom bypasses the preview dialog box and starts making your HDR file immediately.

Creating HDR panoramas

For the last few years, Lightroom has been able to create panoramas with a series of HDR images all at once. Previously, you had to merge each bracketed series of exposures into an individual HDR file and then merge those files into a panorama. Lightroom has automated the entire process and still kept the resulting file as a DNG, letting you tone it with great detail.

I took a series of bracketed exposures (five exposures for each photo, ranging from −2 EV to 2 EV) of rock formations in the desert southwest, although we are going to use only three of the images. I wanted to make sure that I captured all of the tonality of the moment, while making an image large enough to feel like you can get lost in it. Let's see how Lightroom handles the process.

1   Select lesson07 - 016 through lesson07 - 030 (without our previous pano) in the Library module by clicking the first image in the series and Shift-clicking the last image and then Command-clicking/Ctrl-clicking the pano to deselect it.

2   Right-click one of the thumbnails and choose Photo Merge > HDR Panorama. With 15 images being merged to HDR and then merged as a panorama, you might expect it to take quite a while, but it's faster than you'd think.

The result of the HDR pano looks like what you'd expect to see from the merged files, with white areas in the corners. The Spherical projection looks like the best of the three here.

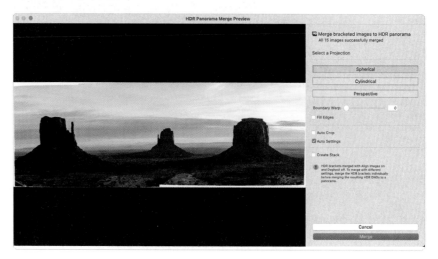

3   The Auto Crop option eliminates too much of the foreground. Boundary Warp or Fill Edges work much better for this image, so deselect Auto Crop and select Fill Edges instead. This corrects the perspective while bringing the edges back.

4   Click Merge, and Lightroom will start merging your HDR pano. The resulting DNG file can be further developed in the Develop module with even more tone.

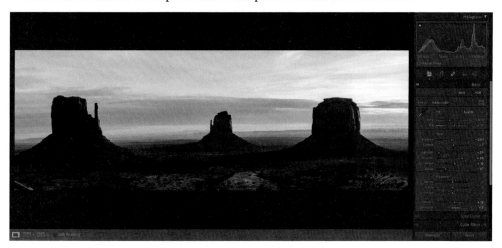

New: View HDR Output in Lightroom

Your camera is capable of capturing an incredible amount of color and tone in your images, known as **dynamic range**. Unfortunately, our computer monitors have been unable to reproduce that information so we can see it on our screens. As technology advances, more and more monitors support high dynamic range, allowing you to see all of this information for editing. For those who own monitors capable of displaying HDR color, Lightroom now has the ability to show you this expanded range of tone, making it easy to edit and share images with a high dynamic range.

In the previous lesson we were able to make an HDR image and an HDR panorama by merging a series of exposures together. While these images do contain this expanded tone, a standard dynamic range monitor is unable to show you just how much you are visually missing in these higher-quality images. We are left to adjust the tonality that is out of range (in the HDR range) and move it back to a range that we can see.

1   Select the lesson07 - 031-HDR image in the HDR and Panorama collection and make sure you are in the Develop module. To the right of the Auto and BW buttons under the Basic panel is a new option. Click the HDR button.

The Histogram panel will split into two sections. On the left, you will see the tonal range that your monitor is capable of seeing, labeled SDR (standard dynamic range). To the right, you'll see a new section of the histogram labeled HDR. This area will show you a histogram of the tone and color that you are not able to see on the monitor.

2   If you have a monitor that supports HDR, go into your display settings and make sure that it is turned on. Here I am using the BenQ SW321C, which adds a toggle switch in the Mac's Displays settings to turn this feature on.

3   When HDR is turned on, the HDR area in the histogram stops being red and shows you the histogram information that resides in the HDR space for the image.

4 If you would like to see exactly where the expanded range is, you can select the Visualize HDR option at the bottom of the Tone area in the Basic panel and an overlay will appear on the image. This allows you to see the areas that

are too bright for an SDR monitor and make any edits to the image quickly.

5 If you would like to simulate what your image will look like on a standard display, select the Preview For SDR Display option in the SDR Rendition Settings area of the panel. You can make adjustments to the image while the tonal range is to SDR.

6 Once you have made all of the changes to your image, you can export the HDR version of the file by selecting the HDR Output option under File Settings in the Export window. Lightroom has added JPEGXL and AVIF—two additional image formats that support HDR output—to the Image Format menu.

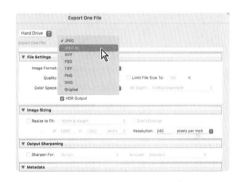

I'm really excited about being able to see everything in HDR, but it will take a little time for a large number of users to reap the benefits of using HDR-capable displays. That said, for those who are already using them, the difference is pretty substantial.

Hardware suggestion: BenQ Photographer Monitors

We spend a ton of time, energy, and money on getting better at photography. We put all of this effort into making the best image we can make, only to have it gone in the swipe of a mobile phone finger. However, if you think about it, your computer monitor is the place where you experience your photography at its fullest potential. I'll shoot a ton, share a few, and print even less than that, but all of them get seen on a monitor.

While many consumer monitors are great for browsing and email, you'll see a drastic change in colors between what you see on a computer monitor, a mobile device, and a print. That consistency across devices is important to me as a creative. Because of that, I have switched to BenQ monitors and have been very happy with their performance.

Now that Lightroom supports the viewing of HDR, BenQ's photographer monitors, such as the SW272U and SW321C, can be used to their fullest potential. Simply switch on the HDR feature in the display settings to take advantage of all of the tones and color that were not available to you previously.

However, the tech was only part of the reason I started a relationship with BenQ. In meeting with their teams, they've often expressed a passion for supporting photographers on their journey. To that end, they have been creating free webinars and how-to content tailored to Adobe applications to get people excited about making things. So I decided to jump in and help them make even more content in the Adobe and Lightroom space as a BenQ Ambassador.

If you want to check out some of the webinars that I am doing or want me to make a specific tutorial that would help you, please feel free to visit *rcweb.co/benqrc* or scan the QR code here. If I can make a tutorial that will help, I'll be happy to do so.

Saving time in Lightroom

One thing I really like about Lightroom is how easy working with images is for the most part. The goal of all this technology is to make it easier for you to realize your vision and get back to making more images. All the skills you've learned help in the process of realizing your vision, but how do we make it go faster? Synchronizing your changes across images is a great start.

Applying previous corrections

Let's correct the series of images in the Timesavers collection a little more intelligently by selecting one of the images and making sure those changes are applied to the rest of the similar images.

1 In the Library module, switch to the Timesavers collection, make sure your Sort is set to File Name, and then select the lesson07 - 002 image.

2 Go to the Develop module, and then type in **5150** for Temp and +**19** for Tint. Let's add a Contrast of +10, Highlights of −67, and a Texture of 40.

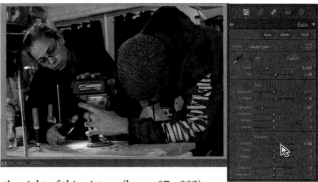

3 In the Filmstrip, select the picture to the right of this picture (lesson07 - 003). Now click the Previous button below the right-side panels. Lightroom copies all the settings you added to the first image and applies them to the second one.

Tip: For you to
correctly use the
Previous feature, you
must immediately
select the next image
that you want to apply
the effect to. If you
select one image and
move to another image,
the Previous button
will not bring over
the effects. It requires
you to be very specific
about the next image
you choose in order for
it to work.

What's even more amazing here is that Lightroom reapplies any AI masking to the
new image for the adjustment. For images that are similar to one another, this will
take a little editing and make it incredibly easy. For images that are different in
composition and tone, it will give you a solid head start.

4   Select the lesson06 - 017 photo
    in the Select People collection
    inside the Lesson 06 Practice
    collection set. In the Develop
    module, decrease the Exposure
    to −0.05.

Remember that we made a series
of masks for this image to change
the contrast in some of their cloth-
ing and the brightness of their faces to make them pop out.

5   Select the first picture that is
    similar to this one in the series.
    In this collection it is the
    second one, lesson06 - 011.
    Clicking the Previous button
    on the right side, Lightroom
    will apply the AI masks to the
    image. The good part? Because
    the masks are AI-based and not
    raster (painted on), it will adjust for the people in the frame and still apply the
    adjustments that you need. That is an incredible time saver!

Synchronizing corrections

Clicking the Previous button to apply corrections to another picture is a great way
to make it easier if you have one or two pictures, but what if you have 50 of them?
For that, you'll want to use the Synchronize command.

1   Click the lesson06 - 011 photo in the Filmstrip.

2   Hold down the Shift key and click the lesson06 - 016 image. The first image that
    was selected will be the source image from which your corrections will
    synchronize, while the other images will receive the adjustments.

3   Click the Sync button below the right-side panels.

4   In the Synchronize Settings dialog box, either click the Check None button in the lower left and select the settings that we changed in the first image or click Check All to be sure all changes made are selected. Once you've selected all of the options to synchronize, click the Synchronize button.

All of the changes that were done in the original image, including AI masks, are now added to the other images, making it so much faster to do general processing of images. If the images were not exposed in a similar manner, you will see some variation. That said, a single change of one slider is much better than having to perform the entire edit. This frees you up to do more creative editing on images to really bring out all of the detail in them as needed.

Creating a Develop preset

Another great way to develop images quickly is by using a preset.

1   Go to the Selective Tools collection and select the lesson07 - 002 image. Apply the Modern 08 Profile from the Profile Browser and set the Temperature to 4293,

Tint to +19, Exposure to –0.35, Contrast to +42, Highlights to –67, Shadows to +36, Whites to +17, and Texture to +40.

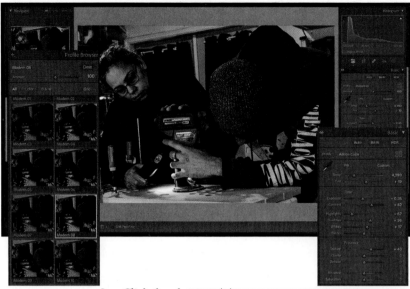

2 Click the plu[...] the right side of the Preset panel's header and choose Create Preset to bring up a dialog box that allows you to save specific settings for the toning of your images. Type **Arcade Weekend** as your preset name, click Check All, and then click Create.

3 Once the preset is saved, you can access it under User Presets in the Presets panel. You can even choose the amount of the individual preset you want applied to the image by adjusting the Amount slider.

4 Navigate to the next image in the Filmstrip and hover your pointer over the Arcade Weekend preset from the Presets panel.

5 As you hover over the individual effects, you will see a preview of what they will look like on the image. Click the preset to apply it.

6 Press the letter G to return to the Grid view in the Library module. Click the Saved Presets menu in the Quick Develop panel, and you'll see that the Arcade Weekend preset appears in the menu, making editing and toning even easier.

Review questions

1 What are the differences between Select Subject, Select Sky, and the Brush when using the Masking tool?

2 How do you reset all of the sliders in the Masking tool's local adjustment tools' options panels?

3 How does the Targeted Adjustment tool work in the HSL, Color, B&W, and Tone Curve panels?

4 What is the difference between the Boundary Warp, Auto Crop, and Fill Edges options in the Merge to HDR and Merge to Panorama dialog boxes?

5 What does the HDR button at the top of the Basic panel do?

6 How do you synchronize changes to one photo with multiple similar photos?

Review answers

1 Select Subject and Select Sky are pixel-based masks that use AI to develop their selections. The Brush tool uses vector-based masks to save space.

2 When using one of the Masking tool's local adjustment tools (the Linear Gradient, the Radial Gradient, or the Brush tool), you can reset all of the sliders in the options panel by double-clicking the Preset label.

3 The Targeted Adjustment tool allows you to drag on specific areas of an image to adjust the colors or tones without knowing exactly which colors or tones will be affected.

4 The Boundary Warp slider attempts to warp the edges of the image to fill in any edge gaps left by the merge. Auto Crop simply crops off any gaps at the edges of the image. Fill Edges uses Content-Aware Fill to fill in the white spaces left at the edges of the merged image.

5 The HDR button allows you to see the full high dynamic range of your image if your monitor supports HDR. You can then adjust the image based on the full dynamic range or preview what it will look like on a standard dynamic range monitor.

6 If you have multiple photos taken in the same lighting, you can make your tonal adjustments to one photo, select all the photos, and then click the Sync button at the bottom of the right panel group. In the Synchronize Settings dialog box, select all the settings you changed in the first image, and click Synchronize.

PHOTOGRAPHY SHOWCASE
FELIX HERNANDEZ

"The most important photo is the one I'm working on, and my best photo is the one I'm going to create tomorrow."

I'm a 47-year-old graphic designer, photographer, digital artist, miniature artist, husband, and father of two, living in Cancun, Mexico.

I manage my photography studio, where I create high-impact images for the advertising industry, branded content for digital media, and personal projects. My specialty is "creative photography"—normally working indoors, shooting scale models and dioramas, doing practical effects as well as digital art. By mixing all these disciplines, I have developed a personal "visual language" that defines my style, which I call "dreamphography." For me, photography is the means by which I can portray not the reality, but all the ideas that arise from my mind.

I'm never in my comfort zone. The kind of photography I do demands that I try, test, experiment, and repeat!

I'm a dreamer, not because I'm seeking to fly high, but because I literally use my dreams as my main source of inspiration for creating. So I don't "dream big"; I dream small and just do.

I have just one ambition on which I'm totally focused: to create. The more I create, the better and happier I feel. Growth, money, fame, and recognition come along if you do what you love for a long enough period of time.

hernandezdreamphography.com
instagram.com/hernandez_dreamphography/

8 CREATING A PHOTO BOOK

Lesson overview

Whether it's produced for a client or as a professional portfolio or designed as a gift or as a way to preserve precious memories, a photo book makes a stylish way to share and showcase your images. The Book module makes it easy to design beautiful, sophisticated book layouts and then publish them without leaving Lightroom. This lesson will give you the skills to create your own professional-looking photo book. In this lesson, you'll learn how to:

- Work with text and photo cells to modify page layout templates.

- Set a page background.

- Place and arrange images in a layout.

- Add text to a book design.

- Use the Text Adjustment tool.

- Save your photo book and custom page and book layouts.

- Export your creation.

 This lesson will take about 90 minutes to complete. To get the lesson files used in this chapter, download them from the web page for this book at *peachpit.com/LightroomCIB2024*. For more information, see "Accessing the lesson files and Web Edition" in the "Getting Started" section at the beginning of this book.

The Book module delivers everything you need to create polished book designs that can be uploaded directly from Lightroom Classic for printing through the on-demand book vendor Blurb, or exported to PDF and output on your own printer. Template-based page layout, an intuitive editing environment, and state-of-the-art text tools make it easy to present your photographs in their best light.

Getting started

Note: This lesson assumes that you already have a basic working familiarity with the Lightroom Classic workspace. If you need more background information, refer to Lightroom Classic Help, or review the previous lessons.

Before you begin, make sure you've set up the LRC2024CIB folder for your lesson files and created the LRC2024CIB Catalog file to manage them, as described in "Accessing the lesson files and Web Edition" and "Creating a catalog file for working with this book" in the "Getting Started" section at the start of this book.

If you haven't already done so, download the lesson08 folder from your Account page at *peachpit.com* to the LRC2024CIB\Lessons folder, as detailed in "Accessing the lesson files and Web Edition" in the "Getting Started" section.

1   Start Lightroom Classic.

2   In the Select Catalog dialog box, make sure the file LRC2024CIB Catalog.lrcat is selected under Select A Recent Catalog To Open, and then click Open.

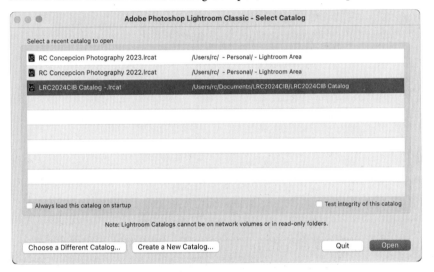

Note: If you can't see the Module Picker, choose Window > Panels > Show Module Picker, or press the F5 key. If you're working on macOS, you may need to press the fn key together with the F5 key, or change the function key behavior in the system preferences.

3   Lightroom Classic will open in the screen mode and workspace module that were active when you last quit. If necessary, switch to the Library module by clicking Library in the Module Picker at the top of the workspace.

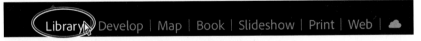

Importing images into the library

The first step is to import the images for this lesson into the Lightroom library.

1   In the Library module, click the Import button below the left panel group.

2 If the Import dialog box appears in compact mode, click the Show More Options button at the lower left of the dialog box to see all of the options in the expanded Import dialog box.

3 Under Source at the left of the expanded Import dialog box, locate and select your LRC2024CIB\Lessons\lesson08 folder. Ensure that all 23 images in the lesson08 folder are selected (checked) for import.

4 In the import options above the thumbnail previews, select Add so that the imported photos will be added to your catalog without being moved or copied. Under File Handling at the right of the expanded Import dialog box, choose Embedded & Sidecar from the Build Previews menu and leave the Don't Import Suspected Duplicates option selected. Under Apply During Import, choose None from both the Develop Settings menu and the Metadata menu and type **Lesson 08, Portfolio** in the Keywords text box. Make sure that your import is set up as shown here, and then click Import.

The 23 images are imported and now appear in both the Library module's Grid view and the Filmstrip across the bottom of the Lightroom workspace.

Assembling photos for a book

► **Tip:** The first time you enter any of the Lightroom Classic modules, you'll see tips that will help you get started by identifying the components of the workspace and stepping you through the workflow. Dismiss the tips by clicking the Close button. To reactivate the tips for any module, choose [*Module name*] Tips from the Help menu.

The first step in creating a book is to gather the photos you wish to include. Since we just imported them, the images for this lesson are already isolated from the rest of your catalog in the Previous Import folder, which is selected as the image source.

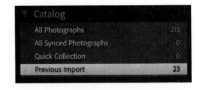

The Previous Import folder is merely a temporary grouping, and you can't rearrange the images inside it or exclude a photo from your project without removing it from your catalog entirely. Instead, use either a collection or a single folder without subfolders as the source for the images in your book; both will let you reorder photos in the Grid view or the Filmstrip. For this exercise, you'll create a collection—you can delete an image from a collection without deleting it from your catalog.

1 Make sure that either the Previous Import folder in the Catalog panel or the lesson08 folder in the Folders panel is selected as the image source; then press Command+A/Ctrl+A or choose Edit > Select All.

2 Click the plus sign (+) button in the Collections panel's header and choose Create Collection. In the Create Collection dialog box, type **Book Portfolio** as the collection's name. Make sure that the Include Selected Photos option is selected and all of the other options are disabled, and then click Create. Your new collection appears in the Collections panel, where it is automatically selected.

3 Choose Edit > Select None. In the Toolbar, set the Sort order to Capture Time, and then click Book in the Module Picker at the top of the workspace.

Working in the Book module

● **Note:** The pictures that are provided here are to be used for mocking up a book in this lesson only. They should not be sent for printing.

Whether you want to commemorate a family moment, save memories from a special trip, or create a vehicle to show your work, a photo book is an attractive and sophisticated way to showcase your photography. The Book module delivers everything you need to create stylish books that can be uploaded directly from Lightroom for printing through the on-demand book vendor Blurb or exported to PDF and printed on your own printer. We'll use some sample pictures of mine to practice here.

Setting up a photo book

In the work area, you may or may not see photos already placed in page layouts, depending on whether you've already experimented with the Book module's tools and controls. You can start this project by clearing the layout and setting up the workspace so that we're all on the same page.

1   Click the Clear Book button in the header bar across the top of the work area. If you don't see the header bar, choose View > Show Header Bar.

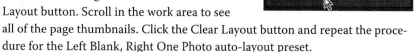

2   In the Book Settings panel at the top of the right panel group, select Blurb Photo Book from the Book menu, and then make sure that the Size, Cover, Paper Type, and Logo Page are set to Standard Landscape, Hardcover Image Wrap, Standard, and On, respectively. The estimated price of printing the book at the current settings is displayed at the bottom of the panel.

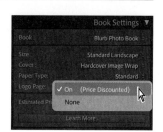

3   If it's not already selected, click the Multi-Page View button at the far left of the Toolbar at the bottom of the work area. In the View menu, disable Show Info Overlay.

4   Choose Book > Book Preferences and examine the options. You can choose whether photos are zoomed to fit their image cells or cropped to fill them, toggle the Autofill feature for new books, and set your preferences for text behaviors. Leave the settings at the defaults and close the Book Preferences dialog box.

The Autofill feature is activated by default; if you just entered the Book module for the first time, you would have seen the images from the collection already placed in the default book layout. An automatically generated layout can be a great starting point for a new book design, especially if you're beginning without a clear idea of exactly what you want.

Note: If you're publishing to Blurb.com, auto-layout is limited to books of 240 pages. There is no auto-layout page limit for books published to PDF.

5   Expand the Auto Layout panel, if necessary. From the Auto Layout Preset menu, choose One Photo Per Page, and then click the Auto Layout button. Scroll in the work area to see all of the page thumbnails. Click the Clear Layout button and repeat the procedure for the Left Blank, Right One Photo auto-layout preset.

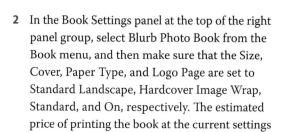

6 Take a look at the book results in the work area; scroll, if necessary, to see all of the page thumbnails arranged on the two-page spreads in the Multi-Page view. If you need more viewing space, hide the left panel group by pressing F7 or by clicking the triangle at the left edge of the workspace. Drag the Thumbnails slider in the Toolbar to reduce or enlarge the thumbnails.

Tip: Blurb offers a discounted price for photo books that incorporate the Blurb logo on the last page.

Lightroom generates a book with a cover, separate pages for each of the images in the collection—placed in the order in which they appear in the Filmstrip—and a last page reserved for the Blurb logo. You can't place a photo on the Blurb logo page, but you can disable it in the Book Settings panel, if you prefer.

Tip: If you want to rearrange the order of images in the Filmstrip before you click Auto Layout, you'll first need to save your book.

The first image in the Filmstrip is placed on the front cover; the last photo in the series becomes the back cover image. The number above each photo in the Filmstrip indicates how many times it has been used in the book; the first and last images have each been used twice—on the cover and also on pages 1 and 45.

Changing page layouts

Using an auto-layout preset can help you get started on your book. Then you can focus on individual spreads and pages to introduce subtlety and variety to the design. For this project, however, you'll build your book layout from scratch.

1 In the Auto Layout panel, click the Clear Layout button.

2 Right-click the Page panel header and choose Solo Mode from the menu.

3 In the Multi-Page view, double-click the front cover (the right side of the spread).

Note: Double-clicking the front cover's thumbnail takes you to Single Page view but shows both front and back covers, with the front cover's photo cell selected, as indicated by the yellow square in the center. The Page panel shows a diagrammatic preview of the default cover template: two image cells (identifiable by central crosshairs) and a narrow text cell positioned along the book's spine.

4   Click the Change Page Layout button (it's black with a gray triangle) to the right of the layout preview thumbnail in the Page panel, or in the lower-right corner of the cover spread displayed in the work area.

5   Scroll down in the page template picker to see all of the available cover layout templates. Gray areas with central crosshairs indicate image cells; rectangles filled with horizontal lines represent text cells. Click to select the third template in the menu. The single crosshairs at the center of the spread shows that this template has a single image cell that extends across both covers, and three text cells: one on the back cover, one on the spine, and one on the front cover.

6   Expand the Guides panel. Make sure that the Show Guides option is selected, then watch the layout in the work area as you toggle each of the guides in turn. Move the pointer over the back cover to see the borders of the text cells.

The Page Bleed guide's wide gray border shows the area to be cut off after printing. A thin gray line borders the Text Safe Area, where your text will be well clear of accidental trimming. The Filler Text guide shows filler text (here, the word *Title*) to mark the position of text cells. Filler text disappears when you click a text cell.

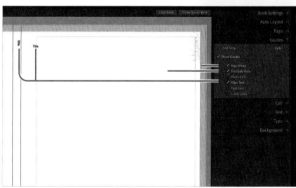

7   Deselect Photo Cells and leave only the three options here selected; then click the Multi-Page View button in the Toolbar.

The first page in a photo book is always on the right side of the first spread; the grayed-out left side represents the inside of the front cover, which is not printed on. Likewise, the last page in a photo book to be published to Blurb must always occupy the left side of the final spread. At this stage, your book consists of a cover and a single double-sided page, the back of which is the Blurb logo page.

8 Right-click page 1 and choose Add Page from the menu. A second spread appears in the Multi-Page view. Right-click page 2 and choose Add Page to copy the same page layout to page 3.

9 Click to select page 2; then click the Change Page Layout button below the lower-right corner of the page. For inside pages, unlike the cover, the page template picker groups layout templates in categories according to style, project type, or the number of photos per page.

Tip: To add a page layout to the Favorites category in the template picker, click the circle that appears in the upper-right corner of the template's thumbnail when you move the pointer over it (seen at right).

10 Click 2 Photos to see the templates with two image cells. Select the fourth template: a layout without text cells that fills the page with two portrait-format images, side by side. In the Guides panel, briefly turn Photo Cells on so that you can see the changes.

Adding page numbers to a photo book

Note: The context menu of a page number cell also lists commands that enable you to hide the page number on a selected page or set the page numbering to start from a page other than page 1.

1 Double-click page 1 to shift to Single Page view, and then select Page Numbers at the top of the Page panel. From the Location menu, choose Bottom Corner, and choose Left and Right from the Display menu. Right-click page 1 and make sure that the Apply Page Number Style Globally option is activated in the menu.

2 Click the new page number cell in the page preview, then expand the Type panel and inspect the default font, style, size, and opacity settings. With Apply Page Number Style Globally activated, any change to these type style settings is made throughout the book; for now, leave them unchanged.

Placing photos in a book layout

Note: When you drag an image onto a page, wait until you see a green + (plus sign) before releasing your mouse button.

You can add photos to a page layout in any of the three views.

1 Click the Multi-Page view button at the left of the Toolbar; then go back to the Library module and set the Sort Order to File Name. Return to the Book module and drag lesson08 - 0019.jpg over the center of the cover spread. Drop it there, and it zooms to fill both covers.

2   Drag the lesson08 - 0007 image from the Filmstrip to page 1 in the Multi-Page view. Place the lesson08 - 0010 and lesson08 - 0011 photos in the left and right image cells on page 2, respectively, and the lesson08 - 0013 image on page 3.

Tip: If you see an exclamation mark badge in the upper-right corner of an image cell, this indicates that the image may not be a high enough resolution to print well at the current size. You can reduce the size of the image in your layout or ignore the alert if you are prepared to accept a lower print resolution.

Changing the images in a photo book

You can remove a photo from a page layout by right-clicking the image in the layout and choosing Remove Photo from the menu. If you simply want to replace a photo, you don't need to remove it first.

Tip: You can easily rearrange the order of the pages in your photo book—or even shuffle entire spreads—in the same way; simply drag them to new positions in the Multi-Page view.

1   Drag the lesson08 - 0015 photo onto page 1, which replaces lesson08 - 0007.

2   In the Multi-Page view, drag the image on page 1 (lesson08 - 0015) onto the photo on page 3 (lesson08 - 0013). The photos on pages 1 and 3 swap places.

You should see the image thumbnail move as you drag, not the page itself. If you move the page instead, drag it back into place and try again, making sure to drag from well inside the photo cell.

Working with photo cells

The photo cells in a page layout template are fixed in place; you can't delete them, resize them, or move them on the page. Instead, you can use the *cell padding*—the adjustable space around a photo within its cell—to position the images in your page layout exactly as you want them.

1 Double-click page 3. The Book Editor switches from Multi-Page view to Single Page view.

2 Click the photo to select it, and then experiment with the Zoom slider. When you enlarge the image too much, an exclamation-point badge appears in the upper-right corner to alert you that the photo may not print well. Right-click the photo and choose Zoom Photo To Fill Cell; the image is scaled so that its shortest edge fills the cell (at a zoom value of 18% for this photo). Drag the photo to position it horizontally within the cell. Drag the Zoom slider all of the way to the left; the minimum setting reduces the image so that its longest edge fits within the image cell. Click well within the borders of the photo and drag it to the top of the cell.

Note: If you don't see the Amount slider, click the triangle above the padding values.

3 Set the photo at the 0% zoom setting. Expand the Cell panel and increase the padding by dragging the Padding Amount slider or typing a new value of 75 pt.

4 Click the white triangle above the Padding value to expand the padding controls. By default, the four controls are linked, so the adjustment you made in the previous step changed all four values. Deselect the Link All option (the checkbox darkens), and set the Bottom padding value to 162 pt.

By starting with the right template and then setting the photo cell padding, you can position an image anywhere on the page, cropped however you wish.

5 In the Cell panel, select Link All, and then drag any of the sliders to set all of the padding settings to zero. Right-click the photo in the Single Image view and choose Zoom Photo To Fill Cell. Drag the image horizontally inside its cell to find a pleasing crop.

6 Click the Spread View button in the Toolbar to see pages 2 and 3 as a spread.

7 Select the image on the left of page 2. Set the linked padding controls to 50 pt, and then unlink them and reduce the Right padding to 15 pt. Repeat the process for the photo on the right of page 2, but this time, reduce the Left padding to 15 pt.

8 Double-click the yellow frame below page 2 to see it enlarged in the Single Image view. In the illustration at right, the left and right photos are zoomed to about 4%. Drag each image inside its cell padding to position it as shown. For a clearer view and to remove the yellow highlight, click the space outside the page to deselect it.

9 In the Toolbar below the Single Image view, click the left navigation arrow to jump to page 1. Then, move the image to the left to center the tool in the center of the picture.

10 Click away from the page to deselect it, and then click the Multi-Page View button in the Toolbar for an overview of the changes you've made.

Setting a page background

By default, all of the pages in a new book share a plain white background. You can change the background color, set up a partially transparent backdrop image, or choose from a library of graphics, and then apply this design to the entire book or just one of the pages.

You can start by adding two more spreads to your book layout.

1 Right-click page 4 and choose Add Page from the menu. To apply the default layout to page 5, right-click page 5 and choose Add Page. Right-click page 6 and choose Add Blank Page.

2 Click to select page 6 in the Multi-Page view, and then click the Spread View button in the Toolbar.

3 Expand the Background panel. Deselect the Apply Background Globally option, and then drag lesson08 - 0012 to the preview pane in the Background panel. Drag the slider to set the opacity of the image to 43%.

4 Select the Background Color option, and then click the adjacent color swatch to open the color picker. Drag the saturation slider at the right of the color picker about two-thirds of the way up its range, and then drag the eye-dropper cursor in the picker to find a muted tone; I chose a color with R, G, and B values of 37, 16, and 16, respectively. Press Return/Enter to close the picker.

5 In the Background panel, activate the Apply Background Globally option, and then click the Multi-Page View button in the Toolbar.

Your background is applied to every page (except the Blurb logo page, where only the color is applied); it can be seen on pages 4, 5, 6, and 7 and behind the images on page 2. On other pages, the background design is hidden behind photo cells.

6 Deselect the Background Color option; then right-click the image in the background preview pane and choose Remove Photo. Deselect Apply Background Globally.

7 Select page 2 in the Multi-Page view, and then reactivate the Background Color option. Click the color swatch to open the color picker, and then click the black swatch at the top of the picker. Press Return/Enter to close the color picker.

Adding text to a photo book

There are several ways to add text to your pages in the Book module, each useful in different situations:

- Text cells that are built into page layout templates are fixed in position; they can't be deleted, moved, or resized, but you can use the adjustable cell padding to position text anywhere on a page.

- A photo caption is a text cell that is linked to a single image in the layout. It can be positioned above or below an image or overlaid on the photo and can be moved higher or lower on the page.

- A page caption is a text cell that is linked to the page as a whole, rather than to any particular image. Page captions span the full width of the page; you can move them vertically and then adjust the cell padding to position the text horizontally, enabling you to place custom text anywhere in your layout.

On a single page, you can add a page caption and a separate photo caption for each image—even if the page is based on a layout template that has no fixed text cells. Fixed text cells and photo captions can be configured for custom text or set to display captions or titles extracted automatically from your photos' metadata.

The Book module incorporates state-of-the-art text tools that give you total control over every aspect of the text styling. Type attributes can be adjusted using sliders or numerical input or tweaked visually with the Text Adjustment tool.

Working with text cells

As mentioned earlier, text cells incorporated in a page layout template are fixed in place. Instead, you can use the adjustable cell padding—the space surrounding the text within its cell—to position text in your page layout exactly as you want it.

1 Click the Multi-Page View button to see your entire book layout; then double-click just below the cover spread to zoom in on the layout. Click in the center of the front cover to select the fixed text cell.

2 Expand the Type panel. Make sure that the Text Style Preset is set to Custom to accommodate manually entered text, rather than metadata from the image.

3 Choose a font and type style from the menus below the preset setting. I chose American Typewriter, Bold. Click the Character color swatch to open the color picker, click the black swatch at the top of the picker, and then press Return/Enter to close the picker.

▶ **Tip:** To select a page or a spread, rather than the text and image cells in the layout, click near the edge of the thumbnail or just below it.

Set the type size to 47 pt, and leave the opacity set to 100%. Click the Align Center button at the lower left of the Type panel.

4 Type the words **Jason's First**; then press Return/Enter and type **Arcade**. Double-click the word *Arcade* to select it, and then type **90** pt in the Size text box to increase the size of the selected text.

5 Keeping the text selected, click the white triangle at the right of the Character color swatch to see the type attribute controls. Set the Character swatch to white. Reduce the Leading—the spacing between the selected text and the line above it—to 73.8 pt. To make the text stand out better, select both lines of text, switch both to white, and then click the Align Right button at the bottom of the panel.

▶ **Tip:** Once you've changed the Leading value, the Auto Leading button becomes available below the text adjustment controls, making it easy for you to quickly reinstate the default setting. The Auto Kerning button works the same way.

6 Click inside the text cell, but away from the text, to keep the cell selected while deselecting the text, and then expand the Cell panel. Deselect the Link All option, and then increase the Top padding to 60 pt.

Fine-tuning type

In the Type panel, Lightroom incorporates a suite of sophisticated, yet easy-to-use, type tools that allow you detailed control over the text styling. You can use the adjustment sliders and numerical input to set type attributes in the Type panel or tweak your text visually in any view using the intuitive Text Adjustment tool.

1 Expand the Type panel and examine the four controls below the Size and Opacity sliders. Be sure to undo any changes you make at this stage.

- **Tracking** adjusts the letter spacing throughout a text selection. You can use tracking to change the overall appearance and readability of your text, making it look either more open or more dense.

- **Baseline** adjusts the vertical position of selected text relative to the baseline—the imaginary line on which the text sits.

- **Leading** adjusts the space between selected text and the line above it.

- **Kerning** adjusts the letter spacing between specific pairs of letters. Some pairings produce optical effects that cause letter spacing to appear uneven; place the text insertion cursor between two letters to adjust the kerning.

2 Select all of the text in the front cover text cell, and then click to activate the Text Adjustment tool to the left of the Character color setting in the Type panel.

3 Drag horizontally across the selection to adjust the text size. The adjustment is applied relatively; the different sizes of text are changed by relative amounts. Choose Edit > Undo or press Command+Z/Ctrl+Z to undo the change.

4 Drag vertically over the selection to adjust the leading, and then choose Edit > Undo or press Command+Z/Ctrl+Z to undo.

5 Hold down the Option/Alt key—to temporarily disable the Text Adjustment tool—and select the words *Jason's First*, leaving the word *Arcade* unselected. Release the Option/Alt key and the mouse button, and hold down Command/Ctrl as you drag horizontally over the selected text to decrease the tracking slightly. Watch the Tracking control in the Type panel as you drag to set a value of −21 em.

6 Release the mouse button. Hold down the Command/Ctrl key and drag vertically over the selected text to shift it in relation to its baseline. Drag it to 6 pt and click away from the text to deselect it.

7 If necessary, press F7, or choose Window > Panels > Show Left Module Panels, to see your front cover text larger. Make sure that the Text Adjustment tool is still

active, and then use your arrow keys to move your cursor between the *d* and *e* in Arcade. Drag to the right over the insertion point. Watch the Type panel as you drag to set a Kerning value of 50 em.

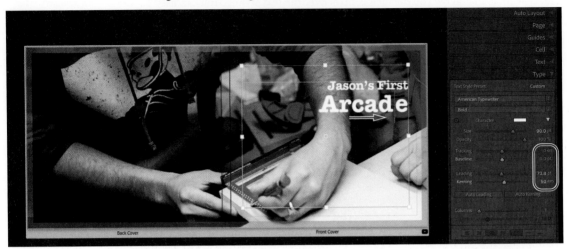

8 Reset your leading for the type by selecting all of the text and dragging the Leading slider until it looks good. Click the Text Adjustment tool in the Type panel to disable it, and then click the Multi-Page View button in the Toolbar to see your entire book layout. Double-click page 1 to zoom to the Single Page view.

Working with captions

Unlike the fixed text cells built into layout templates, page and photo caption cells can be moved vertically; horizontal placement of captions is achieved by adjusting padding. Each page can include one page caption text cell and one photo caption cell for each photo on the page, even if the page template has no built-in text cells.

1 Right-click the header of the Type panel and disable Solo Mode; then, leaving the Type panel open, expand the Text panel.

> **Tip:** If you prefer, you can add a photo or page text caption by selecting the respective option in the Text panel, rather than using the floating buttons.

2 Move the pointer over page 1. The template for this page has no fixed text cell; hence, nothing is highlighted. Click the photo; then click the Add Photo Text button. In the Text panel, the Photo Text controls become active. Press Command+Z/Ctrl+Z to undo the photo caption. Now, click the yellow footer below the photo to switch the Add Photo Text button to the Add Page Text button. Click the Add Page Text button, and the Page Text controls are activated in the Text panel.

> **Tip:** Unlike photo captions, page captions can't be set to display information drawn from a photo's metadata; they can only be used for custom text.

3 To anchor the page caption to the top of the page, click the Top button in the Page Text controls, and then drag the Offset slider to 96 pt.

4 With the page caption active, set up the Type panel as you did for steps 2 and 3 of the "Working with text cells" exercise earlier in this lesson, but use Regular instead of Bold, set the Size to 30 pt, set the Tracking to 3 em, click the Auto

Leading button if it's active, set the color to white, and click the Align Left button. Then type whatever you like in the page caption, using the Return/Enter key to break the lines so that the text is shaped to fit the image, as shown here.

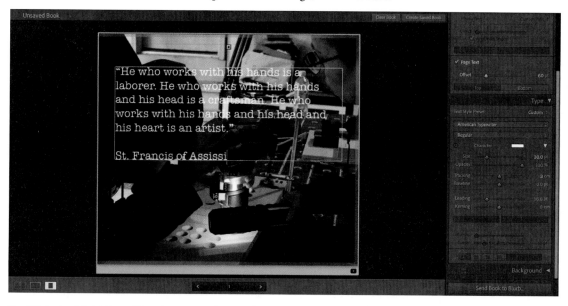

5 Click the Multi-Page View button in the Toolbar.

Creating a custom text preset

You can save your text settings as a custom text preset, so you can apply the same style elsewhere in your book or reuse it in a different project, by choosing Save Current Settings As New Preset from the Text Style Preset menu in the Type panel.

Saving and reusing custom book page layouts

Once you've used cell padding and caption text to modify a page layout, you can save your design as a custom template that will be listed in the Page Layout menus.

1 Expand the Page panel; then watch the layout thumbnail as you right-click the page 1 preview in the Multi-Page view and choose Save As Custom Page.

   The original single-photo layout is now overlaid by a text cell with the proportions and position of the page caption we just created.

2 Click the Change Page Layout button below the lower-right corner of the Multi-Page view's page preview or to the right of the Page panel's layout thumbnail. The saved layout is listed in the Custom Pages category.

Another way to reuse the work you've put into a layout is to copy and paste it directly onto another page in your book, where you can use it as is or make further modifications to the design. You'll find the Copy Layout and Paste Layout commands in the context menu you used in step 1 when you right-clicked the page.

Creating a saved book

Since you entered the Book module, you've been working with an unsaved book, as is indicated in the bar across the top of the work area.

Until you save your book layout, the Book module works like a scratch pad: You can move to another module, or even close Lightroom, and find your settings unchanged when you return. However, if you need to clear the layout to begin another project, all of your work will be lost.

Converting your project to a saved book not only preserves your work but also links your book layout to the particular set of images for which it was designed.

Your photo book is saved as a special kind of collection—an output collection—with its own listing in the Collections panel. Clicking this listing will instantly retrieve the images you were working with and reinstate all of your settings, no matter how many times the book layout scratch pad has been cleared.

1 Click the Create Saved Book button in the bar at the top of the work area, or click the New Collection button in the header of the Collections panel and choose Create Book.

> **Tip:** Adding more images to your saved photo book is easy: simply drag photos onto the book's collection in the Collections panel. To jump directly from the Library to your layout in the Book module, move the pointer over your saved book in the Collections panel and click the white arrow that appears to the right.

2 In the Create Book dialog box, type **Jason's Arcade** as the name for your saved layout. In the Location options, make sure the Inside option is selected with the Book Portfolio collection chosen from the menu, and then click Create.

Your saved book appears in the Collections panel, marked with a Saved Book icon and nested inside the source collection. The image count shows that the output collection includes only five of the photos in the source collection. The bar above the work area shows the name of the book.

Depending on the way you like to work, you can save your book layout at any point in the process—you could create a saved book as soon as you enter the Book module with a selection of images or wait until your design is finalized.

Once you've saved your book project, any further changes you make to the design are auto-saved as you work.

Copying a saved book

Your saved photo book design represents a lot of effort. If you want to try something different without losing what you already have, or add pages and photos without a clear idea of what you'd like to achieve, you can duplicate your saved book and make changes to it without the risk of losing your work thus far.

1 Right-click your saved book in the Collections panel and choose Duplicate Book from the menu.

  If you're happy with your extended design, you can delete the original saved book and then rename the duplicate.

2 Right-click the original saved book in the Collections panel and choose Delete; then confirm the deletion.

3 Right-click the duplicated book in the Collections panel and choose Rename. In the Rename Book dialog box, delete the word *Copy* from the end of the book's name, and then click Rename.

Exporting a photo book

You can upload your book to Blurb.com or export it to a PDF and print it at home.

1 To publish your photo book to Blurb.com, click the Send Book To Blurb button below the right panel group.

2 In the Purchase Book dialog box, either sign in to Blurb.com with your email address and password or click "Not A Member?" in the lower-left corner and register to get started.

3 Enter a book title, subtitle, and author name. You'll see an alert at this stage warning that your book must contain at least 20 pages; the Upload Book button is disabled. Click Cancel, or sign out of Blurb.com first and then cancel.

  Books published to Blurb must have between 20 and 240 pages, not including the front and back covers. Blurb.com prints at 300 dpi; if a photo's resolution is less than 300 dpi, an exclamation point badge (!) appears in the upper-right corner of the image cell in the work area. Click the exclamation point to find out what print resolution can be achieved for that photo. Blurb.com recommends a minimum of 200 dpi for optimum quality.

  For help with printing, pricing, ordering, and other Blurb.com issues, visit the Blurb.com Customer Support page.

4 To export your photo book as a PDF file, first choose PDF from the Book menu at the top of the Book Settings panel. Examine the controls that appear in the lower half of the Book Settings panel. You can leave the JPEG Quality, Color Profile, File Resolution, Sharpening, and Media Type settings at their defaults for now (these will change based on the printer and paper you're using). Click the Export Book To PDF button below the right panel group.

5 In the Save dialog box, type **Jason's Arcade** as the name for the exported book. Navigate to your LRC2024CIB\Lessons\lesson08 folder, and then click Save.

6 To export your Blurb photo book as a PDF file for proofing purposes, leave the Book selection set to one of the Blurb choices, and click the Export Book To PDF button below the left panel group.

Well done! You've successfully completed another Lightroom Classic lesson. In this lesson, you learned how to put together an attractive photo book to showcase your images.

In the process, you've explored the Book module and used the control panels to customize page templates, refine the layout, set a backdrop, and add text.

In the next lesson, you'll find out how to present your work in a dynamic slideshow, but before you move on, take a few moments to reinforce what you've learned by reading through the review questions and answers on the next page.

Review questions

1 How do you modify a photo book page layout?

2 What options are available for page numbering?

3 What is cell padding, and how is it used?

4 What text attributes are affected by the Tracking, Baseline, Leading, and Kerning controls in the Type panel?

5 How can you use the Text Adjustment tool to fine-tune text?

Review answers

1 Click the Change Page Layout button to the right of the layout preview thumbnail in the Page panel or in the lower-right corner of a selected page or spread in the work area. Choose a layout category, and then click a layout thumbnail to apply that template. Use cell padding to tweak the layout.

2 Page numbering can be found in the Page panel, where you can also set the global position for the numbers and whether you want them on both right and left pages. Use the Type panel to set text style attributes. Right-click a page number to apply the style globally, hide the number on a given page, or have the page numbering start on a page other than page 1.

3 Cell padding is the adjustable space around an image or text within its cell. It can be used to position text or a photo anywhere on the page. In combination with the Zoom slider, it also can be used to crop an image any way you wish.

4 Tracking adjusts the letter spacing throughout a text selection, making it look either more open or more dense. The Baseline setting shifts selected text vertically in relation to the baseline. Leading affects the space between selected text and the line above it. Kerning adjusts the letter spacing between specific pairs of letters.

5 Drag horizontally across selected text to adjust the text size. Drag vertically over the selection to increase or decrease the leading (line spacing). Hold down the Command/ Ctrl key as you drag horizontally over selected text to adjust the tracking. Hold down the Command/Ctrl key and drag vertically over a text selection to shift it in relation to its baseline. Hold down the Option/Alt key to temporarily disable the Text Adjustment tool when you wish to change the text selection. Click between a pair of letters to place the text insertion cursor, and then drag horizontally across the text insertion point to adjust kerning.

PHOTOGRAPHY SHOWCASE
TITO HERRERA

"Make the ordinary extraordinary."

I fell in love with photography by looking at magazines like *National Geographic*, *Time*, and *Life*, and finding the beauty in the everyday moments and in telling the stories of "ordinary" people. That beauty has guided my photographic journey from the beginning, as I clearly knew what kind of photos I wanted to take. I still try to guide my work by this simple, self-imposed rule: Make the ordinary extraordinary.

To me, the good photos are not so much about finding fascinating subjects. The truth is that whatever is amazing to someone in one part of the world is completely normal and ordinary to someone in another part, and what makes a subject amazing is not so much the subject itself, but rather the way it's presented by the photographer. A beautiful person or an amazing location can look really bad if not photographed properly, while some of the most mundane things can catch your eyes for hours if photographed from the right angle and with the right light.

The trick is to keep an open mind, to continue to be amazed by the world, to be inquisitive and creative, and to push yourself to see differently. Start by finding the beauty, good light, and interesting subjects in your own backyard. Until you learn to do this, I guarantee you that you won't find them halfway around the world.

It's not about finding amazing subjects; it's about making every subject look amazing.

www.titoherrera.com
instagram.com/titoherrera

JEREMY WADE - RIVER MONSTERS

BEAR GRYLLS

GUNA YALA, PANAMA

NURA, KAZAKHSTAN

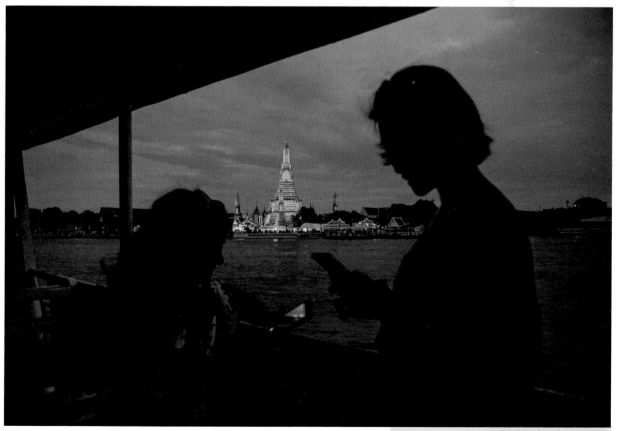

BANGKOK, THAILAND

9 CREATING A SLIDESHOW

Lesson overview

Once you've spent time bringing out the best in your images, showing them off in a slideshow is one of the easiest and most effective ways to share your photos with friends and family or to present them to a client. Choose a template as a starting point, and then customize the layout, color scheme, and timing. Add backdrops, borders, text overlays—even music and video—to create a dynamic presentation that will complement your work and captivate your audience. In this lesson, you'll learn how to:

- Group the images for your slideshow as a collection.

- Choose a slideshow template, adjust the layout, set a backdrop image, and add a text overlay, sound, and motion.

- Save your slideshow and your customized template.

- Export your presentation.

- View an impromptu slideshow.

 This lesson will take about 90 minutes to complete. To get the lesson files used in this chapter, download them from the web page for this book at *peachpit.com/LRClassicCIB2024*. For more information, see "Accessing the lesson files and Web Edition" in the "Getting Started" section at the beginning of this book.

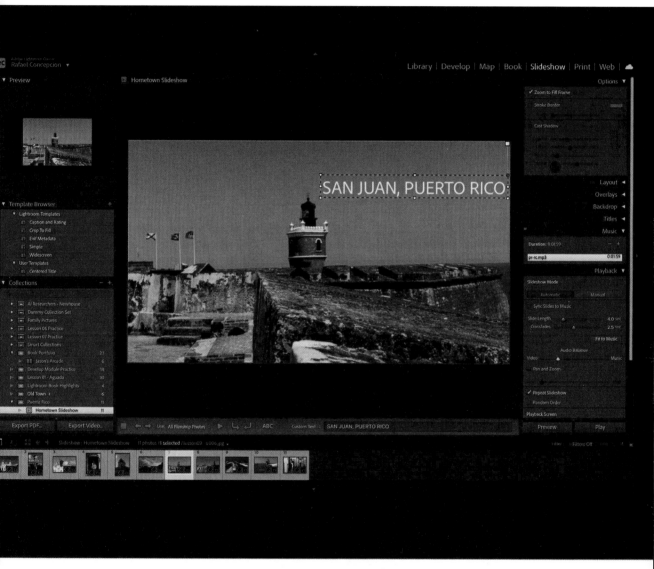

In the Slideshow module you can quickly put together an impressive onscreen presentation complete with stylish graphic effects, transitions, text, music, and even video. Lightroom Classic makes it easier than ever to share your images with family and friends, clients, or the world at large by giving you the option of exporting your slideshow to PDF or video.

Getting started

Note: This lesson assumes that you already have a basic working familiarity with the Lightroom Classic workspace. If you need more background information, refer to Lightroom Classic Help, or review the previous lessons.

Before you begin, make sure you've set up the LRC2024CIB folder for your lesson files and created the LRC2024CIB Catalog file to manage them, as described in "Accessing the lesson files and Web Edition" and "Creating a catalog file for working with this book" in the "Getting Started" section at the start of this book.

If you haven't already done so, download the lesson09 folder from your Account page at *peachpit.com* to the LRC2024CIB\Lessons folder, as detailed in "Accessing the lesson files and Web Edition" in the "Getting Started" section.

1   Start Lightroom Classic.

2   In the Select Catalog dialog box, make sure the file LRC2024CIB Catalog.lrcat is selected under Select A Recent Catalog To Open, and then click Open.

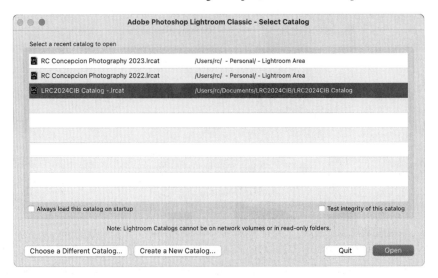

Note: If you can't see the Module Picker, choose Window > Panels > Show Module Picker, or press the F5 key. If you're working on macOS, you may need to press the fn key together with the F5 key, or change the function key behavior in the system preferences.

3   Lightroom Classic will open in the screen mode and workspace module that were active when you last quit. If necessary, switch to the Library module by clicking Library in the Module Picker at the top of the workspace.

Importing images into the library

The first step is to import the images for this lesson into the Lightroom library.

1   In the Library module, click the Import button below the left panel group.

2 If the Import dialog box appears in compact mode, click the Show More Options button at the lower left of the dialog box to see all of the options in the expanded Import dialog box.

3 Under Source at the left of the expanded Import dialog box, locate and select your LRC2024CIB\Lessons\lesson09 folder. Ensure that all 11 images in the lesson09 folder are selected (checked) for import.

4 In the import options above the thumbnail previews, select Add so that the imported photos will be added to your catalog without being moved or copied. Under File Handling at the right of the expanded Import dialog box, choose Embedded & Sidecar from the Build Previews menu and leave the Don't Import Suspected Duplicates option selected. Under Apply During Import, choose None from both the Develop Settings menu and the Metadata menu and type **Lesson 09, San Juan** in the Keywords text box. Make sure that your import is set up as shown here, and then click Import.

The 11 images are imported and now appear in both the Library module's Grid view and the Filmstrip across the bottom of the Lightroom workspace.

Assembling photos for a slideshow

▶ **Tip:** Your slideshow can include video as well as still images.

The first step in creating a slideshow is to gather the photos you wish to include. Since we just imported them, the images for this lesson are already isolated from the rest of your catalog in the Previous Import folder, which is selected.

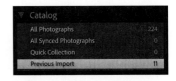

Although you could move to the Slideshow module now, this isn't a good solution. The Previous Import folder is a temporary grouping. The next time you import images into Lightroom, the Previous Import will contain another set of images. Also, the images there cannot be reorganized.

▶ **Tip:** You can reorder photos in a collection by simply dragging the thumbnails in the Grid view or the Filmstrip. Your custom display order will be saved with the collection.

1   With the Previous Import folder still selected, press Command+A/Ctrl+A or choose Edit > Select All. Click the plus sign (+) icon in the Collections panel's header and choose Create Collection from the menu. In the Create Collection dialog box, type **Puerto Rico** as the name for

your new collection. Make sure the Include Selected Photos option is selected and the rest of the options remain unselected; then click Create.

Your new collection appears in the Collections panel, where it's automatically selected. The image count at the right indicates that the Puerto Rico collection contains 11 photos.

▶ **Tip:** The first time you enter any of the Lightroom modules, you'll see tips that help you identify the components of the workspace and understand the workflow order. You can dismiss the tips by clicking the Close button. To reactivate the tips for any module, choose [Module name] Tips from the Help menu.

This is also a good time to point out that as your list of collections increases, it may become harder to find a collection. Directly under the Collections panel's header, there is a search box. Type in any collection name, and it searches all of the collections in the panel for a match (as shown above).

2   With the Puerto Rico collection selected, in the Toolbar below the Grid view, change the Sort menu to File Name (you can reorganize them later, while setting up your slideshow). Press Option+Command+5/Alt+Ctrl+5, or click Slideshow in the Module Picker to switch to the Slideshow module.

Working in the Slideshow module

The Slide Editor view is the main area where you'll work on your slide layouts and preview your slideshow in operation.

In the left panel group, the Preview panel displays a thumbnail preview of whichever layout template is currently selected (or under the pointer) in the Template Browser panel, while the Collections panel provides easy access to your photos.

The Toolbar below the Slide Editor view offers controls for navigating through the images in your collection, previewing the slideshow, and adding text to your slides.

Note: Your preview may look slightly different from the illustration, depending on the size and proportions of your computer display.

Choosing a slideshow template

Each of the preset Lightroom slideshow templates incorporates a different combination of layout settings—such as image size, borders, backgrounds, shadows, and text overlays—that can be customized to create your own slide designs.

1   In the Template Browser panel, expand the Lightroom Templates folder, if necessary, and then move the pointer slowly up and down the list of Lightroom templates. The Preview panel shows you how the selected image looks in each template layout as you move over it. Select a different image in the Filmstrip, and then preview the templates again.

Tip: The default template will be used when you launch the impromptu slideshow from another module. To designate a different template for this purpose, right-click its name in the Template Browser and choose Use For Impromptu Slideshow. A plus sign (+) appears after the name of the new default template.

2   When you're done previewing the options in the Template Browser, click to select the Widescreen template.

3   In the Toolbar below the slide preview, choose All Filmstrip Photos from the Use menu. In the Filmstrip, select the fourth image, lesson09 - 0004.

4   Click the Preview button at the bottom of the right panel group to preview your presentation in the Slide Editor view. When you're done, press the Esc key on your keyboard, or click in the Slide Editor view to stop the preview.

Template options for slideshows

As a convenient starting point for creating your own slide layouts, you can choose from these customizable Lightroom templates:

Caption And Rating This template centers the images on a gray background and displays the photo's star rating and caption metadata on each slide.

Crop To Fill Your photos fill the screen and may be cropped to fit the screen's aspect ratio, so this is probably not a good option for images in portrait format.

EXIF Metadata The slides are centered on a black background and include star ratings, EXIF (Exchangeable Image Format) information, and your identity plate.

Simple This template centers your photographs on a black background and incorporates your custom identity plate.

Widescreen Your images are centered and sized to fit the screen without being cropped; any empty space outside the image is filled with black.

Customizing your slideshow template

For the purposes of this lesson, you won't be adding an identity plate or metadata information to your slides, so the Widescreen template will serve as a good basis for setting up a customized layout.

Adjusting the slide layout

Once you've chosen a slide template, you can use the controls in the right panel group to customize it. For this project, you'll start by modifying the layout and then change the background to set up the overall look of the design before you make decisions about the style and color of borders and overlaid text. The Layout panel enables you to change the size and position of the photo in the slide layout by setting the margins that define the image cell.

> **Tip:** Video clips in a slideshow are placed in your slide layout in the same way as still images, complete with borders and shadows.

1   If the Layout panel in the right panel group is currently collapsed, expand it by clicking the triangle beside its name. Select the Show Guides and Link All options if they aren't already. If your screen has an aspect ratio other than 16:9, choose 16:9 from the Aspect Preview menu.

2   Move the pointer over the lower edge of the image in the Slide Editor view. When the pointer changes to a double-arrow cursor, drag the edge of the image upward. As you drag, white layout guides appear against the background around

the scaled-down image. All four guides move at the same time because the Link All option is selected in the Layout panel. As you drag upward, watch the linked sliders and numerical values change in the Layout panel and release the mouse button when the values reach 64 px.

▶ **Tip:** You could also drag the sliders in the Layout panel, or click the pixel values and type new numbers, to adjust the size of the image in the slide layout. With the settings linked, you need to only drag one slider or enter one value. Remember that the proportions of your slides may differ from what you see in the illustrations in this lesson, depending on the aspect ratio of your computer display.

Now you can increase the width of the slide's top margin to create a space where you can add text later in the lesson.

3   In the Layout panel, deselect the Link All option, and then either drag the Top slider to the right, type over the adjacent pixel value, or drag the top guide in the Slide Editor to set a value of 300 px. Deselect the Show Guides option, and then collapse the Layout panel.

Setting up the slide background

In the Backdrop panel, you can set a flat background color for your slides, apply a graduated color wash, or place a background image—you can even mix all three elements to create an atmospheric frame for your photos.

▶ **Tip:** When all three of the backdrop options are disabled, the slide background is black.

1   In the Filmstrip, select any image other than the last photo in the series.

2   If necessary, expand the Backdrop panel in the right panel group and deselect Background Color at the bottom of the panel. Then select the Background Image option and drag the lesson09 - 0011 image from the Filmstrip into the Background Image well. Drag the Opacity slider to the left to reduce the value to around 50% or click the Opacity value and type **50**.

▶ **Tip:** You can also drag an image from the Filmstrip directly onto the background of any slide in the Slide Editor view.

With the Background Color option disabled, the default black background shows through the partially transparent image, effectively darkening it. However, the background is still competing too much with the featured photos. You can use the Color Wash feature to darken the backdrop a little more. Color Wash applies a graduated wash that fades from whatever color is set in the Color Wash swatch to the background image (or color).

3 Select the Color Wash option. Click the Color
   Wash swatch, and then click the black swatch
   at the top of the Color Picker.

4 Click the Close button at the upper left of the
   Color Picker, and then use the Opacity slider
   to set the color wash opacity to 85%. Set the
   Angle of the wash to 45°. When you're done,
   collapse the Backdrop panel.

With the background photo set to partial transparency, your backdrop design is now a composite
of all three optional elements: a graduated color wash, an image, and the default
background color.

Adjusting stroke borders and shadows

Now that you've established the overall layout and feel for your slides, you can "lift"
the images to make them stand out more against the background by adding a thin
stroke border and a drop shadow. We'll choose a
border color that will provide a contrast to the
predominantly warm, dark backdrop.

1 In the right panel group, expand the Options
   panel. Select the Stroke Border option, and
   then click the color swatch beside it to open the
   Color Picker.

2 To set a pale yellow stroke border, click the R, G, and B percentages at the bottom of the Color Picker in turn to select them and type values of **79**, **81**, and **63**, respectively. Click outside the Color Picker to close it.

3 Use the Width slider to set a width of 1 px or type **1** in the text box.

4 Select the Cast Shadow option in the Options panel and experiment with the controls. You can adjust the opacity of the shadow, the distance the shadow is offset from the image, the angle at which it is cast, and the Radius setting, which affects the softness of the shadow's edge. When you're done, turn off the Stroke Border and Cast Shadow options, as well as all of the options in the Backdrop panel.

Adding a text overlay

In the Overlays panel, you can add text, an identity plate, or a watermark to your slides and have Lightroom display the rating stars you've assigned to your images or the captions that you've added to their metadata. In this exercise, you'll add a simple headline that will be overlaid on the background for every slide.

1 Expand the Overlays panel and select the Text Overlays option. If the Toolbar is not visible just below the Slide Editor view, press the T key. In the Toolbar, click the Add Text To Slide button (ABC).

2 Type **PUERTO RICO** in the Custom Text box, and press Return/Enter. The text appears in the lower-left corner of the slide, surrounded by a bounding box (you may need to click the bounding box to see the text).

3 The settings in the Text Overlays area of the Overlays panel update to show the default font details. Click the double triangle beside the font name and choose a different font and face, if you want. I left it at the default. Leave the text color set

● **Note:** For this exercise, you won't incorporate an identity plate or watermark in your slideshow. For more information on identity plates, refer to the online bonus lesson "Publishing Your Photos" or the Lightroom Classic Help topic "Add your identity plate to a slideshow" in the *Lightroom Classic User Guide*.

to the default white (the swatch at the right of Text Overlays). If it's too bright, decrease the Opacity to 80% to soften the effect.

4 Drag the text upward, and allow it to attach itself to the anchor at the center of the slide's upper edge. Drag the handle at the bottom of the text bounding box upward to scale the text, making it a little smaller, and then use the up and down arrow keys to position the title as shown here.

As you drag text on a slide layout, Lightroom tethers the bounding box either to the nearest of various reference points around the edge of the slide or to a point on the border of the image itself.

5 To see this in operation, drag the text around the slide, both inside and outside the image, and watch the white tether-line jump from point to point. When you're done, return the text to its original position.

Throughout a slideshow, the tethered text will maintain the same position relative either to the slide as a whole or to the border of each image, whatever its shape.

You can use this feature to ensure that photo-specific caption text, for instance, will always appear just below the left corner of each image no matter what its size or orientation, while a title that applies to the presentation as a whole—as does the text in our example—will remain in a constant position onscreen. In the latter case, the text is tethered to one of the anchors around the edge of the slide; in the former, the text would be tethered to an anchor on the border of the feature image.

The color and opacity controls in the Text Overlays area operate just as they do in the Color Wash and Stroke Border areas. On macOS, you can also set up a drop shadow for your text.

6   Collapse the Overlays panel and deselect the text box in the Slideshow Editor.

7   Select the first slide in the Filmstrip and click the Preview button at the bottom of the right panel group to preview your slideshow in the Slideshow Editor view. When you're done, press Esc to stop playback.

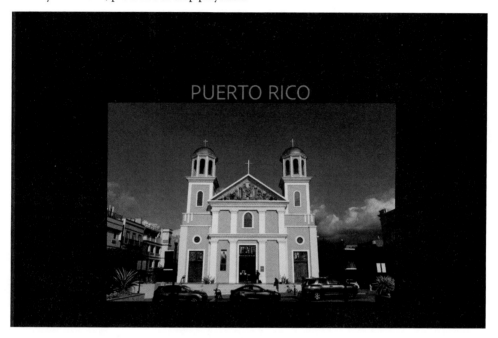

Creating a saved slideshow

Since you entered the Slideshow module, you've been working with an unsaved slideshow, as is indicated in the bar across the top of the Slideshow Editor view.

Unsaved Slideshow   Create Saved Slideshow

Until you save your slideshow, the Slideshow module works like a scratch pad. You can move to another module, or even close Lightroom Classic, and find your settings unchanged when you return, but if you click a new slideshow template—or even the one you started with—in the Template Browser, the "scratch pad" will be cleared and all of your work will be lost.

Converting your project to a saved slideshow not only preserves your layout and playback settings but also links your design to the particular set of images for which it was designed. Your slideshow is saved as a special kind of collection—an output collection—with its own listing in the Collections panel. Clicking this listing will instantly retrieve the images you were working with and reinstate all of your settings, no matter how many times the slideshow scratch pad has been cleared.

Using the Text Template Editor

In the Slideshow module, you can use the Text Template Editor to access and edit the metadata that is stored in your photos and set up text overlays to be displayed on each slide, drawn from that information. You can add custom text and choose from titles, captions, image size, camera info, and a wide range of other options, and then save your choices as a text template preset that will help you streamline and automate your workflow for similar projects in the future.

To call up the Text Template Editor, click the Add Text To Slide button (ABC) in the Toolbar, and then click the double triangle beside the Custom Text box in the Toolbar and choose Edit from the menu.

In the Text Template Editor, you can set up a string of one or more text tokens, place-holders that represent the information items to be drawn from each photo's metadata for display in your slideshow.

In the Preset menu at the top of the editor, you can apply, save, and manage text overlay presets, saved sets of info tokens that are customized for different purposes.

Use the Image Name menu to set up a text string with the current or original filename, copy name, or folder name.

Use the Numbering menu to number the images in your slideshow and display image capture dates in a variety of formats.

Choose from EXIF metadata including image dimensions, exposure, flash settings, and many other attributes.

IPTC metadata includes copyright, creator details, and numerous other options.

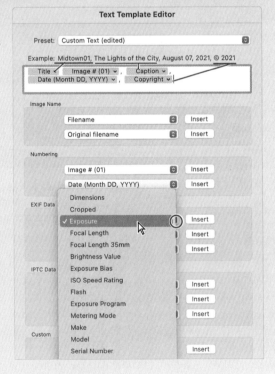

1   Click the Create Saved Slideshow button in the bar at the top of the Slideshow Editor view, or click the plus sign (+) button in the header of the Collections panel and choose Create Slideshow.

2   In the Create Slideshow dialog box, type **Hometown Slideshow** as the name for your presentation. In the Location options, select the Inside option, choose the Puerto Rico collection from the menu, and then click Create.

Tip: The Make New Virtual Copies option is useful if you want to apply a particular treatment, such as a developing preset, to all of the pictures in your slideshow, without affecting the photos in the source collection.

The title bar above the Slide Editor now displays the name of your saved slideshow and no longer presents the Create Saved Slideshow button.

Your saved slideshow appears in the Collections panel, marked with a Saved Slideshow icon and nested inside the original source collection, Puerto Rico. The image count shows that the new output collection, like the source, contains 11 photos.

You can save your slideshow at any point in the process—you could create a saved slideshow as soon as you enter the Slideshow module with a selection of images or wait until your presentation is polished. Once you've saved your slideshow, any changes you make to the layout or playback settings are auto-saved as you work.

For the purposes of this lesson, saving the project at this stage enables you to delete and rearrange slides to refine your presentation, without affecting the source collection. Any image you exclude from the slideshow now will be removed from the Hometown Slideshow output collection but will remain a part of your original Puerto Rico collection.

This could be useful if you also plan to use the photos in the Puerto Rico collection to produce a print layout and a web gallery, for instance. Your original collection remains intact, while the output collection for each project may contain a different subset of images, arranged in a different order.

Refining the content of a slideshow

It's a good idea to finalize the photo set for your slideshow at this point, before you go on to specify playback settings. If you remove an image later, you might need to readjust the time allocated for each slide and transition, especially if your slideshow is timed to match the duration of a sound file.

Tip: Adding more photos to your saved slideshow is easy: simply drag images onto the slideshow's listing in the Collections panel. While your pointer is over your saved slideshow in the Collections panel, click the white arrow that appears to the right of the image count to jump from the Library to your presentation in the Slideshow module.

1 In the Filmstrip, right-click the lesson09 - 0011 image—the photo you used as a background image—and choose Remove From Collection.

Although the photo disappears from the Filmstrip and is not featured on any slide in the presentation, it is not removed from the Slide Background well in the Backdrop panel. The background image has become part of the slide layout, rather than merely one of the selected photos to be displayed.

Even if you fill your slideshow with a different set of photos entirely, the background image will remain in the panel. Your saved slideshow includes a link to the photo that is independent of the output collection or its parent collection.

In the Collections panel, the nested Hometown Slideshow output collection now shows an image count of 10 photos, while its parent collection still contains the original count of 11.

2 In the Filmstrip, drag the lesson09 - 0007 image to a new position between the lesson09 - 0003 and lesson09 - 0004 images, releasing the mouse button when the black insertion bar appears.

Adding sound and motion to your slideshow

One way to make your presentation more dynamic is to add video clips, which are placed on their own slides according to your layout, just like your photos—complete with stroke borders, shadows, and overlays.

Even for a slideshow composed entirely of still images, you can easily create atmosphere and generate emotional impact by adding music and bring your photos to life with filmic pan and zoom effects.

You'll find a sound file named pr-rc.mp3 in your lesson09 folder. This piece of music will underline the timeless, vibrant theme of the slideshow; however, feel free to choose any other file from your music library that you'd like. With only 10 images in the slideshow, a fairly short piece will probably work best.

1 Expand the Music and Playback panels in the right panel group. Click the switch at the left of the Music panel's header to enable the sound-track for your slideshow. Click the Add Music

button, navigate to your LRC2024CIB\Lessons\lesson09 folder, select the pr-rc.mp3 file, and click Choose. The name of the sound file and its duration are displayed in the Music panel.

2   Expand the Titles panel and select both the Intro Screen and Ending Screen options. Deselect the Add Identity Plate option for both screens.

The next step is to fine-tune the slideshow's timing by setting the duration of the slides and the transitions between them to match the length of the music file.

3   In the Playback panel, watch the Slide Length and Crossfades values change as you click the Fit To Music button. If you get a message that it won't fit, lower the Crossfades length. The timing is adjusted to fit the 10 images and two title screens to the duration of the music file.

4   Drag the Crossfades slider to the right to increase the duration of the fade transitions a little, and then click the Fit To Music button once more, keeping an eye on the Slide Length value as you do so. Lightroom recalculates the slide duration so that the slideshow fits the music file despite the lengthened fades.

5   Deselect the Repeat Slideshow and Random Order options, farther down in the Playback panel. In the Filmstrip, select the first image, and then click the Preview button at the bottom of the right panel group to preview the slideshow in the Slideshow Editor view. When you're done, press Esc to stop playback.

    Adding music created a sense of narrative for the presentation; now it's time to add some movement that will help to make it not just a story, but a journey.

6   Select the Pan And Zoom option in the Playback panel. Drag the slider to set the level for the effect about one-third of the way between Low and High. The higher you set the Pan And Zoom slider, the faster and broader the movement; a low setting creates a slow drift that never moves too far from a full-frame view.

7   Make sure the first photo is selected in the Filmstrip, and then click the Play button at the bottom of the right panel group to see the slideshow in full-screen mode. If you want, you can press the spacebar to pause and resume playback. When you're done, press the Esc key to end the slideshow.

For a slideshow that contains more images, use the Add Music button to attach more sound files. If you use multiple sound files, clicking the Fit To Music button will fit your slides and transitions to the combined duration of the music tracks.

▶ **Tip:** You can add up to 10 music files to your slideshow soundtrack; to change the order in which they'll play, drag files to new positions in the Music panel list.

The Sync Slides To Music option disables the Slide Length and Crossfades controls and the Fit To Music button. Lightroom then analyzes the sound file and sets the timing of the slideshow to match the tempo and to respond to prominent sounds in the music.

The Playback panel's Audio Balance slider enables you to mix your soundtrack music with the audio from video clips in your slideshow.

If you have a second display attached to your computer, you'll see the Playback Screen area at the bottom of the Playback panel, where you can choose which screen will be used when you play your slideshow at full screen and whether the other screen will be blank during playback.

Saving a customized slideshow template

Having spent so much time customizing your slideshow template, you should now save it so that it becomes available as a new choice in the Template Browser panel. This is not the same as saving your slideshow, as you did earlier. As mentioned earlier, a saved slideshow is actually an output collection, an arranged grouping of images saved with slideshow settings. In contrast, a saved custom template records only your slide layout and playback settings—it's not linked to any images.

Saving your customized slideshow template will save you a lot of time later should you wish to put together a related presentation or simply use the template as a starting point for creating a new design.

By default, your customized template will be listed with the User Templates in the Template Browser panel.

1   With your slideshow still open, click the Create New Preset button in the header of the Template Browser panel, or choose Slideshow > New Template.

▶ **Tip:** When saving a customized template, it's a good idea to give it a descriptive name. This will make it easier to find as you add more new templates to the Template Browser.

2   In the New Template dialog box, type **Centered Title** as the new template name. Leave the default User Templates folder selected as the destination folder in the Folder menu, and then click Create.

Your new customized template is now listed under User Templates in the Template Browser panel.

Modifying and organizing user templates

The Template Browser offers numerous options for organizing your templates and template folders as described here:

Renaming a template or template folder

You cannot rename the Lightroom Templates folder, any of the built-in templates, or the default User Templates folder. To rename any of the templates or template folders that you have created, right-click the template or folder in the Template Browser and choose Rename from the menu.

Moving a template

If you want to move a template into another folder in the Template Browser, simply drag the template to that folder. If you want to move a template into a new folder, right-click the template and choose New Folder from the menu. The selected template will be moved into the new folder as it is created. If you try to move one of the Lightroom templates, the template will be copied to the new folder but will still remain in the Lightroom Templates folder.

Updating a custom template's settings

If you want to modify one of your own custom templates, select it in the Template Browser and make your changes using any of the controls in the right panel group. To save your changes, right-click the template in the Template Browser and choose Update With Current Settings.

Creating a copy of a template

You may want to create a copy of a template so that you can safely make modifications without affecting the original. If you want to create a copy of the currently selected template in an existing template folder, click the Create New Preset button (+) in the Template Browser panel header. In the New Template dialog box, type a name for the copy, choose the destination folder from the Folder menu, and click Create. If you want to create a copy of the currently selected template in a new folder, click the Create New Preset button (+) in the Template Browser panel header, and in the New Template dialog box, type a name for the copy and choose New Folder from the Folder menu. Then, in the New Folder dialog box, give your new folder a name and click Create. The new folder appears in the Template Browser. Click Create in the New Template dialog box to dismiss it. The copied template will be created in the new folder.

Exporting a custom template

To export your custom slideshow template so that you can use it in Lightroom on another computer, right-click the template name in the Template Browser and choose Export from the menu.

Importing a custom template

To import a custom template that has been created in Lightroom on another computer, right-click the User Templates header or any of the templates in the User Templates menu and choose Import from the menu. In the Import Template dialog box, locate the template file and click Import.

(continues on next page)

Exporting a slideshow

To send your slideshow to a friend or client, play it on another computer, or share it on the web, you can export it as a PDF file or as a high-quality video file.

1 In the Slideshow module, click the Export PDF button at the bottom of the left panel group.

Note: PDF slideshow transitions work when viewed using the free Adobe Reader® or Adobe Acrobat®. However, slideshows exported to PDF will not include music, randomized playback order, or your customized slide duration settings.

2 Review the options available in the Export Slideshow To PDF dialog box, noting the settings for size and quality, and then click Cancel.

3 Repeat the process for the Export Video button. Review the Export Slideshow To Video dialog box, noting the range of options available in the Video Preset menu. Select each export option in turn to see a brief description below the Video Preset menu.

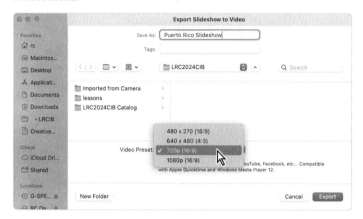

Lightroom Classic exports slideshows in the MP4 movie format so that you can share your slideshow movies on video sharing sites or optimize them for playback on mobile devices. Preset size and quality settings range from 480 x 270, optimized for personal media players and email, to 1080p, optimized for high-quality HD video.

4 In the Export Slideshow To Video dialog box, type a name for your exported video and specify a destination folder. Choose an option from the Video Preset menu, and then click Export.

A progress bar in the upper-left corner of the workspace shows the status of the export process.

Playing an impromptu slideshow

Even outside the Slideshow module you can play an impromptu slideshow. In the Library module, for instance, it is a convenient way to see a full-screen preview of the photos you've just imported.

The impromptu slideshow can be launched from any of the Lightroom Classic modules. The slide layout, timing, and transitions for the impromptu slideshow will depend on the template currently set in the Slideshow module for use with the impromptu slideshow. If you haven't set one, it will use the current settings in the Slideshow module.

▶ **Tip:** To change the slideshow template used for the impromptu slideshow, right-click a template in the Slideshow module Template Browser and choose Use For Impromptu Slideshow.

1 Switch to the Library module. In the Catalog panel, select Previous Import. Use the Sort menu and the Sort Direction button (it should show an "A" above a "Z") in the Grid view toolbar to choose the order in which you'd like to view your images.

2 Select the first photo in the Grid view, and then press Command+A/Ctrl+A or choose Edit > Select All to select all of the images from the previous import.

3 Choose Window > Impromptu Slideshow or press Command+Return/Ctrl+Enter to start the impromptu slideshow.

4 Use the spacebar to pause and resume playback. The slideshow will repeat, cycling through the selected images until you either press the Esc key on your keyboard or click the screen to stop playback.

Tip: In the Library and Develop modules, you can also use the Impromptu Slideshow button in the Toolbar. If you don't see the Impromptu Slideshow button in the Toolbar, choose Slideshow from the content menu at the right end of the Toolbar.

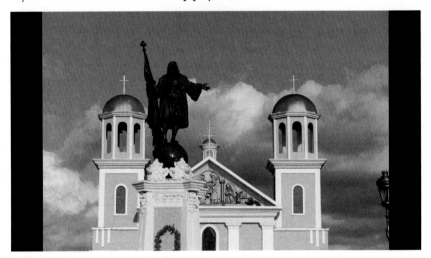

Well done! You have successfully completed another Lightroom Classic lesson. In this lesson you learned how to create your own stylish slideshow presentation. At the same time, you've explored the Slideshow module and used the control panels to customize a slideshow template.

In the next lesson, you'll find out how to present your work in printed format, but before you move on, take a few moments to read through my recommended settings, and then reinforce what you've learned by reading through the review questions and answers on the last page.

Note: You don't have to follow along with this section. At this point, you can see these sections as mere suggestions for what to do with your workflow.

My suggested settings for a slideshow

This lesson was designed to take you through a tour of all of the features in the Slideshow module. It's important to note that while all of the features are there, you aren't required to use every one of them. In fact, when I create slideshows for myself, I often opt for a very stripped-down experience, but with some key changes to make sure that my branding is taken into account. I wanted to take a moment to share those changes with you here.

I tend to want my pictures to be the center of the discussion, so select the Simple template in the Template Browser. In the Layout panel, set the margins to 72 px. In the Options panel, set the stroke border to a dark gray (R=20%, G=20%, B=20%) and the width to 1 px, and make sure that the only thing selected in the Backdrop panel is a black background color. All Overlays panel options are deselected.

Where I do dedicate a little bit of time is adding intro and ending screens in the Titles panel.

If you are presenting a slideshow to a group of people or a client, you want to be sure you make the biggest impact out of the gate. I do not want my slideshow displaying the first image until I am ready to show it. I may want to introduce the project or speak a little before it starts.

The Intro Screen area in the Titles panel allows you to use an identity plate with your branding information. The easiest option is to select Use A Styled Text Identity Plate in the Identity Plate Editor (click the Identity Plate preview and choose Edit to open the it). Here, I chose Helvetica Neue Condensed Bold for my font and just typed in my company's name.

Once your identity plate is set up, you can use the Scale slider in the Titles panel to make the text bigger and fit the presentation. While the text is a good start, I want to personalize this even further.

If you are using Lightroom, there's a good chance you also have Photoshop available to you. I created a logo graphic in Photoshop with my signature (easy to create with a tablet and pen) and one text layer. I saved this graphic as a transparent PNG file (the color fill layer at the bottom is only there to show you how the white type looks).

Back in the Identity Plate Editor in Lightroom, select Use A Graphical Identity Plate instead. Then, click the Locate File button and select the PNG image.

The slideshow now has my own custom branding. Select the Ending Screen option and leave it set to black. Leave Add Identity Plate unselected. When it comes to presentation time, you can start the presentation and immediately pause it. This leaves your name or logo onscreen and lets you introduce yourself or your work before you start the show.

Review questions

1 How can you change which template is used for the impromptu slideshow?

2 Which Lightroom slideshow template would you pick if you wanted to display metadata for your images?

3 What options do you have when customizing a slideshow template?

4 How does tethered text help you design your layout?

5 What is the difference between saving your customized slideshow template and saving the slideshow you've created?

Review answers

1 In the Slideshow module, right-click the name of a slideshow template in the Template Browser and choose Use For Impromptu Slideshow.

2 The EXIF Metadata template centers photos on a black background and displays star ratings and EXIF information for the images, as well as an identity plate.

3 In the right panel group you can modify the slide layout, add borders and text overlays, create shadow effects for images or text (on a Mac only at this point), change the background color or add a backdrop image, adjust the durations of slides and fades, and add a soundtrack.

4 Tethered text is anchored either to the outside edge of the slide, which can be used to ensure that title text appears on every page in the same place, or to the image border, which ensures that photo-specific text will appear in the same place for each photo.

5 A saved custom template records only your layout and playback settings—it is like an empty container that is not linked to any particular set of images. A saved slideshow is actually an output collection—an arranged grouping of images, saved together with a slide layout, text overlays, and playback settings.

10 PRINTING IMAGES

Lesson overview

The Lightroom Classic Print module offers all of the tools you'll need to quickly prepare your images for printing. You can print a single photo, repeat one image at different sizes on the same sheet, or create an attractive layout for multiple images. Add borders, text, and graphics, and then adjust print resolution, sharpening, paper type, and color management with just a few clicks. In this lesson, you'll learn how to:

- Choose and customize a print template, and create a Custom Package print layout.

- Add an identity plate, borders, a background color, and captions created from a photo's metadata.

- Save a custom print template, and save your print job as an output collection.

- Choose print settings, printer driver options, and appropriate color management options.

 This lesson will take about 90 minutes to complete. To get the lesson files used in this chapter, download them from the web page for this book at *peachpit.com/LightroomCIB2024*. For more information, see "Accessing the lesson files and Web Edition" in the "Getting Started" section at the beginning of this book.

The Print module in Lightroom Classic makes it easy to achieve professional printed results, with device-specific soft proofing to help you produce prints that match the color and depth you see onscreen and customizable layout templates for anything from a contact sheet to a fine art mat.

Getting started

● **Note:** This lesson assumes that you already have a basic working familiarity with the Lightroom Classic workspace. If you need more background information, refer to Lightroom Classic Help, or review the previous lessons.

Before you begin, make sure you've set up the LRC2024CIB folder for your lesson files and created the LRC2024CIB Catalog file to manage them, as described in "Accessing the lesson files and Web Edition" and "Creating a catalog file for working with this book" in the "Getting Started" section at the start of this book.

If you haven't already done so, download the lesson10 folder from your Account page at peachpit.com to the LRC2024CIB\Lessons folder, as detailed in "Accessing the lesson files and Web Edition" in the "Getting Started" section.

1   Start Lightroom Classic.

2   In the Select Catalog dialog box, make sure the file LRC2024CIB Catalog.lrcat is selected under Select A Recent Catalog To Open, and then click Open.

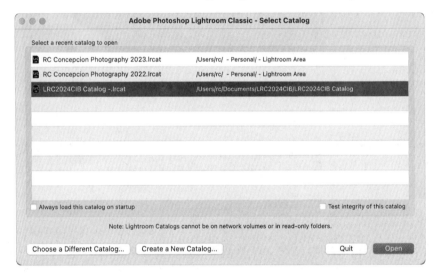

● **Note:** If you can't see the Module Picker, choose Window > Panels > Show Module Picker, or press the F5 key. If you're working on macOS, you may need to press the fn key together with the F5 key, or change the function key behavior in the system preferences.

3   Lightroom Classic will open in the screen mode and workspace module that were active when you last quit. If necessary, switch to the Library module by clicking Library in the Module Picker at the top of the workspace.

Creating a collection from the existing images

We've already imported and worked on many images in this book, so let's select 11 of them and place them into a collection for this lesson.

1   Click All Photographs in the Catalog panel, located near the top of the panels on the left of the Library module.

2 Click the plus sign (+) icon at
the right of the Collections
panel's header and choose Create
Collection. Type **Images to Print**
for the name. Make sure the
Include Selected Photos option
is deselected, select Set As Target
Collection, and click Create.

▶ **Tip:** If you ever
want to change which
collection is used as the
target collection, simply
right-click the collection
in the Collections panel
and select Set As Target
Collection.

3 In the Toolbar, set the Sort order to File Name. Scroll through all of the
photographs looking for images that you believe are good candidates for
printing. When you find an image you want to work with, press the letter B
on your keyboard and it will be sent to the target collection we just specified.
This gives you the freedom to look without having to drag.

4 You can use whichever files you would like to print, but if you want to
follow along with this lesson, you will need the following files: lesson03-019,
lesson05 - 001, lesson05 - 002, lesson05 - 011, lesson06 - 002, lesson06 - 017,
lesson07 - 015, lesson07 - 020-Pano, lesson07 - 031-HDR, lesson08 - 017, and
lesson08 - 0019. Click the Images to Print collection in the Collections panel,
set the Sort order to File Name, and then click Print in the Module Picker at
the top of the workspace to switch to the Print module.

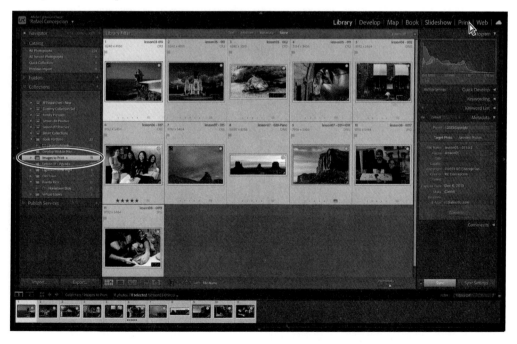

About the Lightroom Classic Print module

In the Print module, you'll find tools and controls for each step in the printing workflow. Change the order of your photos; choose a print template and refine the layout; add borders, text, and graphics; and then adjust the output settings. Everything you need to produce professional-looking prints is at your fingertips.

The left panel group contains the Preview, Template Browser, and Collections panels. Move the pointer over the list in the Template Browser to see a thumbnail preview of each layout template displayed in the Preview panel. When you select a new template in the list, the Print Editor view—at center stage in the workspace—is updated to show how the selected photos look in the new layout.

You can quickly select and rearrange the photos for your print job in the Filmstrip, where the source menu provides easy access to the images in your library, listing your favorites and recently used source folders and collections.

You'll use the controls in the right panel group to customize your layout template and to specify output settings.

The Template Browser contains templates of three distinct types: Single Image/Contact Sheet layouts, Picture Package layouts, and Custom Package layouts.

The first set of Lightroom Templates presets (that start with parentheses) in the menu are Picture Package layouts. They repeat a single image at a variety of sizes on the same page. The second set are Single Image/Contact Sheet layouts, which can be used to print multiple photos at the same size on a single sheet. They range from contact sheets with many cells to single-cell layouts. The custom layout templates enable you to print multiple images at any size on the same page. All of the templates can be customized; you can save your modified layouts under User Templates in the Template Browser.

Once you've chosen a layout from the Template Browser, the Layout Style panel at the top of the right panel group indicates which type of template you're working with. The suite of panels you see below the Layout Style panel will vary slightly, depending on which type of template you have chosen.

The controls in the Image Settings panel enable you to add photo borders and to specify the way your pictures are fitted to their image cells.

For a Single Image/Contact Sheet template, you can use the Layout panel to adjust margins, to adjust cell size and spacing, and to change the number of rows and columns that make up the grid. Use the Guides panel to show or hide a selection of layout guides. For a Picture Package or Custom Package template, you'll modify your layout and show or hide the guides with the Rulers, Grid & Guides panel and the Cells panel. The Page panel has controls for watermarking your images and adding text, graphics, or a background color to your print layout. In the Print Job panel, you can set the print resolution, print sharpening, paper type, and color management options. When you are done looking at each style, click Single Image/Contact Sheet.

About layout styles and print templates

The Template Browser offers a wide choice of built-in Lightroom print templates that not only differ in basic layout but may also include a variety of design features such as borders and overlaid text or graphics. Templates may also differ in output settings: the preset print resolution setting for a contact sheet, for example, will be lower than the resolution set for a template designed for producing finished prints.

You can save time and effort setting up your print job by selecting the print template that most closely suits your purpose. In this exercise you'll be introduced to the different types of templates and use the panels in the right panel group to examine the characteristics of each layout.

1 In the left panel group, make sure that the Preview and Template Browser panels are expanded. If necessary, drag the top border of the Filmstrip down so that you can see as many of the templates in the Template Browser as possible. In the right panel group, expand the Layout Style panel and collapse the others.

2 Choose Edit > Select None, and then select any one of the images in the Filmstrip. The Print Editor view at the center of the workspace is updated to display the selected photo in the current layout.

3 If necessary, expand the Lightroom Templates folder in the Template Browser panel. Move the pointer slowly over the list of preset templates to see a preview of each layout in the Preview panel.

4 Click the second template in the Template Browser: (1) 4 × 6, (6) 2 × 3. The new template is applied to the image in the Print Editor view. Scroll up in the right panel group, if necessary, and inspect the Layout Style panel. You'll see that the Layout Style panel indicates that this template is a Picture Package layout. In the Template Browser, click the Lightroom template (2) 7 × 5. The Layout Style panel indicates that this is also a Picture Package layout.

5 Now choose the 2-Up Greeting Card preset template in the Template Browser. The Layout Style panel indicates that the 2-Up Greeting Card template is a Single Image/Contact Sheet layout, and the Print Editor view at the center of the workspace displays the new template.

6 In the Layout Style panel, click Picture Package. The Print Editor is updated to display the last selected Picture Package layout: (2) 7 × 5. Click Single Image/Contact Sheet in the Layout Style panel and the Print Editor view returns to the last selected Single Image/Contact Sheet layout: 2-Up Greeting Card.

You'll notice that different control panels become available in the right panel group as you move between the Single Image/Contact Sheet and Picture Package layout styles. Panels common to both layout styles may differ in content for each.

7 In the right panel group, expand the Image Settings panel. In the Layout Style panel, click Picture Package and expand the Image Settings panel again. Toggle

between the Picture Package and Single Image/Contact Sheet layouts and notice how the options available in the Image Settings panel change.

You can see that the selected photo fits to the image cell differently for each of these templates. In the Picture Package layout (2) 7 × 5, the Zoom To Fill option is activated in the Image Settings panel so that the photo is zoomed and cropped to fill the image cell, if needed. In the Single Image/Contact Sheet 2-Up Greeting Card, the Zoom To Fill option is disabled and the wide photo is cropped. Take a moment to examine the other differences in the Image Settings panel.

(2) 7 × 5 template   2-Up Greeting Card template

8   Select the Single Image/Contact Sheet layout style. Look at the page count at the right of the Toolbar below the Print Editor view: it reads "Page 1 of 1." Press Command+A/Ctrl+A or choose Edit > Select All to select all 11 images in the Filmstrip. The page count in the Toolbar now reads "Page 1 of 11." The 2-Up Greeting Card template is now applied to all 11 photos, resulting in a print job of 11 pages. Use the navigation buttons at the left of the Toolbar to move between the pages and see the layout applied to each image in turn and the page count change as you move through the pages.

Tip: You can also navigate your multi-page print document by using the Home, End, Page Up, Page Down, and left and right arrow keys on your keyboard, or choosing from the navigation commands in the Print menu.

9   For the last step in this exercise, collapse the Image Settings panel and expand the Print Job panel. You'll notice that in the Print Job panel, the Print Resolution for the 2-Up Greeting Card template is set to 240 ppi. Select the 4×5 Contact Sheet template in the Template Browser. The Print Resolution option in the Print Job panel is disabled and the Draft Mode Printing option is activated.

Selecting a print template

Tip: By default, each photo will be centered in its own image cell. To expose a different portion of an image that is cropped by the boundaries of its cell, simply drag the photo to reposition it within its image cell.

Now that you've explored the Template Browser, it's time to choose the template that you'll customize in the next exercise.

1 In the Template Browser, click the 4 Wide template. Later in this lesson you'll customize your identity plate, but for now, deselect the Identity Plate option in the Page panel to hide the default design.

2 Choose Edit > Select None. In the Filmstrip, Command-click/Ctrl-click the lesson07 - 015, lesson08 - 0017, and lesson08 - 0019 images to select them. The images are placed in the template in the same order in which they appear in the Filmstrip. Drag the images inside their cells to reposition them as you see here.

Tip: Lightroom automatically scales your photos in the print layout template to fit the paper size you have specified. In the Page Setup/Print Setup dialog box, leave the scale setting at 100% (the default) and let Lightroom fit the template to the page—that way, what you see in the Print Editor view will be what you'll get from your printer.

Specifying the printer and paper size

Before you customize the template, you'll need to specify the paper size and page orientation for your print job. Doing this now may save you the time and effort of readjusting the layout later.

1 Choose File > Page Setup or click the Page Setup button at the bottom of the left panel group.

2 In the Page Setup/Print Setup dialog box, choose the desired printer from the Format For/Name menu. From the Paper Size menu, choose US Letter (macOS)/Letter (Windows). Under Orientation, choose the portrait (vertical) format, and then click OK.

Customizing print templates

Having established the overall layout of your print job, you can use the controls in the Layout panel to fine-tune the template so that the images fit better to the page.

Changing the number of cells

For the purposes of this exercise, we need only three of the four preset image cells.

1   If necessary, expand the Layout panel in the right panel group. Under Page Grid, drag the Rows slider to the left or type **3** in the text box to the right of the slider.

2   Experiment with the Margins, Cell Spacing, and Cell Size sliders—making sure to undo (Command+Z/Ctrl+Z) after each change. Select the Keep Square option below the Cell Size sliders. The Cell Width and Cell Height sliders are locked together at the same value. Deselect the Keep Square option.

3   The black lines you might see around the photos are merely guides indicating the image cell boundaries; they will not appear on your printed page. These guides are helpful while you're adjusting the cell size and spacing, but they'll be distracting when you add printable borders to your layout in the next exercise. If necessary, expand the Guides panel below the Layout panel and deselect the Image Cells option; then collapse the Layout and Guides panels.

Note: If you don't see the guides referred to in this step, select the Show Guides option at the top of the Guides panel and toggle each option to see the effect.

Modifying the page layout of a print template

Layout controls for Single Image/Contact Sheet and Picture Package templates

Depending on which type of print template you are working with, you'll find a slightly different suite of panels in the right panel group. The Image Settings, Page, and Print Job panels are available for all template types, but the controls for modifying the page layout differ. If you've chosen a Single Image/Contact Sheet template, you'll customize your layout using the Layout and Guides panels. For a Picture Package template, you'll use the Rulers, Grid & Guides panel and the Cells panel. For Custom Package layouts you'll also use the Rulers, Grid & Guides panel and the Cells panel—where you'll find a few minor differences from the options offered in the same panels for a Picture Package template.

Picture Package templates and Custom Package layouts are not grid-based, so they are very flexible to work with; you can arrange the image cells on the page either by simply dragging them in the Print Editor view or by using the controls in the Cells panel. You can resize a cell by using the width and height sliders or by simply dragging the handles of its bounding box. Add more photos to your layout with the Cells panel controls or Option-drag/Alt-drag a cell to duplicate it and resize it as you wish.

Lightroom Classic provides a variety of guides to help you adjust your layout. Guides are not printed; they appear only in the Print Editor view. To show or hide the guides, select Show Guides in the Guides or Rulers, Grid & Guides panel, or choose View > Show Guides (Command+Shift+G/Ctrl+Shift+G). In the Guides panel, you can specify which types of guides will be displayed in the Print Editor view.

Note: The Margins and Gutters guides and Image Cells guides—available only for Single Image/Contact Sheet layouts—are interactive; you can adjust your layout directly by dragging the guides themselves in the Print Editor view. When you move these guides, the Margins, Cell Spacing, and Cell Size sliders in the Layout panel will move with them.

Using the Layout panel to modify a contact sheet/grid layout

Ruler Units sets the units of measurement for most of the other controls in the Layout panel and for the Rulers guide in the Guides panel. Click the Ruler Units setting and choose Inches, Centimeters, Millimeters, Points, or Picas from the menu. The default setting is Inches.

Margins sets the boundaries for the grid of image cells in your layout. Many printers don't support borderless printing, so the minimum value for the margins is dependent on the capabilities of your printer. Even if your printer does support borderless printing, you may first need to activate this feature in the printer settings before you can set the margins to zero.

Page Grid specifies the number of rows and columns of image cells in the layout. The grid can contain anything from one image cell (Rows: 1, Columns: 1) to 225 image cells (Rows: 15, Columns: 15).

Cell Spacing and **Cell Size** settings are linked so that changes you make to one will affect the other. The Cell Spacing sliders set the vertical and horizontal spaces between the image cells in the grid; the Cell Size controls change the height and width of the cells. The Keep Square option links the height and width settings so that the image cells remain square.

Using the Guides panel to modify a contact sheet/grid layout

Rulers are displayed across the top and at the left of the Print Editor view. If Show Guides is selected, you can also show the rulers by choosing View > Show Rulers (Command+R/Ctrl+R). To change the ruler units, click the setting in the Layout panel.

Page Bleed shades the non-printable edges of the page, as defined by your printer settings.

Margins and Gutters guides reflect the Margins settings in the Layout panel; in fact, dragging these guides in the Print Editor view will move the respective sliders in the Layout panel.

Image Cells shows a black border around each image cell. When the Margins and Gutters guides are not visible, dragging the Image Cells guides in the Print Editor view will change the Margins, Cell Spacing, and Cell Size settings in the Layout panel.

Dimensions displays the measurements of each image cell in its upper-left corner, expressed in whatever units of measurement you have chosen for the Ruler Units.

Using the Rulers, Grid & Guides panel to modify a Picture Package layout

Ruler Units lets you set the units of measurement just as you would in the Layout panel when you're working with a contact sheet/grid template.

Grid Snap helps you to position the image cells accurately on the page in the Print Editor view. As you drag the cells, you can have them snap to each other or to the grid (or turn the snap behavior off) by choosing Cells, Grid, or Off from the Grid Snap menu options. The grid divisions are affected by your choice of ruler units.

Note: If you accidentally overlap your image cells, Lightroom will let you know by showing a warning icon (!) in the upper-right corner of the page.

Page Bleed and **Dimensions** work just as they do in the Guides panel for a Single Image/Contact Sheet layout.

Using the Cells panel to modify a Picture Package layout

Add To Package offers six preset image cell sizes that can be placed in your layout at the click of a button. You can change which of the presets is assigned to each button by clicking its menu triangle. The default presets are standard photo sizes, but you can edit them if you wish.

New Page adds a page to your layout, though Lightroom automatically adds pages if you use the Add To Package buttons to add more photos than fit on a page. To delete a page from your layout, click the X button in the upper-left corner of the page in the Print Editor view.

Auto Layout optimizes the arrangement of the photos on the page for the fewest cuts.

Clear Layout removes all of the image cells from the layout.

Adjust Selected Cell lets you change the height and width of an image cell using the sliders or with a numerical input.

Rearranging the photos in a print layout

Lightroom places your photos in the cells of a multiple-image print layout in the order in which they appear in the Filmstrip (and the Library module Grid view).

If your image source is a collection or a folder without subfolders nested inside it, you can change the placement of your images in the print job by simply dragging their thumbnails to new positions in the Filmstrip. Rearranging photos in this way is not possible if either the All Photographs folder or the Previous Import folder is the selected image source.

Deselect all of the images by clicking one of the other images in the Filmstrip. Once the images are deselected, rearrange the images into a new order, as shown here. With the images reordered, select the first three images in the Filmstrip by Command-clicking/Ctrl-clicking them.

Creating stroke and photo borders

For our Single Image/Contact Sheet layout, the Image Settings panel offers options that affect the way your photos are placed in the image cells, as well as a control for adding a border. In this exercise you'll add a stroke border around each of the three images and adjust the width of the stroke.

1   Expand the Image Settings panel. For the 4 Wide template, the Zoom To Fill option is activated. This means that the photos are cropped in height to fit the proportions of the image cells.

▶ **Tip:** You can change the color of the border by clicking the Stroke Border color swatch and selecting a color from the Color Picker.

2   Select the Stroke Border option, and then drag the Width slider to the right or type **1** in the text box to the right of the slider. For your reference, 1 inch is equivalent to 72 points (pt).

3   In the Layout Style panel, click Picture Package. In the Rulers, Grid & Guides panel, select the Image Cells option to see the borders of the cells. For a Picture Package template, the Image Settings panel offers two controls for borders. An Inner Stroke border is the picture package equivalent of a stroke border. The Photo Border control lets you set the width of a blank frame between the edge of each photo and the boundary of its image cell.

4   Experiment with the Inner Stroke and Photo Border settings.

5   Deselect the Image Cells guides. In the Layout Style panel, click Single Image/Contact Sheet to return to your modified 4 Wide template.

Customizing your identity plate

In the Page panel, you'll find controls for adding an identity plate, crop marks, page numbers, and text information from your photos' metadata to your layout. To begin with, you'll edit the identity plate to suit your layout.

1   Expand the Page panel, and then select the Identity Plate option. The illustration at the right shows a preview of the default Identity Plate on macOS (your macOS or Windows username). Click the triangle in the lower-right corner of the identity plate preview and choose Edit from the menu.

2   In the Identity Plate Editor dialog box, select the Use A Styled Text Identity Plate option. I chose Helvetica Neue, Condensed Bold, and 24 point from the font menus. To change the color of the text, highlight it in the text box to select it, click the color swatch to the right of the font size menu, and choose a new color in

▶ **Tip:** If your text is too long to be fully visible in the text box, either resize the dialog box or reduce the font size until you've finished editing.

Using the Rotate To Fit option

By default, Lightroom will place photos so that they are upright within their image cells. The Rotate To Fit option in the Image Settings panel will override this behavior so that your photos are rotated to match the orientation of the image cells. For presentation layouts you would not want to have images displayed in different orientations on the same page, but in some situations this feature can be very helpful and save on expensive photo paper too! The Rotate To Fit option is particularly useful when you wish to print photos in both portrait and landscape formats on the same sheet, as large as possible and without wasting paper, as shown here.

Another situation where you might choose to use the Rotate To Fit setting is when you are printing contact sheets. As you can see in the next illustration, Rotate To Fit enables you to see all of the photos at the same size regardless of the image orientation.

the Color Picker. Select the text again, if necessary, type **RC CONCEPCION PHOTOGRAPHY** (or a name of your choice), and then click OK.

3   Drag the Scale slider to the right so that the identity plate text is nearly as wide as the image. You can also scale the identity plate by clicking it in the Print Editor view and dragging the handles of its bounding box.

▶ **Tip:** By default, the identity plate will be oriented horizontally. This setting (0°) is indicated at the top right of the Identity Plate area in the Page panel. To reorient your identity plate on the page, click the 0° indicator and choose Rotate Onscreen 90°, 180°, or –90° from the menu. To move your identity plate, simply drag it in the Print Editor view.

4   Select the Override Color option to set the color of the identity plate for this layout only—without affecting the defined color settings for the identity plate.

5   Click the Override Color swatch to open the Color Picker. For the RGB values, type in R: **56%**, G: **7%**, B: **16%**, and then close the Color Picker. The color of the text identity plate is now a deep, slightly desaturated purple.

● **Note:** If you see a hexadecimal value displayed in the lower-right corner of the Color Picker rather than RGB values, click RGB below the color slider.

6   In the Identity Plate pane, use the Opacity slider or type **75** in the text box beside it to set an opacity value of 75% for the identity plate. This feature can be particularly effective if you wish to position your identity plate over an image.

Printing captions and metadata information

In this exercise, you will add a caption and metadata information—in this case, titles for the images—to your print layout using the Page panel and the Text Template Editor.

1 At the bottom of the Page panel, select the Photo Info overlay option, and then choose Edit from the menu at the right. Most of the other options in the Photo Info menu are drawn from the images' existing metadata.

The Text Template Editor enables you to combine custom text with the metadata embedded in your image files and then save your edited template as a new preset, making it easy to add the same items of text information to future print jobs.

▶ **Tip:** You'll find more detailed information on the Text Template Editor in the sidebar "Using the Text Template Editor" in Lesson 9, "Creating a Slideshow."

Descriptions of our lesson photos have been pre-entered in the Caption field of the images' metadata; you'll base your text captions on this metadata.

2 Choose Caption from the Preset menu at the top of the Text Template Editor dialog box.

3 Click to place the insertion cursor before the Caption token in the Example text box. Type **Print Portfolio:** (including the colon), and then add a space between your text and the token.

4 Click to place the cursor after the Caption token in the Example box. Type a space, a hyphen, and another space, and then choose Date (Month) from the second Numbering menu. If the Date (Month) token doesn't appear in the Example box, click the Insert button to the right of the Date menu to add it.

5 Add a space after the Date (Month) token; then choose Date (YYYY) from the second Numbering menu and click the Insert button if necessary. Click Done to close the Text Template Editor dialog box. The images in the Print Editor view are now captioned and dated.

Print Portfolio: Measuring the edge profile of the board - October 2023

6 Click the triangles beside Font Size at the bottom of the Page panel, choose 12 pt from the menu, and then collapse the Page panel.

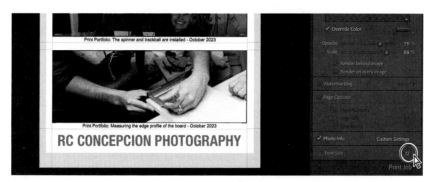

Saving your customized print template

After starting with a preset print template, you've created your own page design by modifying the layout and adding borders, an identity plate, and caption text to the images. You can now save your customized layout for future use.

1 Click the Create New Preset icon (+) in the header of the Template Browser panel, or choose Print > New Template.

2 In the New Template dialog box, type [**Your Name**] **3 Wide Triptych** in the Template Name text box. By default, new templates are saved to the User Templates folder. For this exercise, leave the Folder menu set to the default User Templates as the destination folder and click Create.

3 Your saved template appears in the User Templates folder in the Template Browser panel, where you can access it quickly for use with a new set of images. With your new template selected in the Template Browser, Command-click/ Ctrl-click the lesson05 - 011, lesson07 - 020-Pano, and lesson05 - 002 images in the Filmstrip so you can see how easy it is to create and use your own templates.

Creating a Custom Package print layout

▶ **Tip:** If you'd prefer to work without using a template, start by clicking Custom Package in the Layout Style panel; then click Clear Layout in the Cells panel and drag photos from the Filmstrip directly onto the page preview.

Every Single Image/Contact Sheet template is based on a grid of image cells that are all the same size. If you want a more free-form layout or you prefer to create your own page layout from scratch without using any of the preset templates as a starting point, you can use the Custom Package option in the Layout Style panel.

1 Choose Edit > Select None, or press Command+D/ Ctrl+D on your keyboard. In the Template Browser, select the layout Custom Overlap ×3 Landscape from the list of Lightroom templates.

2 In the Rulers, Grid & Guides panel, select the Show Guides option, if necessary, and then deselect all but the Rulers, Page Bleed and Page Grid guides.

The images in a Custom Package layout can be arranged so that they overlap. The selected template includes three overlapping image cells spread diagonally over a fourth that occupies most of the printable page area.

3   Click to select the central image cell in the layout, and then right-click inside the selected cell. Note the menu options here: the first four commands enable you to move an image forward or backward in the stacking order.

4   For now, choose Delete Cell, leaving you the two corner cells and the large background cell.

5   At the bottom of the Cells panel, select the Lock To Photo Aspect Ratio option. Drag the lesson07 - 031-HDR image from the Filmstrip into the smaller image cell at the upper right and the lesson07 - 020-Pano photo into the larger cell behind it.

6   Click away from the large photo cell to deselect it; then re-select the image and use the controls in the Cells panel to set the Width to 10.19 in. The Height value is adjusted automatically, maintaining the photo's original proportions.

7   In the Cells panel, deselect the Lock To Photo Aspect Ratio option, and then drag the handle at the top of the large cell's bounding box downward to set the height to 3 in (watch the slider in the Cells panel move as you do this). With the Lock To Photo Aspect Ratio option deselected, the image is cropped to fill the altered proportions of its cell.

8   Select the smaller image on the page and set the Width to 5 in and the Height to 4.75 in. Delete the small cell in the lower left, and then hold down the Option/Alt key and drag the square-cropped image to produce a copy. Replace the photo in the copied cell by dragging the lesson07 - 015 image from the Filmstrip.

● **Note:** Depending on your printer, the printable (non-bleed) area may not be centered on the page, as is the case in these illustrations.

9   Drag the three images to arrange them on the page as shown here. Be sure to center the arrangement within the printable area of the page (that is, inside the area defined by the gray border of the Page Bleed guide). To refine the way each image is cropped, hold down the Command/Ctrl key and drag to reposition the photo within the frame of its image cell.

Changing the page background color

▶ **Tip:** To save on printer ink, you may prefer not to print a page with large areas of bold color or black in the background on your home printer, but when you're ordering professional prints, this can be a striking choice.

1   In the Image Settings panel, select the Inner Stroke option. Use the slider or type over the current value to set the width of the stroke to **1.0** pt. Leave the stroke color set to the default white—the white stroke borders will become visible when you set a background color in step 4.

2   In the Rulers, Grid & Guides panel, deselect Show Guides.

3   In the Page panel, select the Page Background Color option. Click the color swatch to the right to open the Color Picker.

4   In the Page Background Color Picker, click the black swatch at the top to sample it with the eyedropper, and then click the Close button (×) to close it.

The new color appears in the Page Background Color color swatch and in the page preview in the Print Editor view. If you need to make further edits to make sure the images fit on the page, now is a good time to do so.

Configuring the output settings

The final step before you're ready to print your layout is to adjust the output settings in the Print Job panel.

1 Expand the Print Job panel in the right panel group. From the Print To menu at the top of the Print Job panel, you can choose to send the job directly to your printer or generate a JPEG file, which you can print later or send out for professional printing. The controls in the Print Job panel vary slightly depending on which of these options is selected.

2 Choose Printer from the Print To menu at the top of the Print Job panel.

Selecting the Draft Mode Printing option disables the other options in the Print Job panel. Draft Mode Printing results in high-speed output at a relatively low quality, which is an efficient option for printing contact sheets or for assessing your layout before you commit it to high-quality photo paper. The 4 × 5 Contact Sheet and the 5 × 8 Contact Sheet templates are preset for Draft Mode Printing.

▶ Tip: The terms *print resolution* and *printer resolution* have different meanings. *Print resolution* refers to the number of printed pixels per inch (ppi); *printer resolution* refers to the capability of the printer, called dots per inch (dpi). A printed pixel of a particular color is created by patterns of tiny dots of the few ink colors available.

Soft proofing photos before printing

Each type of monitor and printer operates within its own *color gamut* or *color space*, which defines the range of colors that can be reproduced accurately by that device. By default, Lightroom uses your monitor's *color profile*—a mathematical description of its color space—to make your photos look as good as possible onscreen. When you print an image, the image data must be reinterpreted for the printer's color space, which can sometimes result in unexpected shifts in color and tone.

You can avoid these surprises by soft proofing your photos in the Develop module before you bring them into the Print module. Soft proofing lets you preview how your photos will look when they're printed; you can have Lightroom simulate the color space of your printer, and even the inks and paper you're using, giving you the opportunity to optimize your photos before printing them.

To activate soft proofing, open a photo in the Develop module and select the Soft Proofing option in the Toolbar, or press the S key on your keyboard. The background surrounding the image changes to white "paper," and a Proof Preview label appears in the corner of the work area. Use the view button in the Toolbar to switch between the Loupe view and a choice of before and after views.

When you activate soft proofing, the Histogram panel changes to the Soft Proofing panel, which provides access to proofing options. The tonal distribution graph is updated according to the currently selected color profile. In the illustration at the right, the graph in the Histogram panel corresponds to the Current image in the illustration above. The graph in the Soft Proofing panel reflects the comparative flatness of the Proof Preview.

To soft proof your photo for a different printer, choose another color profile from the Profile menu in the Soft Proofing panel. If you don't see the profile you want in the menu, choose Other, and then select from the list of installed color profiles in the Choose Profiles dialog box.

The Intent setting determines the rendering intent, which affects how colors are converted from one color space to another. The Perceptual rendering intent aims to preserve the visual relationship between colors so they look natural, though the color values may change. Relative rendering prints in-gamut colors as they are and shifts out-of-gamut colors to the closest printable approximations, retaining more of the original colors, though the relationships between some of them may be altered.

Once you've chosen a printer profile, you can activate the Simulate Paper & Ink option to simulate the off-white of real paper and the dark gray of real black ink. This option is not available for all profiles.

To check whether your colors are in-gamut for the selected profile and rendering intent, use the buttons in the upper corners of the histogram in the Soft Proofing panel. Move the pointer over the Show/Hide Monitor Gamut Warning icon on the left; colors that are outside your display's capabilities turn blue in the Proof Preview. Move the pointer over the Show/Hide Destination Gamut Warning icon on the right; colors that cannot be rendered by your printer turn red in the preview. Colors that are out-of-gamut for both the monitor and the printer turn pink. Click the icons to show the gamut warning colors permanently; click again to hide them.

Click Create Proof Copy to generate a virtual copy that you can adjust without affecting your master settings. If you start adjusting a photo while soft proofing is on without first creating a proof copy, Lightroom asks if you want to create a virtual copy for soft proofing or make the master image a proof.

Working with16-bit output on macOS

If you are running macOS and are using a 16-bit printer, you can activate the 16 Bit Output setting in the Print Job panel. This will result in less image degradation and fewer color artifacts in files that have been extensively edited.

Note: If you select 16 Bit Output and print to a printer that does not support it, print performance is slowed, but quality is not affected.

For detailed information on working with 16-bit output, consult the documentation for your printer or check with the people doing your printing.

The Print Resolution setting that is appropriate for your print job depends on the intended print size, the resolution of your image files, the capabilities of your printer, and the quality of your paper stock. The default print resolution is 240 ppi, which generally produces good results. As a rule of thumb, use a higher resolution for smaller, high-quality prints (around 360 ppi for letter size). You can use a lower resolution setting for larger prints (around 180 ppi for 16" × 20") without compromising too much on quality.

3 The Print Resolution control has a range of 72 ppi to 1440 ppi. For this exercise, type **200** in the Print Resolution text box.

▶ **Tip:** The purpose of the Sharpening feature in the Develop module is to compensate for blurriness in the original photo, while Print Sharpening improves the crispness of printed output on a particular paper type.

Images tend to look less sharp on paper than they do onscreen. The Print Sharpening options can help to compensate for this by increasing the crispness of your printed output. You can choose between Low, Standard, and High Print Sharpening settings, and then specify a Matte or Glossy Media Type. You won't notice the effects of these settings onscreen, so it's useful to experiment by printing at different settings to familiarize yourself with the results.

4 If it's not already selected, choose Low from the Print Sharpening menu.

Using color management

Printing your digital images can be challenging: what you see onscreen is not always what you get on paper. Lightroom Classic can handle a very large color space, but your printer may operate within a more limited gamut.

In the Print Job panel, you can choose whether to have Lightroom handle color management or leave it up to your printer.

Hardware suggestions: Calibrite

If you have ever walked into a big-box store and stared at a wall of large televisions, you can immediately see the problem of color accuracy. Different monitors can display the exact same image but reproduce its color completely differently. The problem is further compounded when you don't know which one of these monitors is the one that is displaying the color that is most faithful to the original creator's intent.

Another problem is that you want to print an image and have its color be as faithful to the original as the color that you see onscreen. Again, different monitors will yield completely different results.

As I see it, the greatest amount of time I spend with my pictures is on my monitor, so I want to make sure I'm looking at them as accurately as possible. That's why I recommend investing in a good hardware calibrator, like ColorChecker Display from Calibrite.

A calibrator hangs over your monitor and reads the color output from it while comparing that to a set of prebuilt colors the calibrator understands. Then, it creates a specific monitor profile and adjusts the colors as best it can for your specific monitor type.

While I'd love to print every image I fall in love with, I don't have the space (or cash) to do that. I'll just create a slideshow on a well-calibrated monitor and experience all of the work as it was meant to be.

Color managed by your printer

The default Color Management setting in the Print Job panel is Managed By Printer. This can be the easiest option, given the continuing improvement of printing technology, but it will produce only satisfactory results. Click the Printer button at the lower right to open the Print/Printer Properties dialog box and specify the paper type, color handling, and other print settings there. On Windows, click Properties in the Print dialog box to access additional printer-specific settings.

Color management controlled by Lightroom

Letting your printer manage color may be acceptable for general printing purposes, but to achieve high-quality results, it's best to have Lightroom do it. If you choose this option, you can specify a printing profile tailored to a particular type of paper or custom inks.

1 In the Print Job panel, choose Other from the Color Management Profile menu.

You can choose this option when the profile you want isn't listed in the Profile menu. Lightroom searches your computer for custom printer profiles, which may be installed by the software that came with your printer or by you, if you downloaded the profile for the specific paper you are using.

2 Depending on your printer and paper stock, choose one or more printer profiles. In this illustration, three profiles for the Canon Pro 1000 using different papers have been selected. Each profile you choose will be added to the Profile menu under Color Management in the Print Job panel for easy access the next time you print.

Once you've chosen a printer profile from the Profile menu, the Rendering Intent options become available in the Print Job panel. The color space of an image is usually much larger than that within which most printers operate, which means that your printer may not be able to accurately reproduce the colors you see onscreen. This may result in printing artifacts such as posterization or banding in color gradients as the printer attempts to deal with out-of-gamut colors. The Rendering Intent options help to minimize these problems. You can choose between two settings:

- **Perceptual** rendering aims to preserve the visual relationship between colors. The entire range of colors in the image will be remapped to fit within the color gamut your printer is able to reproduce. In this way, the relationships between all of the colors are preserved, but in the process, even colors that were already in-gamut may be shifted as the out-of-gamut colors are moved into the printable range. This may mean that your printed image will be less vivid than it appeared onscreen.

- **Relative** rendering prints all of the in-gamut colors as they are and shifts out-of-gamut colors to the closest printable colors. Using this option means that more of the original color of the image is retained, but some of the relationships between colors may be altered.

In most cases, the differences between the two rendering methods are quite subtle. As a general rule, perceptual rendering is the best option for an image with many out-of-gamut colors, and relative rendering works better for an image with only a few. However, unless you are very experienced, it may be hard to tell which is which. The best policy is to do some testing with your printer. Print a very colorful, vivid photo at both settings and then do the same with a more muted image.

3 For the purposes of this exercise, choose Relative.

Tweaking printed color manually

Printed results don't always match the bright and saturated look of the colors you see onscreen in Lightroom Classic—even when you've spent time setting up the color management for your print job.

The problem may be related to your printer, the inks or paper stock you're using, or an incorrectly calibrated monitor. Whatever the cause, you can make quick and easy adjustments with the Brightness and Contrast sliders in the Color Management area of the Print Job panel.

Your Print Adjustment settings are specific to the combination of printer, paper, and ink that you're using. They'll stay in place as long as you're working with the same output settings, and they'll be saved in the Lightroom catalog file with your custom template or saved print job.

▶ **Tip:** Make sure you download the accompanying videos for this lesson, where you'll learn about a few more advanced options, including how to install an ICC profile for a specific paper type and how to use it to make a print. See the "Getting Started" section at the beginning of this book for how to access them.

▶ **Tip:** The tone curve adjustments produced by the Print Adjustment sliders do not appear in the onscreen preview. You may need to experiment a little to find the settings that work best for your printer.

Saving print settings as an output collection

Since you entered the Print module, you've been working with an unsaved print, as indicated in the bar across the top of the Print Editor view.

> Unsaved Print   Create Saved Print

Until you save your print job, the Print module works like a scratch pad. You can move to another module or close Lightroom Classic and find your settings unchanged when you return, but if you select a new layout template, or even the one you started with in the Template Browser, the "scratch pad" will be cleared and all of your work will be lost.

Converting your print job to a saved print not only preserves your layout and output settings, but also links your layout to the particular set of images for which it was designed. Your print job is saved as a special kind of collection—an output collection—with its own listing in the Collections panel. Clicking this listing instantly retrieves the images you were working with and reinstates all of your settings, no matter how many times the print layout scratch pad has been cleared.

Tip: Once you've saved your print job, any changes you make to the layout or output settings are auto-saved as you work.

1 Click the Create Saved Print button in the bar at the top of the Print Editor view, or click the plus sign (+) icon in the header of the Collections panel and choose Create Print.

2 In the Create Print dialog box, type **Print Portfolio** in the Name box to name your saved print job. Make sure that the Inside option is selected and its menu is set to your Images To Print collection; then click Create.

Tip: To add more photos to a saved print job, drag images to the print output collection in the Collections panel.

Your saved print output collection appears in the Collections panel, marked with a Saved Print icon to differentiate it from an image collection, which has a stacked photos icon. The image count shows that the new output collection contains three photos. The title bar above the Print Editor now displays the name of your saved print job and no longer presents the Create Saved Print button.

You can save your print job at any point in your workflow—you could create a saved print as soon as you enter the Print module with a selection of images or wait until your layout is polished.

A print output collection is different from a normal photo collection. A photo collection is a grouping of images to which you can apply any template or output settings you wish. An output collection links a photo collection (or a selection of images from that collection) to a particular template and specific output settings.

For the sake of clarity: an output collection also differs from a custom template. A template includes all of your settings, but no images; you can apply the template to any selection of images. An output collection links the template and all its settings to a particular selection of images.

Printing your job

To achieve the best results when you print, calibrate and profile your monitor regularly, always verify that print settings are specified correctly, and use quality papers. However, there is no substitute for experience. Experiment with a variety of settings and options—and if at first you do succeed, consider yourself very lucky! To send your print job to the printer:

1   Click the Printer button at the bottom of the right panel group.

2   Verify the settings in the Print dialog box and click Print/OK to print your page, or click Cancel to close the Print dialog box without printing.

Clicking the Print button (at the bottom of the right panel group) instead will send your print job to the printer queue without opening the Print dialog box. This is useful if you print repeatedly using the same settings and don't need to confirm or change any settings in the Print dialog.

Congratulations! You've completed another Lightroom Classic lesson. In this lesson you learned how to set up your own sophisticated print layouts.

In the process, you've explored the Print module and used the control panels to customize a print template, refining the layout and output settings and adding a background color, text, borders, and an identity plate to your printed page.

In the next lesson, you'll look at ways to back up and export your Lightroom catalog and images. Before you move on, take a few moments to refresh your new skills by reading through the review questions and answers on the following pages.

> **Tip:** If you don't need to verify your printer settings, click the Print button at the bottom of the right panel group or choose File > Print.

Review questions

1 How can you quickly preview the preset print templates, and how can you see how your photos will look in each layout?

2 What are the three print template layout styles, and how can you check which type of template you have chosen?

3 How do you add custom text or metadata to your print layout?

4 For what purposes is Draft Mode Printing appropriate?

5 What is the difference between a saved print collection, a photo collection, and a saved custom print template?

6 What is soft proofing?

Review answers

1 Move the pointer over the list of templates in the Template Browser to see a thumbnail preview of each layout displayed in the Preview panel. Select your images in the Filmstrip and choose a template from the list; the Print Editor view shows how your photos look in the new layout.

2 Single Image/Contact Sheet layouts can be used to print multiple photos at the same size on a single sheet. They range from contact sheets with many cells to single-cell layouts. Picture Package layouts repeat a single image at a variety of sizes on the same page in cells that can be moved and resized. Custom Package layouts are not based on a grid; they enable you to print multiple images at any size on the same page, and even to arrange them so that they overlap.

   The Layout Style panel indicates whether a layout selected in the Template Browser is a Custom Package, Picture Package, or Single Image/Contact Sheet template.

3 Text can be added to any layout using a styled text identity plate. Custom text or metadata can be added to a Single Image/Contact Sheet layout using the Photo Info option in the Page panel. Choose from a menu of metadata options, or choose Edit to open the Text Template Editor for more options.

4 Draft Mode Printing results in high-speed output at a relatively low quality, which is an efficient option for printing contact sheets or for assessing your layout before you commit it to high-quality photo paper. The contact sheet templates are preset for Draft Mode Printing.

5 A photo collection is a virtual grouping of images to which you can apply any template or output settings you wish, whereas a Saved Print output collection links a selection of images to a particular template and specific layout and output settings. A saved print template preserves your customized layout and output settings but includes no images; you can apply the template to any selection of images.

6 Soft proofing is a way to check onscreen how your photos will look when printed or output for use on the web. Lightroom Classic uses color profiles to simulate the result of printing to specific printers with particular types of ink and paper—or of saving your images to a different color space as you might do with pictures intended for the internet—enabling you to make the appropriate adjustments to your photos before exporting copies or committing to printing.

11 MAKING BACKUPS AND EXPORTING PHOTOS

Lesson overview

Lightroom Classic makes it easy to back up and export all of the images and data connected with your library, streamlining your workflow and minimizing the impact of accidental data loss. You can create backup copies of your photos on external storage during import, make full or incremental backups of your photos and develop settings or have Lightroom back up automatically, and export files in a range of formats, from images optimized for onscreen viewing to archival copies. In this lesson, you'll learn how to:

- Back up the catalog file and your entire image library.

- Make incremental backups and export metadata.

- Export photos for onscreen viewing or archival purposes.

- Export photos to be edited in another application.

- Use export presets.

- Set up automated post-export actions.

 This lesson will take about 90 minutes to complete. To get the lesson files used in this chapter, download them from the web page for this book at *peachpit.com/LightroomCIB2024*. For more information, see "Accessing the lesson files and Web Edition" in the "Getting Started" section at the beginning of this book.

Safeguard your photographs and develop settings against loss using Lightroom Classic's built-in backup tools. Back up just your catalog file or your entire photo library, complete with develop settings and copies of your master files. Export photos in different file formats for multimedia presentations or email attachments, for further editing in an external editor, or to be stored for archival purposes.

Getting started

Before you begin, make sure you've set up the LRC2024CIB folder for your lesson files and created the LRC2024CIB Catalog file to manage them, as described in "Accessing the lesson files and Web Edition" and "Creating a catalog file for working with this book" in the "Getting Started" section at the start of this book.

If you haven't already done so, download the lesson11 folder from your Account page at *peachpit.com* to the LRC2024CIB\Lessons folder, as detailed in "Accessing the lesson files and Web Edition" in the "Getting Started" section.

1 Start Lightroom Classic.

2 In the Select Catalog dialog box, make sure the file LRC2024CIB Catalog.lrcat is selected under Select A Recent Catalog To Open, and then click Open.

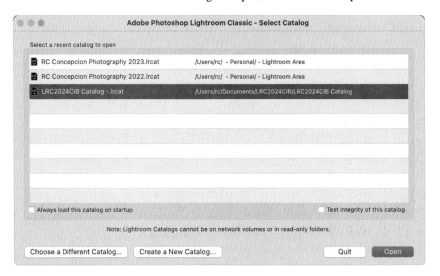

● **Note:** If you can't see the Module Picker, choose Window > Panels > Show Module Picker, or press the F5 key. If you're working on macOS, you may need to press the fn key together with the F5 key, or change the function key behavior in the system preferences.

3 Lightroom Classic will open in the screen mode and workspace module that were active when you last quit. If necessary, switch to the Library module by clicking Library in the Module Picker at the top of the workspace.

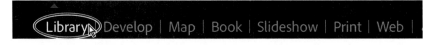

Importing images into the library

The first step is to import the images for this lesson into the Lightroom library.

1 In the Library module, click the Import button below the left panel group.

2 If the Import dialog box appears in compact mode, click the Show More Options button at the lower left of the dialog box to see all of the options in the expanded Import dialog box.

3 Under Source at the left of the expanded Import dialog box, locate and select your LRC2024CIB\Lessons\lesson11 folder. Ensure that all 11 images in the lesson11 folder are selected (checked) for import.

4 In the import options above the thumbnail previews, select Add so that the imported photos will be added to your catalog without being moved or copied. Under File Handling at the right, choose Embedded & Sidecar from the Build Previews menu and leave the Don't Import Suspected Duplicates option selected. Type **Lesson 11** in the Keywords text box. Make sure that your import is set up as shown here, and then click Import.

5 The 11 images are imported from the lesson11 folder and now appear in both the Library module's Grid view and in the Filmstrip across the bottom of the Lightroom Classic workspace. Create a collection called Lesson 11 and place the images in it.

Preventing data loss

The importance of a good backup strategy is often only understood too late. How much damage would be done if your computer were stolen right now? How many files would be irrecoverably lost if your hard disk failed today? How much work and money would that cost you? You can't prevent a disaster from happening, but it *is* in your power to reduce the risks and the cost of recovery. Backing up regularly will reduce the impact of a catastrophe and save you time, effort, and money.

Lightroom Classic delivers a range of options that make it easy to safeguard your photo library; as for the rest of the files on your computer, you really should have your own backup strategy in place.

Backing up the catalog file

The Lightroom catalog file stores a great deal of information for the photos in your library—not only the locations of the image files, but the metadata attached to them, including titles, captions, keyword tags, flags, labels, and ratings, together with all of your developing and output settings. Every time you modify a photo in any way—from renaming the file during import to color correction, retouching, and cropping—all of your work is saved to the catalog file. It records the way your images are grouped and ordered in collections, as well as the publishing history, slideshow settings, web gallery designs, and print layouts associated with them, in addition to your customized templates and presets.

Unless you back up your catalog, you could lose hundreds of hours of work in the event of a hard disk failure, an accidental deletion, or a corrupted library file, even if you do have copies of your original images stored safely on removable media. You can set up Lightroom to initiate a regular backup of your catalog file automatically.

1   Choose Catalog Settings from the Lightroom Classic/Edit menu. On the General tab, choose When Lightroom Next Exits from the Back Up Catalog menu.

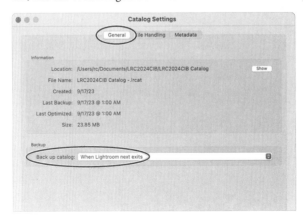

2 Click the Close button/OK to close the Catalog Settings dialog box, and then quit Lightroom Classic. If you get a dialog box asking if you really want to quit Lightroom, click Yes.

3 In the Back Up Catalog dialog box, click the Choose button to change the folder where the backed-up catalog will be stored. Ideally, the backup should be located on a different disk than your original catalog file; for the purpose of this exercise, in the Browse For Folder/Choose Folder dialog box, select your LRC2024CIB folder as the backup directory and click Choose/Select Folder.

4 Make sure the Test Integrity Before Backing Up and Optimize Catalog After Backing Up options are selected. It's a good idea to keep these options selected whenever you back up your catalog; it would defy the purpose of a backup if your original catalog file was not in good working order. Click Back Up.

Each time you back up your catalog, Lightroom Classic will create a complete copy of the catalog file in the directory you specified, inside a new folder with a name composed from the date and time of the backup. To save space on your backup drive, you can either delete your older backup files or compress them. Catalog files compress very effectively; you can expect a compressed catalog to be as small as 10% of the original size. Make sure to decompress the file before attempting to restore your catalog from the backup.

Should your catalog be accidentally deleted or become corrupted, you can now restore it either by copying the backup file to your catalog folder or by creating a new catalog and importing the contents of your backup file. To avoid inadvertently modifying your backup file, it's preferable not to open it directly from the Lightroom Classic File menu.

● **Note:** Backing up the catalog file in this way does not make backup copies of the original image files or the preview images that Lightroom Classic displays in the workspace. The previews will be regenerated as your catalog file is restored from the backup, but you'll need to back up your original image files separately.

5 Start Lightroom Classic. In the Adobe Photoshop Lightroom - Select Catalog dialog box, make sure that the file LRC2024CIB Catalog.lrcat is selected under Select A Recent Catalog To Open, and then click Open.

6 Choose Lightroom Classic > Catalog Settings/Edit > Catalog Settings.

7 In the Catalog Settings dialog box, click the General tab and set your preferred backup frequency by choosing it from the Back Up Catalog menu.

8 Click the Close button/OK to close the Catalog Settings dialog box.

Exporting metadata

The catalog is a central storage location for all of the information associated with every image in your library; exporting and distributing the catalog file's content is another strategy that will lessen the impact if your catalog file is lost or damaged. By saving the information from the catalog file that is specific to each photo to the respective image file on your hard disk—and keeping this exported information in sync with your catalog file, which can be done automatically—you have, in effect, a distributed backup of the metadata and develop settings for each of your photos.

When a photo has changes to its metadata that have not yet been saved to the original image file—such as the Lesson 11 keyword tag you applied to the images for this lesson during the import process—its image cell in the Library module's Grid view and the Filmstrip is marked with the Metadata File Needs To Be Updated icon.

1 If you don't see the Metadata File Needs To Be Updated icon in the Grid view image cells, choose View > View Options. On the Grid View tab in the Library View Options dialog box, select the Unsaved Metadata option under Cell Icons. Click the Close button to close the Library View Options dialog box.

2 Select the first image in the Grid view. Right-click the thumbnail and choose Metadata > Save Metadata To File from the menu. Click Continue to confirm the operation; after a brief processing time, the Metadata File Needs To Be Updated icon disappears from the thumbnail cell.

3 Command-click/Ctrl-click to select the next four photos, and then click the Metadata File Needs To Be Updated icon in the image cell of any of the selected images. Click Save to update the image files on your hard disk.

After a brief processing time, the Metadata File Needs To Be Updated badge disappears from each of the image cells.

If you edit or add to an image's metadata in another application, such as Adobe Bridge or the Photoshop Camera Raw plug-in, Lightroom Classic will show the Metadata Was Changed Externally icon above the thumbnail in the Grid view. To accept the changes and update your catalog file accordingly, choose Metadata > Read Metadata From Files. To reject the changed metadata and overwrite it with the information in your catalog file, choose Metadata > Save Metadata To Files.

You can update the metadata for a batch of modified images—or even for the entire catalog with all its folders and collections—by selecting the images or folders to be updated and choosing Metadata > Save Metadata To Files, as you did in step 2.

You can use the Metadata Status filter in the Filter bar to quickly find those photos in your library with changes made externally to the master files on disk, any image with a metadata conflict (with unsaved changes made by both Lightroom and another application since the file's metadata was last updated) those with unsaved changes made in Lightroom, or images with metadata that is up to date.

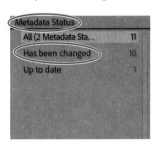

For DNG, JPEG, TIFF, and PSD file formats—which have defined spaces within the file structure where XMP information can be stored separately from the image data—Lightroom writes metadata into the image file itself. In contrast, changes made to camera raw images are written into a separate XMP sidecar file that records the metadata and develop settings exported to the image from Lightroom.

Many camera manufacturers use proprietary and undocumented formats for their raw files, some of which become outdated as new ones appear. Because of this, storing the metadata in a separate file is the safest approach, avoiding the possibility of corruption in the raw file or loss of the metadata exported from Lightroom.

4   From the Lightroom Classic/Edit menu, choose Catalog Settings. On the Metadata tab select Automatically Write Changes Into XMP so that metadata is exported automatically whenever a raw image is modified; the sidecar file will always be up to date with your catalog. Click the Close button/OK.

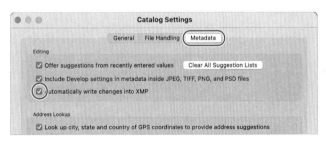

Note that XMP information exported in this way contains only the metadata specific to the individual images: keywords, flags, labels, ratings, and develop settings. It does not include higher-level data relevant to the catalog as a whole, such as information relating to stacks, virtual copies, and settings used in presentations.

Backing up the library

In the first exercise, you backed up your catalog file without any images. In the second exercise, you updated your image files with metadata and develop information from the library catalog. This time, you'll export your entire Lightroom Classic library: images, catalog, stacks, collections—the works!

Exporting images as a catalog

When you export your photos as a catalog, Lightroom creates a copy of the catalog file and gives you the option to make copies of the master files and the image previews at the same time. You can choose to export the entire library, or just a selection of your images, as a catalog. Exporting images in this way is ideal for moving your photos together with all of the associated Lightroom catalog information from one computer to another. You can use the same technique to restore your entire library from a backup after a data loss.

1 In the Catalog panel, click All Photographs; then choose File > Export As Catalog.

   Ideally, you should save your backup files to a hard disk other than the one that stores your catalog and the master image files, but for this exercise, you can save the backup files to your desktop.

2 Type **Backup** in the Save As/File Name text box and navigate to your Desktop folder. Make sure the Build/Include Smart Previews and Export Selected Photos Only (if you selected photos first) options are unselected and that Export Negative Files and Include Available Previews are selected. Click Export Catalog/Save.

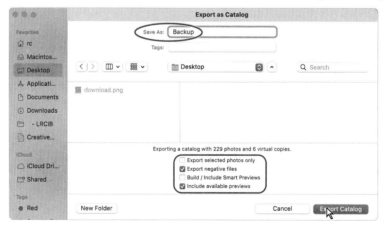

   A progress bar is displayed at the upper left as the new catalog is being created; for such a small catalog, backing up should take only a few seconds. Lightroom copies the image files associated with the catalog to their new location as a background task.

3 When the export process is complete, switch to Finder/Windows Explorer and navigate to your desktop. Open the new Backup folder.

 Note: You may see a different set of folders than is shown in the illustration, depending on which lessons you've already completed.

You can see that the folder structure nested inside the Backup folder replicates the arrangement of folders you see in the Folders panel. All of the master images in your Lightroom Classic library have been copied into these new folders, and the file Backup.lrcat is a fully functional copy of your original catalog.

4 In Lightroom Classic, choose File > Open Catalog. In the Open/Open Catalog dialog box, navigate to the new Backup folder inside your Desktop folder. Select the file Backup.lrcat, and then click Open. If the Open Catalog dialog box appears, click Relaunch. Lightroom will open the backup catalog.

5 Other than the filename in the title bar of the workspace, this catalog will be almost indistinguishable from your original work catalog. Only some temporary status information has been lost; for example, in the Catalog panel you can see that the Previous Import folder is now empty, as is the listing for All Synced Photographs. You can sync only one catalog from Lightroom Classic, so any synced collections in your work catalog will not be marked as synced here.

6 Some of your preferences have been reset to defaults that may differ from the choices you've made for your LRC2024CIB catalog. From the Lightroom Classic/Edit menu, choose Catalog Settings. Click the General tab in the Catalog Settings dialog box. You can see that the backup frequency has been reset to the default. Click the Close button/Cancel to close the Catalog Settings dialog box.

7 Choose File > Open Recent > LRC2024CIB Catalog.lrcat. In the Open Catalog dialog box, click Relaunch. If the Back Up Catalog dialog box appears, click Skip This Time.

Exporting photos

The backup techniques that we've discussed so far all produce backup files that can be read only by Lightroom or another application that is capable of reading and interpreting the exported XMP metadata. If you want to send your work to somebody who doesn't have Lightroom installed on their computer, you'll first need to convert the images to an appropriate file format. This is comparable to saving a Word document as plain text or as a PDF document for distribution; some of the functionality is lost, but at least the recipient can see what you're working on. Your choice of file format will depend on the purpose for which the images are intended.

- To export a photo for use as an email attachment intended to be viewed onscreen, use the JPEG file format and minimize the file size by reducing the resolution and dimensions of the image.

- To export an image to be edited in another application, convert the photo to either the PSD or TIFF file format at full size.

- For archival purposes, export the images in their original file format or convert them to DNG.

Exporting JPEG files for onscreen viewing

For this exercise, you'll use a saved preset to edit the lesson images before you export them so that you'll be able to see at a glance that your develop settings have been applied to the exported copies.

1 Select the Lesson 11 collection in the Collections panel, and choose Edit > Select All. From the Saved Preset menu at the top of the Quick Develop panel, choose User Presets > Arcade Weekend.

2 With all 11 images still selected in the Grid view, choose File > Export from the main menu. You can also right-click any of the images and select Export > Export, or click the Export button at the lower left.

3 Under Export Location in the Export dialog box, choose Specific Folder from the Export To menu, and then click the Choose button to specify a destination folder (see illustration after step 4). Navigate to your desktop and click Choose/Select Folder.

● **Note:** If you are asked whether Lightroom should overwrite the information embedded in the image files, click Overwrite Settings.

4 Select the Put In Subfolder option and type **export** as the name for the new subfolder. Deselect the Add To This Catalog option.

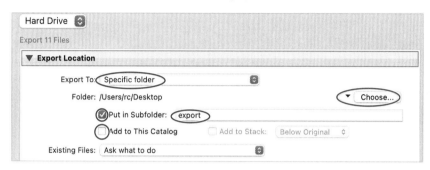

5 Under File Naming in the Export dialog box, select the Rename To option, and then choose Date - Filename from the menu.

6 Scroll down in the Export dialog box, if necessary, so that you can see the File Settings, choose JPEG from the Image Format menu, and set a Quality value of around 70% to 80%—a range that generally makes an acceptable compromise between image quality and file size. Choose sRGB from the Color Space menu. The sRGB color space is a good choice for images intended to be viewed on the web or in circumstances in which you are unsure what form of color management is used, if any at all.

7 In the Image Sizing controls, select the Resize To Fit option and choose Width & Height from the menu. Enter **1,500** for both width (W) and height (H) and choose Pixels from the units menu. This will proportionally scale each image so that its longest side is 1,500 pixels. Our lesson images are all larger than this, so you won't need to select Don't Enlarge to avoid smaller images being upsampled. Set Resolution to 72 Pixels Per Inch, although resolution settings are generally ignored for onscreen display. The reduction in file size is the result of reducing the total number of pixels that make up the image.

8 In the Output Sharpening settings, select the Sharpen For option, choose Screen, and set the Amount to Standard. Under Metadata, choose the Copyright Only option. Note the other options available under Metadata; even with the All metadata option selected, you can still protect your privacy by removing GPS location information. Deselect Watermark. Choose Show In Finder/Show In Explorer from the After Export menu under Post-Processing.

Note: To have Lightroom notify you by playing a sound when the export process is complete, choose a sound from the menu under Completion Sounds on the General tab in the Preferences dialog box.

9 Click Export, and then watch the progress bar on the left side of the top panel in the workspace. When the export process is complete, your Export folder on the desktop will open in macOS Finder/Windows Explorer.

Using export plug-ins

You can use third-party Lightroom plug-ins to extend almost any aspect of Lightroom Classic's functionality, including the export options.

There are export plug-ins that enable you to use the Lightroom export interface to send images to particular online photo sharing sites and social networking sites, or even other applications. For example, a Gmail plug-in enables you to create an instant Gmail message and attach your photos as they are exported.

Other plug-ins add search criteria to the Filter bar, enable you to automate and compress backups, help you to create photo-collages or design and upload web galleries, give you access to professional effects and filters, or let you work with Photoshop-style layers in the Develop module.

Click the Plug-In Manager button in the lower-left corner of the Export dialog box, and then click Adobe Add-Ons to browse online. There, you'll find plug-ins from third-party developers offering additional functionality or helping you to automate tasks, customize workflows, and create stylish effects.

You can search the available Lightroom plug-ins by category, browsing for camera raw profiles, develop presets, export plug-ins, and even web gallery templates.

10 In Windows Explorer, show the Preview Pane or click Slideshow View to see a preview of the images in the folder. In the macOS Finder, select an image in Column view or in Gallery View to see its preview. You can see that the Arcade Weekend preset was applied to these copies of the lesson photos before the export process. The copies are 1,500 pixels wide and have much reduced file sizes.

11 Delete the images from the Export folder. In Lightroom, with the 11 images still selected, choose Edit > Undo Preset: Arcade Weekend to revert to the originals.

Exporting as PSD or TIFF for further editing

Now let's see how to export an image we'll open in an external editor.

1 In the Grid view, choose Edit > Select None, and then double-click the lesson11 - 0008 image. At the top of the Quick Develop panel, in the right panel group, choose Creative > Desaturated Contrast from the Saved Preset menu.

2 Choose File > Export. In the Export dialog box, notice that all of your settings from the previous exercise are still in place. Deselect the Rename To option.

3 In File Settings, choose TIFF from the Image Format menu. When saving in TIFF format, you have the option to apply ZIP data compression—a lossless

▶ **Tip:** To export more images using the same settings that you used for the previous export (and without opening the Export dialog box) choose File > Export With Previous.

form of compression—to reduce the resulting file size. From the Color Space menu, choose AdobeRGB (1998).

▶ **Tip:** Lightroom can automatically export an image in the appropriate file format, open it in the external editor, and add the converted file to the Lightroom library. To do so, choose your preferred external editor, file format, color space, bit depth, compression settings, and file naming options on the External Editing tab of the Preferences dialog box. Then, in the Lightroom Classic workspace, choose Photo > Edit In, and then choose your preferred external image editing application from the menu.

When you intend to edit an image in an external application after exporting it, you should use the AdobeRGB (1998) color profile rather than the sRGB color profile. The AdobeRGB (1998) color profile has a larger color gamut, which results in fewer colors being clipped and the original appearance of your images being better preserved. The ProPhoto RGB color gamut is even larger, capable of representing any color from the original raw image. However, to correctly display images using the AdobeRGB (1998) or ProPhoto RGB color profiles onscreen, you need an image editing application capable of reading these color profiles. You'll also need to turn color management on and calibrate your computer display. Without taking these measures, your images will look bad onscreen with the AdobeRGB (1998) color profile—and even worse with ProPhoto RGB.

4 Change the image format to PSD. Choose 8 Bits/Component from the Bit Depth menu. Unless you have a particular need to output 16-bit files as part of your workflow, 8-bit files are smaller and compatible with more programs and plug-ins but do not preserve fine tonal detail as well as 16-bit files. Lightroom actually operates in a 16-bit color space, but by the time you're ready to export images, you've usually already made any important corrections or adjustments that were necessary, so you won't lose much in terms of editing capability by converting the files to 8-bit for export. Still, we'll set it to 16 bits here.

5 In Image Sizing, deselect Resize To Fit and set the Resolution to 240 pixels per inch. That will give us plenty of resolution we need for further editing and allow us to print at a large size.

6 Leave the Output Sharpening and Metadata settings unchanged. If you have Adobe Photoshop installed on your computer, choose that application from the After Export menu in the Post-Processing options. Alternatively, choose Open In Other Application, and then click Choose to select your preferred image editor. Click Export.

7 Wait until the export is complete and the photo has opened in the external editor. The image has been exported with the Creative preset Desaturated Contrast that you applied in the Quick Develop panel. Its dimensions are still more than 34" × 22".

8 Quit the external editor, delete the file from the Export folder in the macOS Finder/Windows Explorer window, and then return to Lightroom Classic.

Exporting as original or DNG for archiving

If you want to export a raw file for archiving or convert it to a DNG, do the following:

1 Navigate to the Lesson 01 - Aguada collection in the Collections panel and select lesson01-0003.

2 Choose File > Export. In the Export dialog box, under Export Location, deselect Put In Subfolder and choose to export the image to the desktop.

3 To export a raw file, in File Settings, choose Original from the Image Format menu. Note that there are now no other File Settings, Image Sizing, or Output Sharpening options available; Lightroom exports the original image data unaltered. To embed the sidecar information in the file, choose DNG instead.

> **Note:** When you choose to export images in DNG file format, you have additional options that affect the way the DNG files are created, but the original image data remains essentially unchanged.

4   In the Post-Processing options, choose Show In Finder/Show In Explorer from the After Export menu; then click Export.

5   When your raw file has been exported, the folder opens in Finder/Windows Explorer. In the Finder/Windows Explorer window, note that an XMP sidecar file has been saved together with the copy of the raw image file, which was originally provided *without* an XMP file. The XMP file records changes to the image's metadata (the keywords you added at import) as well as its detailed editing history (any develop adjustments you made).

6   In Finder/Windows Explorer, delete both files from the Desktop folder, and then return to Lightroom Classic.

Using export presets

Lightroom Classic provides presets for commonly performed export tasks. You can use any preset as is or as a starting point for setting up your own.

If you find yourself performing the same operations over and over again, you should create your own presets to automate your workflow.

1   Navigate back to the Lesson 11 collection in the Library module. In the Grid view, select any of the images and then choose File > Export.

2   In the list of presets on the left side of the Export dialog box, choose For Email from the Lightroom Presets (click the words, not the checkbox).

3 Examine the settings associated with this preset. With the current File Settings, an exported file will be an sRGB JPEG file with a Quality setting of 60. Under Image Sizing, the exported image is set to be scaled down so that its longest side will be 500 pixels. Output Sharpening and Watermarking are unselected, and the Metadata options are set to export copyright details only. Note that there are no export location settings or post-processing settings.

Lightroom will export the image directly to an email, so there are no export location settings. Post-processing options are also unnecessary—Lightroom automatically generates an email and attaches the photo, and your email is sent from within Lightroom, with no need to launch an email client.

▶ **Tip:** For more detail on exporting photos as email attachments, see "Sharing your work by email" in Lesson 1, "A Quick Tour of Lightroom Classic."

4 In the list of presets on the left side of the Export dialog box, click to select the Burn Full-Sized JPEGs export preset.

5 Note the changes in the export settings. CD/DVD is now selected in the Export To menu at the top of the Export dialog box, instead of Email (so, once again, export location settings are redundant). Under File Settings, the JPEG Quality setting has been set to 100.

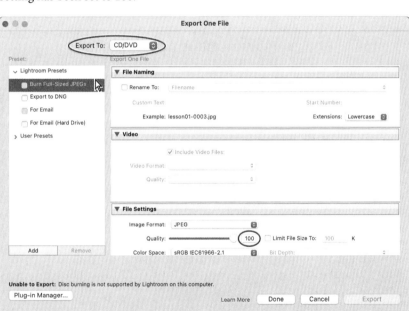

6 Scroll down to examine the rest of the preset options. Under Image Sizing, the Resize To Fit option is unselected, and the file will be exported with all of its metadata, except for People tags and GPS location information.

You can adjust any of the preset settings if you wish and then save your custom configuration as a new preset by clicking the Add button below the Presets list. Once it is saved, you can close the dialog.

Creating user presets

You can save your customized export settings as a new user preset. Export presets are always available from the File menu (File > Export With Preset), where you can start your export without opening the Export dialog first. Let's create a preset that will export an image suitable for posting to Facebook. The preset will save an image to the desktop at 1,400 pixels on the long edge, that has a JPEG quality of 100, and that uses the sRGB profile.

1 From your Lesson 11 collection, select the lesson11 - 0007 image. Click the Export button at the lower left of the Library module.

2 To export the image, follow the settings outlined in the image to the right. The only settings that need changing are:

• Top Export To: Hard Drive

• Export To: Specific Folder

• Folder: Desktop

• File Settings: JPEG

• Quality: 100

• Color Space: sRGB

• Resize To Fit: Long Edge

• Pixels: 1,400

• Resolution: 72 pixels per inch

All of the other settings can stay unselected.

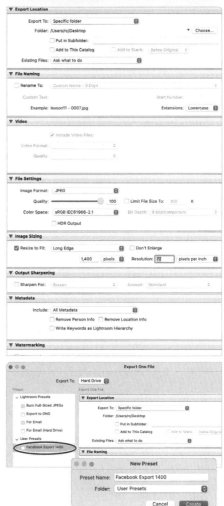

3 Click the Add button at the lower left of the Export dialog box and give the preset a name—I'm going to call this one "Facebook Export 1400"—and click Create. Now that we have the preset set, click Cancel in the Export dialog box.

With the image still selected, right-click it, scroll down to Export, and you'll see the new Facebook preset in the list. This will make it easier to save pictures with just the right settings whenever you need them.

Using Multi-Batch Export

Imagine you have a series of images and you need to publish them to Facebook, make high-resolution exports to deliver to your client, make low-resolution versions to email to the client, and convert to DNG for your backup. Previously, you achieved this by creating a series of export presets and then doing each export separately, one by one. Now, you have the ability to export one set of images with several different presets simultaneously—a boon to photographers' workflows everywhere.

In the Preset list on the left side of the Export dialog box, each preset has a checkbox in front of it. Simply click the checkboxes for the presets you want to use, and when you click Export, Lightroom will export your images with all of the presets at once.

Congratulations! You've completed this lesson on backing up your Lightroom Classic files and exporting your images. You've learned how to use the built-in catalog backup feature and to save metadata to your files. You've backed up all of your images by exporting them as a catalog, and you've exported them individually for viewing onscreen, for further editing, and for archiving. You have also used and created your own export presets. Before you move on to the next lesson, take a moment or two to review some of your new skills by reading through the questions and answers on the next pages.

Review questions

1 What are the two basic components of your photo library that need to be backed up?

2 How can you move a selection of images or your entire image library with all of the associated catalog information from one computer to another?

3 How can you tell if any updated metadata has been saved to a file?

4 How would you choose between file formats for exporting your photos?

5 How do you create your own export preset?

Review answers

1   The two basic components of the image library that need to be backed up are the original image files (or master files) and the library catalog file, which records all of the metadata and the complete editing history for every image in the library as well as information about collections, user templates and presets, and output settings.

2   On one computer, use the Export As Catalog command to create a catalog file together with copies of the original images and the available previews. On the other computer, choose File > Open Catalog, navigate to your exported file, select the exported .lrcat file, and open it.

3   In Grid view and in the Filmstrip, any images that have metadata to be saved will display the Metadata File Needs To Be Updated icon. You can also find any files that need to be updated by using the Metadata Status filter in the Filter bar.

4   The appropriate choice of a file format depends on the intended use of the exported images. To export images for onscreen viewing as email attachments, you'd use the JPEG file format and minimize the file size. To export an image to an external image editing application, you'd use PSD or TIFF and export the image at full size. For archival purposes, export the images in their original format or convert them to DNG.

5   Open the Export dialog box, change the settings to your liking, and then click the Add button at the lower left of the dialog box. In the New Preset dialog box, name your preset, and click Create.

INDEX

Contributors

 Rafael "RC" Concepcion is an award-winning photographer, podcast host, educator, and author of 15 best-selling books on photography, Photoshop, Lightroom, and HDR. He is a digital post-production specialist and assistant teaching professor at the S.I. Newhouse School for Visual Communications at Syracuse University.

He is an Adobe Certified Instructor in Photoshop, Illustrator, and Lightroom, and he worked with Adobe to write the Adobe Certified Expert exams for Photoshop CS6, Lightroom 4, and Lightroom 5. RC has more than 25 years of experience producing content in the creative, IT, and e-commerce industries. He has presented at seminars and workshops around the world. RC's production company, First Shot School, creates educational content and video productions for clients such as Intel, Dell, Epson, Nikon, Canon, Samsung, Nokia, Sandisk, Western Digital, G-Technology, Google, and Creative Live.

Production Notes

Adobe Photoshop Lightroom Classic Classroom in a Book 2024 Release was created electronically using Adobe InDesign. Art was produced using Adobe InDesign and Adobe Photoshop.

References to company names in the lessons are for demonstration purposes only and are not intended to refer to any actual organization or person.

Team credits

The following individuals contributed to the development of this edition of *Adobe Photoshop Lightroom Classic Classroom in a Book 2024 Release*:

Writer: Rafael "RC" Concepcion

Compositor: Cindy Snyder

Technical Editor: Cindy Snyder

Copyeditor: Cindy Snyder

Proofreader: Kim Wimpsett

Indexer: Rachel Kuhn

Keystroker: Megan Ahearn

Cover Illustration: Holly-Marie Cato, behance.net/hcato

Interior design: Mimi Heft

Adobe Press Executive Editor: Laura Norman

Adobe Press Production Editor: Tracey Croom

Typefaces used

Adobe Myriad Pro and Adobe Warnock Pro are used throughout the lessons. For more information about OpenType and Adobe fonts, visit www.adobe.com/products/type/opentype.html.

Photo credits

Photographic images and illustrations supplied by Rafael "RC" Concepcion, Binuk Varghese, Joe Conzo, Mary Bel, Tito Herrera, Sara Lando, Latanya Henry, Gregory Heisler, Amy Toensing, Felix Hernandez, and Adobe Systems Incorporated. Photos are for use only with the lessons in the book.

Special thanks

This book wouldn't have been possible without the help, guidance, and support of some truly amazing people: Cristela, Jennifer, and Sabine Concepcion; Albert J. Fudger; Cindy Snyder; Latanya, Linwood, and Tatiana Henry;, Ken Falk; Kim and Denise Patti; Meredith Payne Stotzner at Adobe Systems; Bonnie Scharf; Matt Davis; Sara Lando; Gabriel Ruiz; Nate and Shana Boyer; and Becca and Nate Peña. To my team at the S.I. Newhouse School of Public Communications at Syracuse University: Dean Mark Lodato, Soo Yeon Hong, Regina Luttrell, Olivia Stomsky, Hal Silverman, Gregory Heisler, Stanley Bondy, Donna Till, Tula Goenka, and Amy Toensing. Thank you for all of your help and support. An extra special thanks to my newfound work-sis, Alexis Trujillo. It has been a joy to work with you!

This book is dedicated to my longtime editor and friend Cindy Snyder. For over 16 years, you have been the person who has made me sound way smarter than I actually am. I could not have done any of this without you. Thank you.

Conclusion

I want to thank you so much for spending your time learning Lightroom Classic with me. It has been an absolute pleasure to be able to share how to use this immensely powerful program with you. I hope that you've come to realize that the folks at Adobe have made this program simple, intuitive, and quite fun to get to know, in the hopes that it inspires you to go out and make the best pictures you can dream of.

If you are interested in learning how Lightroom Classic integrates with Photoshop, make sure you check out my other book in this series, *Adobe Photoshop and Lightroom Classic for Photographers Classroom in a Book*. Also, feel free to stop by Syracuse University for a chat!

Finally, I would love to see what kinds of images you are making or be able to help you in any way that I can. If you'd like to stay in touch, please feel free to find me on Twitter, Instagram, or Facebook. My username everywhere is *aboutrc*.

You can see more of my work at *www.aboutrc.com*.

Now let's get out there and make some pictures!

The fastest, easiest, most comprehensive way to learn
Adobe Creative Cloud

Classroom in a Book®, the best-selling series of hands-on software training books, helps you learn the features of Adobe software quickly and easily.

The **Classroom in a Book** series offers what no other book or training program does—an official training series from Adobe Systems, developed with the support of Adobe product experts.

To see a complete list of our Classroom in a Book titles covering the 2024 release of Adobe Creative Cloud go to:
peachpit.com/CC2024

Adobe Photoshop Classroom in a Book 2024 Release
ISBN: 9780138262525

Adobe Illustrator Classroom in a Book 2024 Release
ISBN: 9780138263829

Adobe InDesign Classroom in a Book 2024 Release
ISBN: 9780138263911

Adobe After Effects Classroom in a Book 2024 Release
ISBN: 9780138316488

Adobe Animate Classroom in a Book 2024 Release
ISBN: 9780138317713

Adobe Photoshop Lightroom Classic Classroom in a Book 2024 Release
ISBN: 9780138318147

Adobe Premiere Pro Classroom in a Book 2024 Release
ISBN: 9780138318567

Adobe Photoshop, Illustrator, and InDesign Collaboration and Workflow Classroom in a Book
ISBN: 9780137908462

Adobe Creative Cloud Classroom in a Book
ISBN: 9780137914708

Adobe Acrobat Classroom in a Book, 4th edition
ISBN: 9780137983636

 Adobe Press